Beyond Traditional Tenure

༺༺༺༺༺༺༺༺༺༺༺༺༺༺༺༺༺༺༺༺༺༺༺

A Guide to Sound Policies and Practices

Richard P. Chait
Andrew T. Ford

Beyond Traditional Tenure

Jossey-Bass Publishers

San Francisco • Washington • London • 1982

BEYOND TRADITIONAL TENURE
A Guide to Sound Policies and Practices
        by Richard P. Chait and Andrew T. Ford

Copyright © 1982 by: Jossey-Bass Inc., Publishers
                     433 California Street
                     San Francisco, California 94104
                            &
                     Jossey-Bass Limited
                     28 Banner Street
                     London EC1Y 8QE

Library of Congress Cataloging in Publication Data

Chait, Richard.
        Beyond traditional tenure.

        Bibliography: p. 273
        Includes index.
        1. College teachers—Tenure—United States.
I. Ford, Andrew T. II. Title.
LB2836.C54   378'122   81-23606
ISBN 0-87589-519-0   AACR2

Manufactured in the United States of America

JACKET DESIGN BY WILLI BAUM

FIRST EDITION

Code 8209

The Jossey-Bass
Series in Higher Education

Preface

       Academic tenure is too prevalent a practice to disappear and too consequential a policy to disregard. About 85 percent of all American colleges and universities have a tenure system, and 59 percent of all full-time faculty have tenure. Commitments to these faculty members cannot be abrogated, and tenured personnel are not likely to relinquish that status or accede to any policy that precludes tenure for the next generation of scholars and teachers. Consequently, tenure undoubtedly will continue to be a prominent feature of the academic landscape; and, over the next several decades, tenure policies, practices, and decisions will influence significantly the quality of a faculty, the nature of a curriculum, the attractiveness of a profession, and the flexibility and financial liquidity of an institution. For these reasons, all members of the academic community—especially faculty, administrators, and trustees—have a substantial stake in tenure policies and policy execution.

The essence of the debates about tenure, however, will shift dramatically. As the economics and demographics of higher education severely test the adaptability of traditional tenure to new and adverse circumstances, passionate, rhetorical exchanges about the merits and demerits of tenure will not be particularly useful. Practical concerns about tenure as a term and condition of employment will assume far greater significance than philosophical discourses about tenure as a hallowed precept. The more vital questions will concern policies and strategies that either enhance the effectiveness of conventional tenure systems or promise a better alternative.

So far, only a very few new four-year colleges and some two-year colleges have adopted an *alternative* to tenure. These schools employ faculty members solely on a term contract basis. Other colleges and universities, by eliminating traditional tenure systems, have elected to modify various provisions of conventional tenure policies. Among the *modifications* enacted are non-tenure-track appointments, extended probationary periods, suspension of the "up-or-out" rule, tenure quotas, and periodic evaluation of tenured faculty members. Still other colleges and universities—either in addition to or instead of the various modifications—have attempted to strengthen the administration and improve the execution of traditional tenure policies and such related policies as peer review, faculty compensation, faculty development, and manpower planning.

To date, no one has systematically surveyed, analyzed, and evaluated these options as actually adopted by different colleges and universities. We do so here, using actual case studies of several institutions. We describe the new policies and practices, assess the strengths and weaknesses of the changes, and consider generally whether these options are suitable and transferable to other campus environments. We conclude with specific and workable recommendations designed to improve the management of human resources, regardless of the particular policy a college uses to employ faculty.

This book, then, differs materially from other works on

academic tenure. First, we do not confine our discussion to traditional tenure but have extended it to encompass an alternative
policy, modifications of conventional policy, and the relationship between tenure and other major personnel policies. Second, we treat tenure as a personnel policy and not as dogma; we
concentrate on the pragmatic, day-to-day aspects of tenure policy and policy execution. And third, we rely principally on applied research and not on abstract arguments. The conclusions
and recommendations we present derive primarily from the successes and setbacks of colleges and universities that have actually eschewed, modified, or strengthened classical tenure policies.

  The information and advice we offer should be helpful
and valuable to all constituencies of the academic community.
Anyone concerned with the vitality of a particular college, university, or the entire profession must be concerned about the
vitality of the faculty. At the risk of only a slight overstate-
ment, we contend that the reputation of a faculty and the reputation of a college are nearly synonymous. Few matters affect
faculty and therefore colleges as directly or as profoundly as
academic tenure. Rightly or wrongly, most faculty members
view tenure as essential to economic and psychological security
and to the conduct of research and instruction. Hence, decisions
to alter the substance or the procedures of traditional tenure
policies on any campus should—for selfish as well as intellectual
reasons—concern faculty everywhere. Trustees and administrators would be well advised to proceed cautiously and to be well
informed about the advantages and disadvantages of contemplated changes before taking any actions to "tinker" with tenure. No other issue can be quite as sensitive or explosive among
academicians. In that regard, the case studies we present should
be particularly instructive.

  The need for administrators and trustees to understand
conventional and nontraditional tenure policies extends far beyond the immediate and personal concerns of the faculty and
the daily operations of the university to the long-range objectives of the institution. Tenure decisions represent sizable, long-
term financial and programmatic commitments that largely define the caliber of a faculty and the dimensions of a curriculum

and also influence the costs of instruction. Perhaps no other decisions so fundamentally shape a college's future. By extension, the policies and practices that govern tenure decisions are equally crucial. Changes that lead to more effective personnel policies and more efficient personnel practices redound broadly to the benefit of the university. Conversely, the introduction or perpetuation of unsound policies and unwise practices can inflict widespread damage. Decisions to abandon, modify, or fortify classical tenure policies and practices are simply too important to make without knowledge of the changes adopted by other colleges and universities and without an assessment of the results.

We tapped many sources to identify those colleges and universities that had eschewed tenure altogether or had altered conventional tenure policies. We visited national associations such as the American Association of University Professors, the American Council on Education, and the Association of Governing Boards. We conducted a computer search of published and unpublished materials; we reviewed the literature on academic tenure; and, between 1974 and 1980, we questioned about 700 senior administrators who attended the Institute for Educational Management, a six-week management development program conducted each summer at Harvard University.

As might be expected, the more radical the reform, the sparser the sample base, and the more conservative the change, the broader the base proved to be. The choices among colleges without a tenure system were, therefore, most limited, whereas the choices among colleges with nontenure tracks or extended probationary periods, for example, were comparatively plentiful. As we selected campuses for case studies, we deliberately attempted to encompass a broad spectrum of institutions—from small, private liberal arts colleges to comprehensive public universities; from new, experimental colleges to mature, traditional universities. Additionally, we attempted to select institutions that had sufficient experience with a particular policy change to permit some conclusions about the effectiveness of that innovation. To enrich the diversity of the sample and the inventory of policy options, we also examined faculty handbooks, policy

manuals, staff reports, in-house newsletters, and student news-
papers from other colleges and universities.

As we proceeded, we were persuaded that the more we
learned about traditional tenure systems, the better equipped
we would be to evaluate any variations. Consequently, we selected and visited three campuses that satisfied several criteria
we believe to be indicative of an effective tenure system. In the
process of these case studies, we discovered several elements of
sound practice common to all three schools. In all, we visited
twenty campuses and reviewed policies and procedures from
scores of other institutions. (To provide the most up-to-date information, we conducted telephone interviews during the spring
of 1981 with key contacts on the campuses where we developed
case studies.)

On the campuses we visited, we normally interviewed the
senior academic officers (such as the president, the provost, and
college deans) and a dozen or so faculty members—some tenured, some untenured; some supportive, some critical of the
policy. Wherever appropriate and possible, we also met with a
local AAUP officer and a college trustee. In each instance, we
sought to determine whether the institution's policy worked
well. The obstacles to evaluation are formidable, since most colleges lack stated policy objectives as well as criteria and procedures to gauge the policy's impact. Despite these barriers, we
analyzed the advantages and disadvantages of all the policies
and practices under discussion, drawing our conclusions from
personal interviews, policy statements, observable results, and
available data. Inevitably, though, these assessments are judgments—ideally, informed judgments. We have, in essence,
adopted a method to evaluate personnel policies similar to
Blackburn's (1980, p. 11) approach to the evaluation of faculty
development programs: "Program evaluation is a process rather
than a procedure. It deals with the formation of judgments
about programs using criteria or standards of comparison and
descriptions of what occurred and resulted in the program."

The first chapter, "Tenure in Context," provides a historical backdrop for the discussions of traditional tenure and departures from that tradition. We describe both the pressures to

change classical tenure systems and the counterforces to preserve that tradition. After we assess the relative strength of
these forces, we offer some observations about the future of
academic tenure, a matter of concern to all academicians.*

Chapter Two reviews in detail the employment policies of
three colleges, opened in the 1970s, that elected to forgo academic tenure entirely and to appoint faculty instead to multiyear contracts, with reappointment based on performance and
professional growth and development. In Chapter Three, we ap-
praise the drawbacks and benefits of nontenure systems as practiced by these three schools and then develop some conclusions
about the effect of term contracts on faculty turnover, innovation, faculty morale and performance, academic freedom, faculty recruitment, and retrenchment. Although hardly representative of the academic mainstream, these three colleges have
now had extensive experience with "Life Without Tenure" and
widespread exposure as "renegades" from traditional tenure
policies. Their experiences should prove enlightening to those
legislators, trustees, administrators, and faculty who have wondered whether there are alternatives to academic tenure and
whether the cure is any better than the disease.

Chapter Four considers policies that establish tenure-
track positions for some faculty and non-tenure-track positions
for other faculty. Since personnel assigned to the "off-track"
positions are usually ineligible for a permanent appointment to
the faculty, the policy guarantees in effect that the college or
university will never be totally tenured. We describe the three
most common types of non-tenure-track positions—nonrenew-
able, indefinitely renewable, and renewable for a limited period
—and examine some campuses where these policies operate. Because nontenure tracks are relatively commonplace, we focus
on a particularly imaginative and, we think, broadly applicable
variation that affords tenure-ineligible faculty especially generous sabbatical leaves as an inducement to forgo tenure and as a

---

*Inasmuch as we confine this study to changes in traditional tenure
policies per se, we do not address the matter of early retirement, a topic
capably treated by Jenny, Heim, and Hughes (1979) and by Patton (1979).

means to correlate risks with rewards. We also examine a college that established a nontenure track, not to exceed 10 percent of the total full-time faculty, and simultaneously introduced growth contracts for all faculty, tenured as well as untenured. Off-track appointments will almost certainly become more and more popular. As colleges and universities add nontenure tracks, the critical issues will be to determine those circumstances that warrant tenure-ineligible appointments and to delineate terms and conditions of employment that are fair to the individual and at the same time beneficial to the institution. The chapter closes with specific recommendations on both matters.

In Chapter Five, we assess policies designed to defer the tenure decision and thereby slow the march of untenured faculty members toward the tenured ranks. We consider three research universities where probationary periods may stretch as many as four to six years *beyond* the seven-year limit recommended by the AAUP. We then address a broader and perhaps ultimately more significant concern as we suggest some strategies academic administrators might employ to utilize the probationary period most effectively whatever its duration may be. Some schools, primarily liberal arts colleges, have adopted a more extreme and open-ended measure than extended probationary periods to postpone the tenure decision. These colleges have suspended the "up-or-out" rule, a fundamental proviso of traditional tenure systems. We analyze the strengths and weaknesses of both these modification of traditional tenure policies.

Chapter Six examines the advisability of tenure quotas—predetermined limits or general guidelines designed to control the percentage of faculty on tenure at one time. When the allowable limit has been reached, no more faculty may be awarded tenure unless and until a tenured member of the faculty leaves the institution. Tenure quotas, controversial though comparatively common, are a somewhat facile solution to a complex problem. Fixed limits on tenure levels, often advocated by trustees, will precipitate for administrators both political problems and practical disadvantages, as the three cases presented in this chapter illustrate. Not without benefits, tenure guidelines may reasonably be *an element* of a tenure system.

Frequently, however, an absolute limit on tenure levels emerges as *the* tenure policy. The chapter concludes, therefore, with a discussion of the proper role of tenure guidelines as one policy variable among many.

In Chapters Seven through Nine, we turn from less conventional policy options to the administration of more traditional tenure systems and personnel policies closely related to academic tenure. Many "problems" associated with tenure policies can, we contend, be alleviated by more effective policy execution. Chapter Seven analyzes the policies and practices of three well-respected schools where, we believe, classical tenure policies work quite well. Selected on the basis of criteria described in the text, these rather different institutions exhibit certain common approaches and practices that seem to characterize effective tenure systems. Colleges and universities committed to conventional tenure systems—indeed, all schools committed to effective personnel administration—would, we believe, do well to incorporate the sound practices and procedures we observed on all three campuses.

Whatever a college's fundamental employment policy for faculty, a reasonable and sensible approach to faculty evaluation will prove invaluable. Thoughtful and judicious personnel decisions demand adequate and appropriate evaluative data for each candidate under consideration. Chapter Eight addresses faculty evaluation both before and after the tenure decision. We develop a general and broadly applicable framework for faculty evaluation that covers the purposes, areas, criteria, standards, and sources of evidence for performance appraisals. We also examine policies and practices expressly adopted for periodically assessing tenured faculty members.

Faculty evaluations should influence decisions by academic administrators on the distribution of rewards and, when necessary, the application of sanctions. In a very real sense, the allocation of rewards (and sanctions) translates policy into action and rhetoric into reality. Unless successfully managed, a great deal can be lost in the translation. In Chapter Nine, we devote considerable attention to salary administration and the conditions necessary for an effective merit pay program. At the same time, we recognize and emphasize that the range of available rewards reaches well beyond remuneration. A broad spectrum of rewards creates conditions conducive to achievement and hence satisfaction. We define these opportunities and rewards as faculty development, and we construct a merit- rather than a need-based framework for the operation of faculty development programs. Incentives span from a grant to support research, a colloquium, or a new curriculum to a reduced work load, an enriched laboratory, or an enlarged department. Faculty members eager to gain recognition may prefer as rewards public statements and symbols of appreciation or private expressions of praise. In all cases, administrators must endeavor to correlate performance with "payoffs" and to ensure that the rewards tendered a faculty member are responsive to that individual's desires. Chapter Nine proposes strategies to meet these crucial objectives. The chapter ends with a discussion of available sanctions, which extend from oral reprimands and modest raises to loss of privileges and ultimately to dismissal for cause.

The final chapter furnishes a general guide to "audit" the effectiveness of any academic personnel system and provides guidance likely to improve personnel policies and policy administration. At the outset, we describe an appropriate personnel data base and some tools and techniques to analyze the data. The balance of the chapter advances some specific recommendations to manage circumstances where changes in policy or changes in administrative personnel seem necessary. In that context, we comment on prospective policy changes that clash with the recommendations of the AAUP, and we confront the matter of censure by the AAUP, an important consideration on many campuses. Lastly, we offer some observations about distinguishing between ill-advised policies and sound policies ineffectively administered.

Two appendices are included. The first document states the promotion and tenure policies of the Harvard Business School, which we find to be a model statement in terms of completeness, clarity, and candor. While each college and university must determine its own criteria and standards, we believe all institutions would do well to formulate as thorough and logical a policy statement. The second appendix presents a sample print-out from a simulation model of faculty flow. Relatively simple to use, such models provide a wealth of data essential to manpower planning.

We hope that the material contained in this book will stimulate and enlighten down-to-earth discussions about traditional as well as nontraditional tenure policies. Educators, legislators, and trustees who are curious about policy options now have an inventory and an evaluation of innovations attempted elsewhere. Deliberations by faculty senates, administrative councils, trustee committees, and statewide boards about new and presumably better policies need no longer occur within an information vacuum where speculation and misapprehension thrive. Facts and analyses can be added to discussions typically dominated by prejudice and predisposition. Decisions can be informed by the experiences of other colleges and universities and by a first-hand assessment of the results. And while we focus primarily on academic tenure, we try, wherever possible, to offer advice that leads toward sound personnel policies, effective policy administration, and a more constructive work environment—objectives that all colleges and universities undoubtedly share.

The nature of the research we conducted necessarily entailed interviews and conversations with countless faculty members, administrators, and trustees at dozens of colleges, universities, and associations. We deeply appreciate the valuable time, thoughts, and data these individuals supplied. We are especially grateful for the indispensable support provided for this project through a grant from the Exxon Education Foundation.

January 1982   Richard P. Chait
                                              University Park, Pennsylvania

                                                          Andrew T. Ford
                                                   Meadville, Pennsylvania

Contents

The Authors

Richard P. Chait is associate provost of The Pennsylvania State University. He was graduated Phi Beta Kappa from Rutgers University (1966) with a B.A. degree in history and then earned an M.A. (1968) in history and a Ph.D. in educational administration (1972) from the University of Wisconsin at Madison. From 1970 through 1973, he served as assistant to the president of Stockton State College, a new college he helped plan and develop. From 1973 to 1977, Chait administered the Institute for Educational Management (IEM) at Harvard University, which offers management development programs for college and university administrators. Over the next three years, he was chairman of the institute's faculty and an assistant professor at the Harvard Graduate School of Education. He continues to serve as a faculty member at IEM.

Chait has been a consultant to dozens of colleges, universities, agencies, and philanthropic foundations on topics related to academic management and personnel policies. He is a consulting editor of *Change* magazine, a college trustee, and an associate of the Cheswick Center, a nonprofit corporation to improve the performance of boards of trustees.

Andrew T. Ford is dean of the college at Allegheny College in Meadville, Pennsylvania. He received his B.A. degree in history from Seton Hall University in 1966. He next attended the University of Wisconsin at Madison, where he received an M.A. (1968) and a Ph.D. (1971) in history, with a minor in the Chinese language. His doctoral dissertation dealt with the diplomacy of the Boxer Uprising. He joined Stockton State College in 1971 as an assistant professor of history and subsequently became assistant to the vice-president for academic affairs. From 1975 to 1978, he served as academic programs coordinator for the New Hampshire College and University Council, a consortium of thirteen regionally accredited higher education institutions. Prior to joining Allegheny College in 1981, he was vice-president for academic affairs at the Rhode Island School of Design.

Ford's principal interests lie in long-range planning, academic management, and faculty development. He studied public-sector mediation at Rutgers University and has negotiated several collective bargaining agreements with faculty unions. He has consulted widely on personnel management, faculty development, and academic resource sharing.

Chait and Ford have worked together on several consulting projects and coauthored several articles, including "Affirmative Action, Tenure and Unionization: Can There Be Peaceful Coexistence?" in D. W. Vermilye (Ed.), *Lifelong Learners—A New Clientele for Higher Education: Current Issues in Higher Education 1974* (San Francisco: Jossey-Bass, 1974); "Academic Tenure," a filmstrip and companion pamphlet (Washington, D.C.: Association of Governing Boards of Universities and Colleges, 1977); and "Can a College Have Tenure . . . and Affirmative Action, Too?" *Chronicle of Higher Education* (Oct. 1, 1973).

To our wives, Diane S. Chait and Anne M. Ford

Beyond Traditional Tenure

A Guide
to Sound Policies
and Practices

1.

Tenure
in Context

‌Whenever controversies swirl around a particular campus or throughout the academic community, the issue of academic tenure can usually be spotted close to the eye of the storm. Whether the discussions concern the quality of instruction, the nature of the curriculum, research productivity, financial solvency, affirmative action, or countless other matters, academic tenure somehow emerges as an integral issue—and for good reason. Tenure governs the fundamental employment relationship between the institution and the dominant segment of the academic work force—namely, the faculty. Not unexpectedly, therefore, tenure policies and practices will influence and affect most aspects of the academic enterprise.

Despite the centrality of tenure, faculty, administrators, trustees, and other parties to the deliberations are often con-

1

fused about the provisions, purposes, and consequences of tenure. Ironically, in an environment that stresses scholarship and research, some individuals argue about tenure more from intuition than from information, and when data controvert personal prejudices, the data are frequently discredited or discarded. In short, strongly held opinions often seem more plentiful than carefully researched conclusions or thoughtfully developed theories.

Even more basically, members of the profession disagree about definitions of terms and of problems. Without consensus on these elementary questions, small wonder that the tenure debate generates more heat than light. In many ways, discussions about academic tenure resemble discussions about the nation's economic ills. What defines a recession, a depression, an "acceptable" level of unemployment, or an "acceptable" rate of inflation? Is the problem unemployment, inflation, productivity, federal regulation, monetary policies, balance of trade, or some combination thereof? In the academy, we struggle to define academic freedom, academic tenure, economic security, institutional flexibility, and financial exigency, to name only a few terms. We are, likewise, uncertain whether enrollment declines, evaluation procedures, incentive structures, insufficient accountability, ineffectual managers, or, again, some combination thereof causes the "tenure problem." Indeed, many academicians rightly or wrongly see no problem.

Tenure Defined

Discussions of academic tenure generally rely on a "definition" offered in 1940 by the American Association of University Professors (AAUP) and the Association of American Colleges (AAC), as part of their "Statement on Academic Freedom and Tenure": "Tenure is a means to certain ends—specifically, (1) freedom of teaching and research and of extramural activities and (2) a sufficient degree of economic security to make the profession attractive to men and women of ability. Freedom and economic security—hence, tenure—are indispensable to the success of an institution in fulfilling its obligations to its students and to society" (American Association of University Professors, 1977, p. 2). This statement seems more a partisan characterization, however, than a definition. Tenure is no more freedom and economic security than marriage is bliss. Although these conditions *may* result from the arrangement, the actual arrangement and the possible outcomes are not one and the same. These same conditions may be attainable through other means. Can tenure really be called "indispensable to the success of an institution" when a number of institutions enjoy "success" without benefit of tenure? Under the AAUP's definition, we would have to label the adoption of an alternative to tenure as an irrational and preposterous decision to eschew a condition necessary to success. As reported in the next chapter, the careful deliberations by clearheaded individuals at colleges that elected to forgo tenure belie that proposition.

We prefer a later, more impartial definition developed by the Commission on Academic Tenure cosponsored by the AAUP and the AAC: "[Tenure is] an arrangement under which faculty appointments in an institution of higher education are continued until retirement for age or physical disability, subject to dismissal for adequate cause or unavoidable termination on account of financial exigency or change of institutional program" (AAUP/AAC Commission on Academic Tenure, 1973, p. 256).

Typically, faculty reach the tenure decision after a period of probationary service. Although the AAUP and the AAC recommend a seven-year trial period, probationary service commonly ranges from three to seven years and currently averages five and a half years at four-year colleges and almost six years at universities (Atelsek and Gomberg, 1980). As a rule, one year before the end of the probationary period, the college or university assesses each candidate for tenure, with the burden initially on the faculty member to demonstrate worthiness for permanent status. At most institutions, then, with some two-year colleges excepted, tenure represents—at least theoretically—an earned privilege and not a rightful expectation.

Under conventional policy, a faculty member denied tenure may not remain at that institution beyond the conclusion of the probationary period; the candidate either moves up into the tenured ranks or moves out of the institution. Hence, this provision is typically called the "up-or-out" rule. Most tenure decisions are thus timed so as to allow unsuccessful candidates adequate opportunity, usually a year, to relocate. Successful candidates are not, as many laymen erroneously believe, guaranteed a lifetime appointment. On most campuses, employment can be severed for some or all of the reasons stipulated in the AAUP/AAC Commission on Academic Tenure's definition. Moreover, within the confines of applicable law and collectively negotiated agreements, institutions are free to define and determine the precise grounds that warrant dismissal of tenured faculty. (See Chapter Nine.)

Forces for Change

Whatever the precise definition, there has always been some opposition to tenure. The classical argument condemns it as a one-sided commitment that binds the institution to the individual, but not the individual to the institution. A tenured faculty member may, without penalty, leave a college at almost any time; yet, it is argued, the college remains relatively powerless to remove the faculty member. From this perspective, tenured status effectively shields faculty, however incompetent, from accountability and thereby guarantees, as a practical matter, "lifetime" employment. More recent attacks on tenure stress different issues, reflecting different circumstances and contemporary concerns. Each argument adds momentum to the evaluation of old policies and the quest for new ones.

Campus Unrest. In the 1960s and 1970s, many college campuses served as headquarters for student activism and as convenient targets for violent protests. As classes were canceled and property destroyed, many law makers, urged by taxpayers, introduced measures to discipline students and reform the university. Professors, they claimed, had too many privileges, too much security, and too little work. The time was ripe to review tenure policies. In short order, three reports on campus unrest—by the Scranton Commission, the American Council on Education, and the U.S. Department of Health, Education, and Welfare (HEW)—all recommended that tenure be reevaluated.

Faculty Unionism. The spread of faculty unionism prompted a second impetus to change. In 1966, only twenty-three institutions, with a total of 5,200 faculty, had been unionized. Six years later, the numbers had jumped to 311 institutions and 87,000 faculty; and by 1979, to 524 institutions and 142,000 faculty (Carnegie Council on Policy Studies in Higher Education, 1980, p. 307). Quite naturally, unions endeavored to gain greater job protection more immediately for more employees. As tenure privileges on some campuses were extended to librarians, registrars, counselors, and other staff members, tenure appeared to be more a conventional matter of employment security than a unique measure to ensure academic freedom (Chait, 1975). Since economic security could be provided by union contracts as well as by academic tenure, some critics wondered why faculty should have both. Similarly, many observers argued that state and federal laws now adequately ensured academic freedom. As a result, since both economic security and academic freedom were adequately protected by other provisions, critics declared tenure an outmoded concept that provides protection redundant at best and excessive at worst.

"Steady State." The onset of the "steady-state" or "no-growth" era constitutes the most powerful current stimulus for reassessment of traditional tenure policies. When the climate and prospects for the academic industry started to deteriorate in recent years, more and more people questioned whether the old rules would be appropriate for the new ball game. Would tenure, as a long-term fiscal and curricular commitment, prove to be ill suited to a period of uncertainty and austerity and incompatible with the need for financial liquidity and program flexibility? Furthermore, as conditions and predictions worsen and the pressures on institutions to adapt and survive intensify, administrators, trustees, and to a lesser extent faculties can be expected to search more ardently for new personnel policies as part of the "solution" to a wide range of difficulties. Traditional tenure policies, already under scrutiny, will be even more severely challenged; and alternatives and modifications, already under consideration, will be even more intently pursued, especially where colleges must minimize commitments and reduce costs.

The cost of a tenure decision can easily approach one million dollars if the faculty member has a thirty-five-year career at the institution. On a year-to-year basis, tenured faculty cost more than untenured faculty, since tenured faculty tend to be more senior and therefore more highly salaried. In a study of age discrimination and retirement, the American Association of University Professors (1978a) estimates that the salary of a sixty-five-year-old professor is twice that of a new assistant professor. At the University of Rochester, for example, the actual salary for a sixty-five-year-old professor in 1977-78 was approximately 1.8 times that of a new assistant professor (Oi, 1979). Tenured faculty, then, appear to have a greater, and perhaps firmer, claim on institutional resources than nontenured faculty do. The elimination of tenure, however, will not lower personnel costs unless simultaneously the administration removes some senior faculty from the payroll, since length of service (presumably leading to increased compensation) and not tenure accounts for increased costs. On the other hand, leaders of an institution faced with a precarious future may wish to abandon tenure, or at least limit or halt grants of tenure, as a means to curtail long-term financial obligations.

Curricular Inflexibility. Tenured faculty hold a strong grip on academic programs, since colleges and universities are labor-intensive organizations without an interchangeable labor force. Trained as specialists, faculty are, in effect, tenured as specialists within a particular department, school, or college. Academic tenure does not mean that a classicist may be required some day to perform as a physicist or that a professor may be required to serve instead as an admissions counselor, a development officer, or a publications editor. In short, to tenure a classicist is to tenure classics; and, by extension, the curriculum cannot be altered markedly unless there are some changes of academic personnel.

In a period of spectacular growth, programmatic obligations and constraints were less noticeable and less consequential. Continued expansion inherently furnished opportunities for flexibility and innovation. By contrast, in steady state—or, worse, in contraction—each commitment becomes more significant for scarcity enhances value; fewer opportunities make each

one more precious. Where a largely tenured faculty offers a curriculum or product mix out of phase with market demands,
the college's ability to compete for students may suffer and enrollments may decline. Fearful of these prospects, some administrators, trustees, and legislators press for employment policies
that do not marry an institution to a particular program or discipline quite as irrevocably as tenure does.

Faculty Immobility. While tenure has always conveyed a
long-term financial and programmatic commitment, many such
commitments were, in fact, of a comparatively short duration in
the late 1960s and early 1970s, when faculty enjoyed much
greater career mobility. In the mid-1960s, the net total faculty
in the United States increased by about 10 percent, or twenty
thousand positions annually; currently, net additions hover
close to zero, and net reductions seem likely until the end of
the century, especially if the ratios of faculty to students increase (Carnegie Council on Policy Studies in Higher Education, 1980, p. 305; Cartter, 1976, p. 153). Fewer vacancies
mean reduced mobility. Thus, movement from one institution
to another by faculty with earned doctorates has dropped from
about 8 percent in the mid-1960s to about 1 percent currently.
Faculty do not go elsewhere because, in the main, there is no-
where else to go. Tenured faculty are permanent indeed.

As steady state approached, probationary faculty continued to reach the tenure threshold, and many of these faculty
earned tenure. In 1972, the American Council on Education
(ACE) reported that 42 percent of all institutions with tenure
systems granted tenure to all eligible candidates, and 72 percent
granted tenure to at least six of every ten candidates. By 1974,
tenure was conferred a bit less generously: 65 percent of the institutions surveyed granted tenure to more than 60 percent of
the eligible pool (El-Khawas and Furniss, 1974). Of 12,000 full-
time faculty considered for tenure at four-year colleges and universities during the 1978-79 academic year, 58 percent received
tenure and 22 percent remained eligible for reconsideration at a
later time; presumably, the other 20 percent were denied permanent positions (Atelsek and Gomberg, 1980, p. 8).

As more faculty entered the tenured ranks and fewer departed, tenure levels increased. Between 1972 and 1974, the proportion of institutions where at least half of the faculty held tenure increased from 43 to 59 percent. Between 1974-75 and 1975-76, the percentage of tenured faculty nationally increased from 53.6 percent to 55.2 percent (National Center for Education Statistics, 1977, p. 2). Four years later, the proportion of tenured faculty at public institutions had surpassed 60 percent in twenty-one states; thirty-eight states reported that tenure levels at public and private institutions together exceeded 50 percent (American Council on Education, 1980, p. 126). While faculty enter the tenured ranks at a steady pace, the outflow seems reduced to a trickle. If, as we expect, Congress extends beyond age seventy or altogether eliminates mandatory retirement, the potential term of employment for tenured faculty will lengthen, and turnover will be still further reduced or postponed. With no special clairvoyance, academicians and lay trustees can foresee a clogged, stagnant pipeline—a vision that heightens the pressure to abandon or modify conventional tenure policies.

Faculty Age Distribution. Compounding the problem, American colleges and universities employ a relatively youthful faculty. Pressed to expand rapidly in the 1960s, institutions of higher education appointed newly minted Ph.D.s, advanced doctoral students, and M.A.s to the faculty. As a result, the modal age of tenured faculty stands today at thirty-six to forty-five. Because of restricted career mobility and relaxed retirement laws, nearly all these faculty will remain within academe and with the same employer for the next two or three decades. Thus, Kerr (1980, p. 10) predicts that by the year 2000 the modal age will be fifty-six to sixty-five, and more faculty will be over age sixty-six than under age thirty-five.

Affirmative Action. With faculty mobility hampered by market conditions and institutional adaptability circumscribed by tenure commitments, few colleges or universities will for the foreseeable future be well positioned to add or advance faculty, a critical aspect of most affirmative action programs. Inasmuch as market conditions are not easily altered, proponents of affirmative action may attack tenure policies instead. More than ten

years ago, Florence Moog (1971, p. 983) cited the tenure system as "the major barrier to the female scholar" beyond the
doctorate. Two years later, Chait and Ford (1973, p. 16) broadened the argument: "A faculty solidified by tenure stands at
cross-purposes with affirmative action, which requires a more
fluid circumstance to be effective. To appoint more blacks, Chi-
canos, women, and other persons previously victimized by discrimination requires vacancies. In the current no-growth era,
vacancies must arise largely from turnover, not from expansion.
Tenure, however, limits turnover. Thus, the immovable object
meets the irresistible force." To the degree that women and minority group members accept these contentions, advocates of
affirmative action may assert, as Moog did, that "the way to
solve the problem is to abolish the tenure system as it stands today" (p. 983).

The confluence, then, of economic uncertainties, no
growth, and limited turnover constrains institutional flexibility
and reduces institutional responsiveness, to use recent catchwords. As a long-term financial and programmatic commitment,
academic tenure imposes further constraints. If the arguments
for change, singly and collectively, gain more currency, more in
stitutions may entertain, and some may adopt, proposals to dis-
mantle or recast the tenets of classical tenure. There are, though,
potent counterforces to the momentum for policy changes.

Forces for Status Quo

However powerful the sentiment for change may be on
certain campuses, we would hardly classify tenure as an endan-
gered species. Tenure represents a deep-seated doctrine of the
profession, even though the concept did not emerge as a formal
precept until the AAUP promulgated a "Declaration of Principles" in 1915. To be sure, an unprecedented combination of circumstances has challenged and perhaps even tarnished the sanctity of academic tenure. Nevertheless, an obituary would be
most premature.

The forces that safeguard and sustain traditional tenure
include the following (adapted from Chait, 1979a):

Prevalence of Tenure. Tenure represents too prevalent a practice to be easily withdrawn or overthrown. About 85 percent of all colleges and universities utilize a tenure system, and these institutions employ about 95 percent of all full-time faculty. For the 1980-81 academic year, the National Center for Education Statistics reported that 59 percent of all full-time instructional faculty held tenure. There is little reason to believe that these 233,000 individuals will relinquish tenure (O'Toole, 1979, who did relinquish it, is quite exceptional) or that institutions may legally revoke that status. Add to this group some 2.3 million elementary and secondary school teachers, the vast majority of whom hold permanent positions. Any move to abolish tenure would threaten the entrenched self-interests of many individuals, professional associations, and labor unions and therefore engender widespread and steadfast resistance.

Tenure's prevalence safeguards tenure's existence in another way. Put most simply, as long as most colleges and universities offer tenure, most colleges and universities will offer tenure. With respect to faculty recruitment and institutional reputation, the *perceived* risks of deviating from accepted practices are greater than most institutions are prepared to assume.

Resilience of Tenure. Tenure has already proved quite resistant to external attack. As noted earlier, academic tenure was especially vulnerable to public challenge from the late 1960s through the early 1970s. Approximately twenty states introduced legislation to reform, curtail, or eliminate tenure. Only one bill passed, and it affected only prospective faculty at the community colleges of Virginia. If tenure at public colleges and universities survived legislative assaults then, it should survive occasional confrontations now, when relations between the campus and the statehouse are not nearly as strained.

Legality of Seniority. Viewed as a typical seniority system, tenure has not been unraveled by equal employment opportunity legislation, even though tenure may hinder affirmative action. In numerous court cases from other industries and at least one from education, seniority systems have been upheld, despite disproportionately adverse effects on racial and ethnic minorities (*Chance* v. *Board of Examiners,* 534 F.2d 993

(2d Cir. 1976); *Jersey Central Power and Light Co.* v. *Local Union 327 etc. of International Brotherhood of Electrical Workers,* 508 F.2d 687 (3d Cir. 1975); *Waters* v. *Wisconsin Steelworkers,* 502 F.2d 1309 (7th Cir. 1974); *Watkins* v. *United States Steelworkers of America, Local 2369,* 516 F.2d 41 (5th Cir. 1975)). Affirmative action will neither overthrow nor overturn academic tenure.

Support of Unions. As the era of steady state or decline unfolds and more institutions are forced to retrench, faculty unions will press harder to protect tenure within the shelter of collective bargaining agreements. No faculty union has negotiated away tenure. (In 1973, when bargainers for the American Federation of Teachers at the University of Hawaii presented for ratification a contract introducing nontenure employment tied to five-year contracts, the rank and file repudiated by a three-to-one margin the contract and the union.) To the contrary, most unions seek to fortify the concept of tenure and the procedural safeguards. When times turn hard and economic gains are less probable, unions generally want greater security and oppose attempts to weaken or rescind protections already obtained.

The Current Debate

With so little information available about alternatives to and modifications of conventional tenure policies, both the champions of change and the supporters of the status quo are free to transform speculations into assertions and assertions into "facts" in order to bolster a particular point of view. Some advocates of change contend that "out there somewhere" there must be a better way. Unhappy with a known quantity, these "revolutionaries" believe that some as yet ill-defined alternative to tenure will prove to be superior to classical tenure. Less radical advocates of change doubt that such drastic departures from tradition are necessary, inasmuch as academic tenure represents a fundamentally sound, albeit slightly flawed, concept. A policy revision here and a procedural alteration there would, in their view, be sufficient to minimize the modest drawbacks and maximize the substantial benefits that academic tenure offers. Finally, supporters of the status quo maintain that the alternatives to tenure are neither irresistibly attractive nor universally practicable; the cures, indeed, may be no better than the supposed disease. The very fact that there has been no stampede to abandon tenure and adopt an alternative suggests to defenders of the status quo that no better way exists.

All these arguments trade on some misconceptions about traditional tenure and a degree of ignorance about the available alternatives and modifications. Misinformation and lack of information about what is "out there" can be tailored and exploited to suit any bias. Until someone charts the territory beyond traditional tenure, the debate will continue to be based more on conjecture and prejudice than on information and analysis. As a profession, then, we need a comprehensive guide to the various policy options and an assessment of the strengths and weaknesses each choice presents. In the chapters that follow, we attempt to furnish such a guide.

2.

Institutions
Without Tenure

In 1716, the Harvard Corporation voted to limit the appointment of tutors to no longer than three years unless "continued by a new election." More than a century later, Josiah Quincy, president of Harvard, reflected on the reasons for this decision to introduce term appointments. First of all, he reported, the corporation apparently believed that talented faculty appointed "without limit of time" (a term still used at Harvard) might be lured elsewhere, whereas those without "the ability to become eminent in a profession would be fixed on the college for life." Moreover, term contracts with the option of reappointment were considered an effective means "to excite tutors from time to time to greater care and fidelity in their work" (quoted in Metzger, 1973, pp. 117-118). These two rationales foreshadowed contemporary attacks on tenure. The first translates today as "Those who are good have no need for tenure, and those who have need for tenure are no good" (Metzger, 1973, p. 117). The second suggests, in the language of modern management, that term contracts offer "performance incentives" and "periodic opportunities to demand accountability."

Today, term contracts constitute a commonplace aspect of a conventional tenure system. Nearly all colleges and universities with traditional tenure policies furnish probationary faculty an appointment letter that, in essence, constitutes a contract for services over a specified period of time. A newcomer to the campus and the profession typically receives a one-year or perhaps a two-year contract. Contingent on satisfactory performance and available resources, a series of multiyear contracts follow until the tenure decision. Likewise, part-time, adjunct, and clinical faculty usually receive term appointments as brief as one semester or as long as several years. Term contracts, then, are neither new nor rare. What is novel and unusual within the realm of contemporary academic practices is the use of contracts *to the exclusion of tenure.*

Contract systems that exclude tenure operate on relatively few campuses; and, as the three case studies presented here illustrate, those colleges most likely to eschew tenure altogether are a distinct breed. Such schools tend to be new, small, innovative, and communal. With a resolve to be different and unfettered by past precedents or faculty unions, new colleges are obviously freer to invent and implement novel personnel policies. Each system has a different name and at least one different wrinkle. There are, for example, growth contracts, learning contracts, rolling contracts, and variable-length contracts. The different catchwords aside, all these systems share a common element: an appointment for a specific and limited period of time, with no assurance (or proscription) of continued employment beyond the expiration date of the contract.

While campuses without tenure systems are undeniably unique, the value of the case studies we selected extends to conventional colleges and universities as well. To be sure, no administration or legislature may rescind tenure commitments already conferred; yet some schools may decide that they will no longer award tenure, an action taken by the Virginia Community Colleges in 1972. As a college or university contemplates the substitution hereinafter of term contracts for traditional tenure, the experiences of the three colleges we examined may be instructive. Moreover, many colleges offer term contracts to some faculty members and tenure-track positions to others (see Chapter Four), and more colleges will probably adopt such a policy over the next several years. On campuses where some faculty serve on non-tenure-track term contracts, the successes and setbacks of colleges with contract systems may be quite relevant, and some policies, procedures, and practices employed at these schools may be transferable to other environments.

Hampshire College

Like many four-year colleges without a tenure system, Hampshire College in Amherst, Massachusetts, has a self-proclaimed and widely acknowledged distinctiveness. "Colleges are not all alike," wrote then president Charles Longsworth in the 1976-77 catalog, "but few are as different as Hampshire."* Opened to students in 1970, Hampshire resulted from a planning process started in 1958 by faculty from Amherst, Mount Holyoke, and Smith Colleges and the University of Massachusetts. The planners envisioned the college as a "new departure in higher education," operated in cooperation with the four other schools in the Pioneer Valley. The college would strive to help students achieve independence, self-reliance, and responsibility and be an institution responsive to new ideas, opportunities, and needs. Hampshire has been described by outside observers as a college with "no grades, student-designed examinations, and free choice of courses. Students invented courses, taught some, designed their own majors, and followed their own bents. It was a college in which the central paradigm was to keep the options open" (Grant and Riesman, 1978, p. 359).

---

*Quotations from college handbooks, catalogs, and policy statements are not fully documented because they are too numerous and often undated and unpaged.

The presence of a tenure system did not at first appear inimical to these goals. To the contrary, *The New College Plan,* a blueprint for Hampshire published in 1958, stated: "The college must offer salaries on a scale at least equal to that of any of the sponsoring institutions, tenure in accordance with the joint recommendations of the American Association of University Professors and the Association of American Colleges, substantial help in the purchase of homes or rental of apartments, and regular research and study leaves" (quoted in Patterson and Longsworth, 1966, p. 184). In a refinement of *The New College Plan,* written in 1966, Franklin Patterson (subsequently named Hampshire's first president) and Charles Longsworth (a later president) reaffirmed the need for the terms and conditions of employment enumerated in 1958: "The present leadership of Hampshire cannot improve on what was said eight years ago" (Patterson and Longsworth, 1966, p. 184). The only departure from tradition was a notion that there would be only two faculty ranks: tenured full professors would comprise about one quarter of the faculty; the balance would be assistant professors, young men and women in the early stages of an academic career. There were to be no or very few mid-career associate professors.

Only two years later, the dominant view had shifted—so much so that the academic deans appointed to plan the college's curriculum and structure proposed that faculty appointments be based on renewable contracts rather than a tenure system. After considerable debate, the Hampshire board of trustees, which included the presidents of the four sponsoring institutions, acted favorably on this recommendation. Rather than assert the new policy as a matter of trustee prerogative, the board placed the regulations for appointment and reappointment before the Academic Council, a college-wide governance body comprised of the entire faculty as well as student and staff representatives. The council's constitution, adopted in 1970, incorporated the term contract policy. Thus, the *Faculty Handbook* reads: "No appointment will be without limit of time; each appointment will define a position which terminates according to contract, after a specified time."

Why did Hampshire opt for a contract system? The *Faculty Handbook* offers the most direct answer. "The college proposes to adopt policies and procedures of appointment in fullest possible accord with its principal aims: a search for the best sense of liberal education, a response to the deep concerns of students and faculty, and a commitment to innovation and change. To establish fixed and permanent binding procedures for appointment would be inconsistent with those aims. . . . The basis of this policy [term appointments], which is unusual in academic arrangements, is the unusual nature of the college itself. Hampshire is an experimenting college in its earliest evolving phases. It has not constructed, nor does it expect to construct, a rigid framework of disciplines and curriculum. Continuing review of goals and procedures essential to the progress of the college will be effective only if staff positions are periodically redefined." In other words, to fulfill its special mission as a college responsive and open to change, Hampshire needed flexibility to appoint new faculty or to remove outdated or underutilized faculty. The college did not aim to substitute faculty members merely for the sake of a new face. Rather, Hampshire's architects wanted the opportunity to reclaim and redefine positions so that the curriculum could be fluid and adaptable to student interests. And, of course, without any required courses, student choice controlled enrollment patterns.

The concept of a permanent faculty assigned to departmental slots also seemed conspicuously at odds with the objective of ready adaptability. Symptomatic of this concern, the chapter on "Academic Programs" in *The Making of a College* (Patterson and Longsworth, 1966) begins with the following quote from Kingman Brewster, then president of Yale: "Not only do professors get tenure, but courses, fields, disciplines, and, above all else, departments get tenure. At least a professor is mortal; departments go on forever" (p. 63). Hampshire has neither tenure nor departments.

Beyond the desire to minimize commitments to people and programs, there existed a related apprehension: the extent to which a permanent faculty could, over time, sustain the experimental nature of the college. As Robert Birney, Hampshire's

vice-president (until 1978), later recalled, the college's founders
were afraid that "with the settling in of permanent faculty, the
spirit of innovation would be lost." All too quickly, Hampshire
could become a captive of its creators, a place where innovation
became convention and dare gave way to dogma. Hampshire
hoped that term contracts would counteract that tendency. In a
report on "Employment by Faculty Contract," issued in October 1975, Birney noted that from the outset "an intimate connection was posited between the maintenance of Hampshire
College as an experimenting institution and the contract system.
. . . It was especially appealing, therefore, to test the contract
system as a device for maintaining vitality and a spirit of renewal among the faculty."

The original contract system, operative at Hampshire until 1980, permitted initial appointments of three to five years in
length, depending on the candidate's academic experience, and
reappointments of three, five, or seven years. The reappointment process, which had to be concluded at least seventeen
months before a contract expired, began with an announcement
in the student newspaper and college bulletin that the faculty
member would be considered for reappointment. The announcement invited students, faculty, and staff to submit written comments about the faculty member's performance and promise.
Only signed letters were accepted; and these letters, as well as
all other elements of the dossier, were available to the candidate, the school faculty, appropriate academic administrators,
and the College Committee on Faculty Reappointments and
Promotions. (The CCFRAP consisted of five faculty members,
at least three of them in the senior ranks, elected for two years
by the faculty; two students elected for one year by the students; and the dean of the faculty ex officio.) The candidate
added a personal statement of goals and objectives for the next
contract period. In principle, this statement derived from conversations with the school dean and faculty colleagues about the
college's and school's needs and the particular role the candidate for reappointment might fulfill to meet those needs. After
reviewing the dossier and discussing the candidate, the school
faculty rendered a recommendation, usually by secret ballot;

the school dean prepared a separate appraisal. These recommendations were forwarded to the CCFRAP, which, after due deliberation, submitted a recommendation to the president (with copies to the dean and the candidate). The committee's report had to contain a synopsis of the discussion, a record of the vote, and, where reappointment had been recommended, a suggested contract length. The president reviewed the dossier, consulted other people as appropriate, and made a final decision. Reappointment decisions were based on judgment of professional competence, promise as a teacher and scholar, and value to the college and community. Predictably, Hampshire placed primary emphasis on performance as a teacher.

In the fall of 1975, Birney issued the first of a series of progress reports on the steps Hampshire had taken "to create a high-quality college, using the most promising ideas to define the nature of liberal arts education." The first report revealed that the college had reappointed sixty-seven of seventy-five faculty members (89 percent) between 1970 and 1975. Birney offered four observations about employment by contract at Hampshire: "[The policy] (1) has resulted in low turnover and hence offers fewer prospects of employment to young faculty members seeking appointments; (2) is probably better than the tenure system vis-à-vis retention prospects of young faculty members in their first position; (3) does not seem to have lessened the long-term employment prospects of senior faculty; and (4) has not yet been tested for its relationship to the security of academic freedom."

Although Birney indicated that term contracts appeared "to have the endorsement of faculty, students, and administrators," President Longsworth wondered why the system had failed to generate turnover, a principal policy objective. Perhaps Hampshire's experience with contracts had been too brief to be predictive, or perhaps the combination of self-selection by faculty and careful selection by the college had yielded a faculty perfectly suited to Hampshire's needs. Uncertain about these hypotheses and troubled by the low rate of turnover, Longsworth appointed, in the late spring of 1976, a task force of eight faculty and one student "to define the main issues and problems with the college's policy on faculty employment by contract." In stark contrast to Birney's appraisal, the task force stated: "The most striking and worrisome conclusion from the discussions is that the contract system and other reappointment policies and procedures have the overall impact of lowering the quality of the faculty. Reappointment was felt to be most difficult for both the best and the worst candidates for reappointment. The general tendency, therefore, is not to identify, support, and promote excellence but rather to encourage mediocre performance and favor the middling strata of faculty." Among many recommendations, the task force proposed a greater commitment to faculty development and the adoption of a "tenure-like" decision point followed by longer-term contracts.

Shortly after the task force submitted its report in July 1976, the college's attention shifted to the search for a new president. After a year in office, Adele Simmons, Longsworth's successor, resurrected the report and appointed a number of committees to investigate issues addressed and recommendations offered in the report. Although the original task force had met for only two days, the members of that group evidently grasped both the problems at hand and appropriate remedies, for well over half the recommendations developed by the task force were endorsed by the new committees, ratified by the faculty in 1979, and enacted by the board of trustees in 1980. (Recommendations from a committee on faculty development are still under consideration. The task force urged that deans "be held accountable for the development of the faculty both individually and as a whole.")

The policy modifications, summarized in Table 1, incorporated three principal changes. The first modification lodged primary responsibility for initial reappointment decisions with the appropriate school, since the faculty and dean of a school could now bypass the CCFRAP and transmit recommendations directly to the president. Reviewed for reappointment in the second year of a three-year contract, new faculty scarcely have an opportunity to contribute substantially to the college. Therefore, the faculty and dean of the school were deemed best positioned to evaluate a candidate for a first reappointment. The

Table 1. Hampshire College's Contract System.

	Original	Revised
FIRST APPOINTMENT	Three, four, or five years.	Three years only, with a fourth and terminal year if not reappointed.
FIRST REAPPOINTMENT		
Contract length	Three, five, or seven years.	Four years only, with a fifth and terminal year if not re-appointed.
Review process	School recommendation to CCFRAP; CCFRAP to president; president to board.	School recommendation to president. CCFRAP optional for school and candidate.
SECOND REAPPOINTMENT		
Contract length	Three, five, or seven years.	Ten years or nonreappointment.
Review process	Same as first reappoint-ment.	No change except president will meet with CCFRAP if there is disagreement on reappointment decision.
SUBSEQUENT REAPPOINTMENTS		
Contract length	Three, five, or seven years.	Ten years, or nonreappointment, or three-year proba-tionary contract if candidate has received one or more ten-year contracts. Candidates completing third ten-year contract eligible only for three-year contract.
Review process	Same as for first reappoint-ment.	See second reappointment review process.
CONFIDENTIALITY	Not permitted by school or CCFRAP. President allowed, but not encouraged to re-ceive confidential informa-tion.	Students allowed to submit confidential material at school level, with material summarized for open file. President not allowed to receive confidential material.

change also responded to a perceived tendency for the schools to "kick upstairs" to the CCFRAP borderline cases for an initial reappointment.

The second major revision eliminated the choice of variable-length contracts on reappointment and substituted the option of either nonrenewal or a contract of prescribed length. For the first reappointment, contracts would be for four years with a terminal fifth year as necessary. Requiring a ten-year contract or none at all transformed the second reappointment into a "tenure-like" decision, as the task force had recommended. The faculty's decision to propose ten-year contracts reflected a widespread concern best articulated by a self-described "refugee" from a tenured position at a midwestern university. While critical of conventional tenure, the professor acknowledged that Hampshire was "in danger of perpetuating mediocrity because there is no crunch decision." Even Birney, generally regarded as an advocate of the contract system, remarked: "If some people here were under a tenure system, they would not have a prayer."

At the same time that the task force recommended ten-year contracts as a means to provide greater security for senior faculty, it also cautioned against too much security for faculty in the later stages of a career—"probably around age fifty-four." Understandably, the relatively youthful faculty of a rather new college feared that older faculty would, perhaps, be less vibrant and less amenable to change. In short, old wood would be deadwood. Thus, the faculty proposed and the board agreed that after the third ten-year contract faculty would be eligible only for three-year appointments.

The move to a ten-year cycle also promised to reduce the annual caseload for faculty review committees. The task force had complained that "the current system also has an adverse impact on the faculty's quality by diverting inordinate faculty time away from teaching, advising, scholarship, and other forms of professional development. The involvement of so many faculty in the review of over twenty of their colleagues a year seriously drains important resources from the main educational functions of the college." Longer contracts would lessen the work load for faculty generally and permit the CCFRAP to examine more thoroughly fewer candidates for reappointment.

The third change concerned confidentiality and open files. Whether a perceived or a real threat, the very prospect of retaliation by faculty members inhibited student participation in the review process. Students were understandably reluctant to contribute critical letters of reference to a file open to the candidate lest the faculty member seek revenge in the classroom. Under the new policy, the dean of the school summarizes confidential evaluations submitted by students and places a synopsis of student opinion, without the authors' names, in an open file.

While students were assured greater confidentiality, the faculty were not. In fact, confidentiality for faculty was somewhat reduced. In the past, the president could solicit or the faculty could volunteer confidential information. While few faculty ever communicated directly and privately with the president on reappointments, the opportunity to do so concerned the faculty at large. Thus, the new policy states: "Confidentiality of any kind at the president's level is considered inappropriate and counter to the overall purpose of the reappointment policy." In other words, Hampshire has barred "privileged communication" between the president and a faculty member on a reappointment decision.

With all peer evaluations open to the candidate and to colleagues, many faculty members, quite predictably, tend to submit "sanitized" recommendations or none at all rather than write a negative evaluation. Referees today and candidates for reappointment tomorrow, faculty fear retribution as well as strained relationships. As a result, according to Birney, a file may be composed predominantly "of praise, however faint, while the [faculty] vote shows negative judgments. The school dean may be well aware of serious reservations held about the candidate, but search in vain for an expression of them in the file material itself."

Evergreen State College

In 1966, a Temporary Advisory Council on Public Higher Education in the State of Washington recommended the establishment of a new four-year college. "It was not the intent of the legislature," the council chairman stated, "that this be just another four-year college." In this regard, the legislature had little cause for disappointment. Evergreen (located in Olympia, Washington) is hardly "just another college."

Opened to students in 1971, Evergreen, like Hampshire, emphasizes innovation and flexibility. There are no academic departments: students select a mix of Coordinated Studies (interdisciplinary programs) and Contracted (independent) Study. There are no faculty ranks; all appointments are to the rank of "faculty member" without "hierarchical distinctions in titles." At first, although no longer, there were no permanent deans; the positions rotated among faculty every three years, with each dean assigned responsibility not for a faculty or set of academic programs but for a "desk" with particular tasks and activities, such as recruitment, curriculum, or space and facilities. "If the structure does not support our goals," the *Faculty Manual* assures, "it will be changed, and changed, and changed until it does."

Foremost among Evergreen's goals stands a commitment to "protect, stimulate, support, and reward good teaching." In 1970, a Planning Faculty of some fifteen persons decided to "eschew the tenure system because experience at other institutions had shown that it was difficult to maintain a primary commitment to the continuous improvement of teaching skills under such a system." As one of the college's original faculty members quipped about his experience at institutions with tenure systems, "I have had the honor of counting some of the worst teachers among my best friends." At Evergreen, things would be different. There would be no tenure system to augment the pressure to publish rather than teach or to achieve scholarly repute rather than serve students. Faculty at Evergreen would concentrate on learning the art and craft of teaching and not "on publishing or worrying about not publishing."

Moreover, the original faculty at Evergreen considered tenure antithetical to the college's pedagogical approach. Evergreen was to be characterized by team teaching, coordinated programs, and open dialogue among faculty. Each year, new teams, new "learning communities," would form around an interdisciplinary theme and serve as a basis for Coordinated Studies. Tenure would foment competition on a campus that valued collaboration. How could credit be distributed for a team effort? How could the concepts of community and teamwork flourish within a caste system based on rank and tenure? For these reasons, Evergreen's faculty planners also recommended that the college eschew merit pay.

To the recollection of most early faculty and staff, the board of trustees had some reservations about both the absence of tenure and the absence of merit pay. With no tenure decisions to make at Evergreen, some trustees feared that the board would forfeit a critical opportunity to shape and direct the college's development. Tenure decisions would afford, indeed mandate, regular occasions for the board to discuss and decide matters of academic programs and priorities. The board also worried that a contract system might generate more personnel decisions and therefore more possibilities for litigation or decisions by third parties outside the college community. Despite these concerns, the board was generally persuaded that a contract system would maximize flexibility and conform to the college's espoused values of teamwork and responsiveness to change.

The issue of merit pay was a bit more troublesome. Both the president, Charles McCann, and the board believed the college should be able to reward distinguished service financially. The faculty argued that merit pay violated the principles of egalitarianism. Ultimately, the faculty apparently persuaded the board that a retreat from a merit pay plan would be an appropriate trade-off for the faculty's concession on tenure.

Under Evergreen's contract system, faculty are employed for three-year terms. No contracts are longer, none shorter. Throughout the contract period, faculty maintain a portfolio, "a cumulative . . . intellectual and professional history." The portfolio forms the basis for discussions with the dean relevant to personal growth and development during the contract period. According to college policy, the portfolio shall include:

1. Both the self-evaluation and the dean's evaluation from the previous year.

2. All evaluations of your work by your faculty colleagues.
3. All evaluations you have written about the work of your faculty colleagues.
4. All evaluations of you by staff members.
5. All evaluations you have written about the work of staff members.
6. All evaluations of your work by your students.
7. All evaluations you have written of your students' work, both transcript and unofficial in-house evaluations.
8. Copies of your Coordinated Studies program covenants or group contract agreements between you and your students.
9. Copies of individual contracts you have drawn with students.
10. A thoughtful and critical self-evaluation of the past year's work, based largely on the documentation available in the portfolio. This essay should assess your successes, your low points and disappointments, and the areas in which you hope to make improvements during the following year in your performance within your teaching mode, within the faculty, within the larger Evergreen community, with the non-Evergreen world, within your established fields of expertise, and in exploring virgin academic territories.

As the documentation list for a faculty portfolio suggests, the emphasis at Evergreen, as at Hampshire, rests on broad participation in evaluation. All constituencies evaluate one another.

In the spring of the first and third years, evaluations focus on growth and development. The primary purpose "is to provide reinforcement and continuous feedback in respect to each faculty member's commitment to the teaching arts, the basis on which all Evergreen faculty appointments are made." Thus, portfolio reviews and conversations with the dean are viewed as occasions to identify areas of strength and weakness and to design the means to remedy deficiencies, especially those that might, in the future, serve as grounds for nonreappointment. Shortcomings of that nature must be addressed directly, in the dean's oral and written evaluations of the faculty member.

In the winter of the second year of a contract period, a "Reappointment Evaluation" occurs. Here attention turns toward whether the faculty member has demonstrated sufficient growth and development to warrant another contract. All reappointment decisions must be based exclusively on the following criteria:

1. Willingness and ability to teach in both Coordinated Studies and Contracted Studies.
2. Adherence to a faculty team agreement or covenant.
3. The keeping of a faculty portfolio and participating in annual faculty-dean evaluations.
4. Participation in Coordinated Studies faculty seminars.
5. Willingness and ability to devote at least one third of a three-year contract to the development of interdisciplinary competence.
6. Participation in Evergreen State College activities, in addition to teaching.
7. The completion of student credit reports and student evaluations in a timely fashion in accordance with current academic policies.

If, after reviewing the portfolio, the dean and the president decide not to renew a contract, the faculty member to be terminated must receive a written statement of reasons, and the reasons must not be new. No faculty member, in other words, may be terminated for reasons not cited in the Growth Evaluation for the year prior to the Reappointment Evaluation. When a faculty member appeals a negative decision, the faculty member and the institution each select two members of the college community who, in turn, choose a neutral third party, either from inside or outside the college. The arbiter hears arguments, serves as judge, and renders a decision binding on both parties. Significantly, college regulations stipulate that "the burden of proof lies with the institution." Assured a statement of reasons and due process, and spared the burden of proof, all faculty at

Evergreen enjoy rights normally accorded elsewhere only to tenured faculty or to faculty dismissed in mid-contract.

The preamble to the college's personnel policies notes that "Faculty evaluation at Evergreen should become a pleasure rather than a chore." Whether or not the process proved to be a pleasure, the outcome for nearly all faculty by the fall of 1980 had at least one pleasant result—continued employment. Of 250 faculty reappointment decisions from 1971-72 through 1979-80, only nine contracts (4 percent) were not renewed.

As a new, nontraditional institution, Evergreen—like Hampshire—manifests a set of circumstances that seems to militate against nonrenewal. First, personal growth and development dominate as the ethos and *raison d'être* of the college. By and large, Evergreen presumes that all faculty (and students) possess the wherewithal needed for personal growth and intellectual development. If the college provides the proper environment, adequate resources, and wise counsel, and if the faculty member (or student) makes an earnest effort, self-improvement should result. If not, one must ask whether the institution, the individual, or both have failed. In light of Evergreen's commitment to "self-actualization," there is a natural inclination to search for ways of altering the work environment to tap an individual's potential more effectively. Thus, Evergreen tends more to look for, and work toward, personal growth among current faculty than to look for new faculty.

The college's educational philosophy poses another problem perhaps endemic to institutions marked by interdisciplinary study and interdisciplinary faculty formations. Typically, faculty ply a "trade" and gain an identity as a chemist, sociologist, or the like. Over time at Evergreen, these disciplinary distinctions and identities recede, quite by design. In a sense, the "one-time" historian starts to ask, "Who am I?" At the same time, parties to the reappointment decision begin to ask whether the traditional standards and criteria applied to evaluate a historian are appropriate for the nontraditional role fulfilled by the "one-time" historian at Evergreen. Conventional yardsticks may require conversion tables, and even then the measures may apply only slightly or not at all.

Such special circumstances notwithstanding, the college had become concerned about selectivity by the fall of 1976. President McCann told us: "Sometimes I say to myself, 'My God, we have instant tenure!' " A faculty member we interviewed offered a similar perception: "It was pretty easy to give up tenure because in fact we got instant tenure in another sense." And Edward Kormondy, the vice-president and provost, observed: "Some people are carried and reappointed as the college awaits amplification of criteria for reappointment." A number of ad hoc committees, or what Evergreen terms Disappearing Task Forces (DTF), began examining various aspects of the contract system during that academic year. In the fall of 1977, the college adopted several modifications put forward by the DTFs.

The revised policy maintained the requirement that faculty be given reasons for nonreappointment and that the college carry the burden of proof. Reappointment criteria were clarified and expanded. For the first time, Evergreen explicitly proclaimed excellence as the standard: "The evaluation process, through which reappointment decisions are made, has at its heart a concern for excellence in all aspects of the academic enterprise; and each faculty member will be evaluated in terms of his or her growth as a teacher, colleague, and member of the Evergreen community." Against this standard, the college enumerated thirteen criteria, where there had been seven, to be considered in the evaluation process:

1. Program design and leadership.
2. Seminar leadership.
3. Individual contract design and leadership.
4. Lecturing.
5. Laboratory, studio, or workshop leadership.
6. Timely evaluation writing of students and colleagues.
7. Student counseling and academic advising.
8. Writing and adhering to a faculty covenant (growth contract).
9. Participating in faculty seminars.
10. Keeping a faculty portfolio and participating in the annual faculty-dean evaluations.

11. Demonstrating mastery of one's fields of specialization, willingness and ability to encounter other disciplines, and acceptance of the collaborative assumptions of the coordinated studies mode.
12. Devoting at least one third of a three-year contract to the development of interdisciplinary competence through teaching in the Coordinated Studies mode.
13. Participating in Evergreen activities, such as DTFs, curriculum development and evaluation, and the Evergreen council.

Three additional criteria, applied to faculty on renewed contracts, addressed the special responsibility of experienced faculty to help their colleagues improve as teachers through a variety of means, including a new set of faculty seminars.

The 1977 changes also described the evaluation process more fully. The second-year review was labeled a reappointment evaluation, while the first- and third-year reviews were termed evaluations for improvements. Deans received latitude to spend more time and effort on reappointment reviews and less on evaluations for improvement, whereas previously deans had been required to accord equal weight to all reviews.

Most significantly, at the second-year review, the new policy added a third option to the options of nonrenewal and a three-year reappointment. The college could now offer a one-year extension to the current three-year contract as a means of warning that marginal performance, unless remedied, would likely result in a notice of nonrenewal one year later and termination at the conclusion of the fourth year of service. This so-called reappraisal contract must enumerate the faculty member's performance deficiencies, and these, in turn, must have been cited in the immediately previous annual evaluation.

According to Byron Youtz, who succeeded Kormondy as vice-president and provost in 1977, the option of a reappraisal contract and the more precise language of the changes have contributed to improved evaluations of faculty by deans. Clearer criteria have helped deans identify weaknesses, while the reappraisal option has provided a mechanism for reevaluation of weak faculty a year later rather than three. The availability of a reappraisal contract could, however, moderate the impact of the second-year reappointment evaluation. Where the second-year review once forced a renewal or denial decision, the reappraisal contract now offers a convenient escape clause, a chance to defer the decision another year. Thus, as Hampshire moves toward a definitive decision, a "crunch point," Evergreen appears headed in quite a different direction.

Although no faculty member has been denied reappointment since 1977, five have been "counseled out," and another five (four of whom had been at Evergreen over five years) received reappraisal contracts in January 1979, a year after the policy changes were adopted. Only one of the five received a three-year reappointment the subsequent year; three took the opportunity to resign, and one died. These results, Youtz argues, have laid permanently to rest any lingering worries about instant tenure at Evergreen.

University of Texas at Permian Basin

Few colleges could be more different from Hampshire and Evergreen than the University of Texas at Permian Basin (UTPB). The contrasts begin with appearance. Hampshire and Evergreen occupy lush, green, picture-postcard campuses. The UTPB facilities stand almost lonely on the sandy, barren plains of western Texas between Odessa and Midland. Only oil derricks punctuate the horizon.

Beyond cosmetics are significant substantive differences. UTPB, a part of the University of Texas System, opened to students in 1973 as an upper-division and graduate institution with several professional programs as well as the basic disciplines. Unlike Hampshire and Evergreen, which aspired to be national models of innovation in the liberal arts, UTPB had a more modest, some would say more down-to-earth, purpose: to make state-supported baccalaureate and graduate programs available to a sizable population center which would otherwise be 125 miles from the nearest senior college. Despite these dissimilarities, UTPB also decided to eschew academic tenure, at least as

conventionally defined, although the process, reasons, and results of UTPB's decision differed markedly from those of
Hampshire and Evergreen.

Early in the planning process, a few administrators decided that UTPB would not award traditional tenure. Unlike the
deliberations at Hampshire and Evergreen, no faculty participated in the exploratory discussions or the final decision at
UTPB. In 1970-71, Billy Amstead, the first president, and V. R.
Cardozier, then academic vice-president and now president,
searched for a policy somewhere between what they considered
the equally unacceptable extremes of no tenure and traditional
tenure. "Term tenure" seemed to strike a proper balance. And
so words heretofore not joined in academe were juxtaposed to
establish a shorthand description of a unique personnel policy.

What is term tenure? A simple answer would be that it is
a seven-year contract, but it is not quite that simple. All new
faculty at UTPB start with annual contracts. Normally, after six
years as an assistant professor or after two years as an associate
professor, the faculty member stands for term tenure. (In September 1980, twenty-eight of sixty-two full-time faculty held
term tenure.) Faculty denied term tenure receive a terminal
one-year contract; successful candidates are offered a seven-year
term tenure appointment. As a matter of university policy, "the
prerogatives accompanying term tenure during that seven-year
period are the same as those with conventional tenure." At the
end of the sixth year of term tenure, another evaluation occurs.
With each renewal of term tenure, the faculty member apparently gains added job security, since policy stipulates that "with
each review, there must be increasingly compelling reasons for
not reappointing a faculty member to term tenure."

In the view of Amstead and Cardozier, traditional tenure
systems—even with periodic evaluations—fail to provide an adequate performance incentive and sufficient accountability. The
likelihood of dismissal is too slight, the faculty's sense of security too strong, and the procedure for removal too cumbersome.
Term tenure would provide *periods* of security and privilege,
which could be extended as performance warranted. The foremost effect of term tenure, however, would be to encourage

professional growth among faculty. As Cardozier declared, "While we do not anticipate that the faculty evaluations conducted following one term of tenure, as a basis for reappointment to another term, will result in many faculty terminations, we think that these evaluations will cause faculty members to do a thorough self-appraisal and try to improve their professional performance at least every seven years." Thus, term tenure intends to be more constructive than punitive, more a means of stimulating faculty growth than of increasing faculty turnover. Questions of institutional flexibility were distinctly secondary to questions of intellectual vitality. In contrast to Hampshire and Evergreen, there was little discussion about the institution's capacity to change or respond to new markets.

The administration and board of regents of the University of Texas System did not officially approve term tenure until February 1974, some six months after the first classes had begun. At the same time, the board accepted a contract-based appointment policy for faculty at the University Cancer Center in Houston. In anticipation of the board's action, the AAUP chapter at the University of Texas at Austin had expressed strong reservations about term tenure as a policy and, more significantly, as a precedent. Sensitive to these concerns, the board of regents emphasized term tenure as an experiment limited to UTPB and the Cancer Center. There was no battle plan to establish a beachhead and then launch a broad attack against tenure on the other campuses. Instead, the board merely wished to encourage diversity and experimentation much as critics of statewide systems had suggested.

Although the board did not act until February 1974, the college had started to recruit faculty as early as 1972. Cardozier recalls that when UTPB entered the marketplace, faculty candidates generally expressed enthusiasm for term tenure: "We were in no way handicapped in the recruitment of faculty by our tenure plan." To many candidates employed elsewhere as junior faculty, term tenure offered a potential escape from tenure quotas that had already foreclosed the possibility of a permanent position. Illustrative of the dilemma, an assistant professor of physics admitted, "Term tenure was an inducement to come

here. I could have remained at [a SUNY campus] or accepted a
position at [a flagship land-grant school]. At both places, the
chances for tenure were nil." Most graduate students in search
of a first appointment criticized tenure and decried encounters
with "slothful, outdated old-timers protected too long by tenure." As for the pressure to perform intended by term tenure,
one professor noted, "The biggest sword over my head is not
term tenure; it's the one I put there myself." In all, Cardozier
remembers only four individuals who cited term tenure as a
principal reason for deciding not to accept a position at UTPB.

Enthusiasm for term tenure vanished rather suddenly after
appointment. Once the college opened and faculty gathered as a
whole, opposition mounted. By May 1975, the faculty senate
had passed unanimously a resolution to discontinue both term
tenure and the exclusion of UTPB faculty from the tenure status
accorded faculty members at other component institutions of
the university system. Many faculty contended that term tenure
had never been fully explained or that explanations provided to
some faculty differed from explanations provided to others.
The faculty resented their exclusion from the initial policy formulation and the administration's reluctance to consider reforms
and modifications. More broadly, some faculty felt generally
disenfranchised and removed from policy deliberations. In part
as a means to obtain a greater role in governance, the faculty
formed an AAUP chapter. Even taken together, though, these
concerns were not so significant or so widespread as to produce
the dramatic shift in faculty attitudes toward term tenure. Rather, the primary cause of the turnabout was the institution's
"no-reasons" policy.

The university system views the nonrenewal of term tenure contracts as nonreappointments, much like the nonreappointment of probationary faculty members under traditional
tenure policy. The *Regents' Rules and Regulations* dictates that
no reasons be provided for nonreappointment. Faculty denied
term tenure at any time thus would be offered no explanation
for the decision. From the faculty's viewpoint, this policy effectively eliminates due process, the promise of added security,
and the need for "increasingly compelling reasons" to deny re-

appointment. As long as no reasons need be provided, any reason, however arbitrary or capricious, could motivate nonrenewal and suffice as justification. Nearly all faculty members
expressed a sentiment similar to a comment offered by an asso
ciate professor of literature: "No reasons. That's the key to faculty opposition."

In preparation for an attack on term tenure, the faculty
assembly polled the membership; seventy-five of eighty-two
faculty responded. Was the term tenure policy discussed prior
to appointment? Fifty-four answered yes, thirteen no, and eight
could not recall. Did the university make clear that termination
could occur without "determination of just cause and giving of
reasons"? Seven recalled such an explanation, fifty-eight did
not, and ten could not remember. With respect to policy alternatives, 87 percent preferred some form of continuous tenure;
and, among those faculty, 86 percent supported the notion of
periodic review. With one exception, all respondents favored the
principles of termination for "cause" and a statement of reasons, whatever the other terms and conditions of employment
might be.

On the matter of preemployment "disclosure," Cardozier
reported to the university system's office: "The deans confirmed the fact that all prospective faculty were apprised of the
plan before their appointment. Hence, none was deceived. They
knew that in accepting an appointment at UT–Permian Basin
they were tacitly accepting the term tenure plan."

The shift in faculty opinion about term tenure hardly sur-
prised Cardozier. Indeed, the change seemed understandable
and predictable. "Now that [the faculty] are well settled in a
position in an institution that does not have tenure quotas, they
do not find appealing the idea of regular evaluation and the possibility of termination every seven years after earning initial
term tenure. When the question of lifetime tenure versus term
tenure is placed before a faculty in the faculty senate, I do not
find it strange that they would vote for lifetime tenure. In fact,
I would find it strange that, given the option, any group of faculty would voluntarily choose a seven-year contract over a lifetime tenure contract. It's a normal human reaction."

In the spring of 1976, the faculty senate submitted to the board of regents a petition to abolish term tenure and introduce traditional tenure. The faculty reiterated support for "continuous scrutiny of professional performance by our peers" and a "means for discontinuing . . . truly incompetent teachers." The petition concluded: "We do not seek a lifetime job. The protection we do seek is due process, the establishment of just cause, and a statement of reasons to safeguard against arbitrary and irresponsible termination." The unanimous faculty resolution and the results of the faculty poll notwithstanding, thirteen faculty members presented to the board a formal endorsement of term tenure as "a concept that we found stimulating for our career efforts because it ensures a continued search for excellence in both teaching and research without stultifying." Many of these faculty members would be among the first to be reviewed for term tenure; yet, they stated, "We still find the concept attractive enough to voice our support for it." Cardozier and the university system's administration recommended that, at the very least, the experiment be allowed to run for a full seven-year cycle from the date (1975) the first faculty gained term tenure. Until then, in their judgment, there could be no basis for a thoughtful, empirical evaluation of the policy. Late in 1976, the board denied the petition and reaffirmed its commitment to allow the term tenure experiment to run at least one seven-year cycle before evaluating it.

The review procedure for term tenure (see Table 2) resembles a conventional tenure review process, except for a provision that the faculty review committee interview the candidate. The school deans collectively appoint the review committee, originally drawn from the faculty at large and now limited to faculty with term tenure. All faculty members are evaluated as teachers. Classroom observations by peers and administrators, expressly encouraged as a matter of policy, are not uncommon. Student evaluations are available only to the faculty member unless the instructor chooses to share the results with the committee.

Research activity at UTPB is optional. Faculty may elect to commit up to 20 percent of work load to research. At the

Table 2. Criteria and Procedure for Term Tenure Review at
University of Texas at Permian Basin

Basic Criteria
1. Teaching effectiveness
2. Student advisement
3. Research and other scholarly activity
4. University committee work
5. Contribution to the discipline
6. Leadership effectiveness
7. Assistance to newer faculty
8. Community service
9. Consulting (paid or gratis)

General Procedure
1. Faculty member meets with faculty review committee to present evidence of success in the criterion categories and to answer questions regarding these categories.
2. Faculty member's professional file is reviewed by each committee member.
3. Committee discusses the evidence gathered in the processes above.
4. If it is deemed advisable, individual committee members interview specific persons to clarify or obtain additional data for review.
5. An overall rating is made within the following options:

    A. Research to be considered:
        (1) criteria 1 & 2 to have possible   50 points
             (a point total of 30 necessary)
        (2) criterion 3 total possible   20 points
        (3) criteria 4-9 total possible   30 points
        Total necessary for reappointment   65 points

    B. No research option:
        (1) criteria 1 & 2 to have possible   60 points
             (a minimum of 36 necessary)
        (2) criteria 4-9 total possible   40 points
        Total necessary for reappointment   65 points

6. Committee and school dean submit separate recommendations to the president.

Memo from the tenure review committee to President V. R. Cardozier, July 8, 1980.

time of term tenure review, these faculty must submit evidence
of scholarly productivity. Interestingly, the *Faculty Handbook*
prescribes that "Faculty members who have chosen not to allocate a portion of their time to research shall submit no evidence
of research activity. This is not to suggest that none of them
will engage in research, for it is likely that a number of them
will do so. But if anyone so classified is permitted to submit research evidence, then the stage is set for judging negatively others in the same category who submit no research evidence."
UTPB thus acknowledges that not all faculty possess the same
set of activity interests. Some prefer only teaching, while others
prefer a mix of teaching and research. UTPB allows faculty
some freedom to allocate time in accordance with interests and
then weights evaluation for term tenure in accordance with the
faculty member's decision.

UTPB completed the first seven-year cycle with this system in the summer of 1980. At that time, all four eligible faculty members received a second term tenure appointment. In
1981, twelve more faculty members will be eligible for a term
tenure renewal, after which, President Cardozier reports, the
university will review the system. Although a definitive assessment of term tenure at UTPB may be premature, some observations are warranted now.

First, whatever the "real" story about who told which
faculty candidates what about term tenure, there can be no
doubt that the college and the faculty would have been better
served had all prospective employees been furnished a detailed,
written policy statement. Prior to appointment, faculty might
even have been asked to sign an affidavit to the effect that they
had read and understood the policy. Instead, the university ran
the risk that oral explanations would not always be consistent
and accurate, not because of deliberate deception but as a result of miscommunication or even forgetfulness. Irrespective of
particular policy, *any* institution would be well advised to provide such information to faculty no later than at the time an appointment is offered.

Second, especially in a state system that does not provide
reasons for nonrenewal, term tenure bears a far greater resem-

blance to a seven-year contract than to traditional tenure. Even
the *Regents' Rules and Regulations* conspicuously refers to
UTPB's policy as a seven-year term appointment. The word *tenure* does not appear anywhere with reference to UTPB. We
agree, therefore, with the faculty senate's view that "if the use
of the phrase *term tenure* is not deceptive, it does clearly mis-
represent the nature of term appointment plan." (Thus, we decided to include discussion of term tenure in our analysis of
contracts in Chapter Three.) Hampshire and Evergreen present
no such ambiguities, and faculty suffered no disillusionment
about the nature of the employment arrangement. The only real
difference between a seven-year contract and UTPB's term tenure is the confusion caused by the latter phrase.

Third, while Cardozier recognized that most faculty
members presented with a choice would prefer conventional
tenure to term tenure, none of the college's founders anticipated that faculty opposition would swell so quickly or extend
so widely. Nor did anyone foresee that the policy debate would
dampen enthusiasm, divert energy, and exacerbate the tensions
and anxieties normally associated with the start of a new enterprise. Compared to the experience at Hampshire and Evergreen,
UTPB's decision to adopt a policy before appointing any faculty supports the theory that the degree of participation in the
decision-making process significantly affects the degree of success realized in the implementation of an innovation.

At least from the advantaged perspective of hindsight,
one might have anticipated faculty opposition to a system that
offered little employment protection, no statement of reasons,
and no due process for nonrenewal of term tenure. Indeed, sensitivity to these issues might have been especially keen since
Perry v. *Sindermann* (408 U.S. 593 (1972)), a lawsuit initiated
by a faculty member dismissed from nearby Odessa Junior College, was en route to the United States Supreme Court while
UTPB recruited its first faculty. This suit by a faculty member
with ten consecutive one-year contracts surely signaled the increased concern among faculty for due process and adequate
protection. The case, decided in the faculty member's favor a
year before UTPB opened, suggested the likelihood of consid-

erable resistance to a policy that offered no reasons and no due process.

As a postscript, we should note that in 1979 the AAUP censured UTPB on two counts. First, it alleged that the university had improperly dismissed two faculty members on the grounds of financial exigency "without having shown that there were no other steps less severe than termination of these appointments for alleviating the institution's financial situation." Second, the investigating committee also alleged that the university had violated the academic freedom of an associate professor denied term tenure in 1977 because of "the administration's displeasure with his outspoken role in university service." In both cases, the committee objected to the lack of adequate due process. While the AAUP did not censure UTPB expressly for adopting term tenure, it charged that the policy, retained "over the overwhelming opposition of the faculty and administered as it has been, is fundamentally incompatible with the standards for academic freedom and tenure that are set forth in the 1940 *Statement of Principles*" (American Association of University Professors, 1979, p. 249).

The AAUP, of course, believes that any deviation from its 1940 statement endangers the sanctity of academic tenure and academic freedom and thereby imperils the very essence of the academic profession. At Hampshire and Evergreen, the faculty and the administration and at UTPB the administration and some faculty believe otherwise.

3.

Life
Without Tenure

⌐╜╜╜⌐

The three colleges examined in Chapter Two eschew tenure and offer contracts for appointments of limited duration. What can we conclude about the effects and effectiveness of such a policy? Some of the conclusions presented here are well documented; others are more speculative, most often because of the absence of sufficient data that relate policy to outcome. Institutions with term contracts, like most other colleges and universities, formulate, maintain, and alter personnel policies with vague objectives in mind and few appropriate data in hand (Cohen and March, 1974).

None of the institutions we visited or studied, Hampshire excepted in part, established any systematic means to monitor or measure the effects of a contract system on the college. (We speak here of simple evaluation and not of some sophisticated social science research paradigm.) In several instances, for example, data on renewal and turnover rates were assembled for the first time when we requested the information. Prospective faculty are not polled on the extent to which the presence of a contract system influences the decision to accept or decline an offer of appointment. Surveys to discover the attitudes and experiences of incumbent faculty are few and most often undertaken through faculty initiative. No school we examined charts the rate at which individual courses or degree programs are substantially revised or replaced, although these indexes (plus others cited in Chapter Ten) would provide some measure of institutional flexibility, purportedly one of the policy objectives. Almost everyone has a feel, a sense, an opinion, or an impression. Almost no one has data. Necessarily, therefore, many of the conclusions and observations we present draw on other sources —interviews, insights, and policy analysis—which, we trust, contribute to informed judgments.

Effects on Faculty Turnover

Contract systems do not produce significant faculty turnover as a result of nonreappointments.

From 1970 through 1979, Hampshire College renewed 159 of 187 contracts (85 percent); from 1971-72 through 1979-80, Evergreen renewed 241 of 250 contracts (96 percent); UTPB would not furnish comparable data. National data confirm the experiences of Hampshire and Evergreen: nearly all institutions renew nearly all contracts. A 1972 survey by the American Council on Education (El-Khawas and Furniss, 1974) found that 87 percent of the institutions with contract systems renewed at least nine of every ten contracts that expired in 1971. For the academic year 1973-74, 93 percent of the institutions renewed at least nine of every ten contracts. (About one third of all two-year colleges and 6 percent of all four-year colleges had contract systems in 1973-74. Thus, the data on rate of renewal reflect largely the experiences of junior and community colleges.) By contrast, in 1973-74, only one of every two colleges with a tenure system awarded tenure to at least eight of every ten candidates, and 23 percent of the institutions surveyed tenured fewer than six of every ten candidates.

The data on term contracts do not reflect "forced resignations" prior to reappointment decisions, nor do the data on tenure success rates reflect terminations or "forced resignations" prior to the tenure decision. To date, thirty faculty members at Evergreen and sixteen at Hampshire have resigned. Since the colleges do not record the reasons for resignations, we cannot determine the number of forced or prompted resignations. Yet, even if *all* these resignations were considered involuntary (certainly a gross overestimation) and therefore treated as nonreappointments, the rate of renewal would still be 78 percent at Hampshire and 86 percent at Evergreen. In 1973, the AAUP/AAC Commission on Academic Tenure (Keast Commission) noted that faculty contracts "seem to be renewed almost as a matter of course" (p. 12). Some eight years later, the commission's statement appears to be equally valid.

It would be easy to make too much of nonrenewal rates for contract systems, much as academicians tend to overemphasize tenure ratios on campuses with tenure systems. Nonrenewal rates for contract systems assume disproportionate significance for two reasons. First, where few hard data exist, analysts focus on what data there are. Second, and perhaps more important, contract systems were conceived and advertised as an effective means to ensure turnover. Contracts would offer at regular intervals opportunities to exercise discretion, cut losses, minimize long-term commitments, and maximize institutional flexibility. Nearly all proponents of a contract system stress these advantages, which, for the most part, derive from the opportunity to end the employment of one professor in order to appoint another. In that way, the contract system would avoid many of the drawbacks of conventional tenure.

Contracts unquestionably present the occasion to exercise discretion and make personnel changes; yet, equally clearly, not many institutions exercise the option to do so. Why not? The case studies suggest some reasons, such as open files and fear of retribution. There are, however, some additional explanations.

False Expectations of Growth. Hampshire, Evergreen, and UTPB were conceived in the late 1960s and early 1970s. At the time, especially at new colleges, there was a vision of growth and expansion. There was a presumption that from time to time faculty would elect to leave the institution for a more attractive appointment elsewhere. Indeed, there existed an expectation that faculty would choose *among* new opportunities. Thus, voluntary attrition, as well as and surely as much as non-reappointments, would foster turnover. Decisions not to renew, moreover, would be less difficult to render and easier to accept, for the sting of nonreappointment would be salved by a ready invitation to join another faculty.

At both Hampshire and Evergreen, faculty and staff recognize in retrospect that the contract system was forged as policy in the light of market conditions of the past rather than those of the future. With an optimism and evangelism characteristic of Hampshire, an early arrival among the faculty recalled: "We assumed that people would have other job opportunities and that they would move on to spread innovation across other colleges." At Evergreen, there was also an assumption that after five or six years faculty would "self-select out," exhausted by such an intense educational experiment. Now, one professor laments, "Those who want to leave can't, particularly the white males."

A Shared Burden of Proof. Consistent with the college's Gestalt, the term contract policies we inspected place a premium on professional growth and development. At least tacitly, the campus community assumes that there will be professional development and that the college will contribute both recommendations and resources to promote that growth. Merely to identify weaknesses and offer no suggestions or support for remediation would be contrary to the college's general philosophy. The institution must share with the professor the burden of faculty development. There follows logically a tendency to ask whether the individual or the institution should bear primary responsibility for someone's failure to develop at a satisfactory pace. At Evergreen, as an example, some deans attributed lack of adequate progress largely to "the fact that the faculty-help program has not worked well" or to "the fact that the college has not fulfilled its obligation to faculty." They worried that Evergreen had not yet decided on a clear mission or communicated to faculty "what it's really about." In that context, how could faculty possibly develop a coherent growth plan? As one professor asked, "How do you see, let alone evaluate, in a fog?" Under conventional tenure systems, institutions usually bear fewer of these burdens and tend not to ask on a case-by-case basis whether the college has failed the faculty member. More likely, the reverse question would be posed: Has the faculty member failed the college?

Elusive Evaluations. The very nature of these institutions confounds the task of faculty evaluation. Although UTPB has a research option, faculty at all three schools are expected, above all else, to teach and advise students. These crafts have traditionally been considered more difficult to assess than scholarship. To complicate the matter, faculty, at Hampshire and Evergreen particularly, "try new things"—new approaches and new courses, often outside the professor's home discipline. There is a consensus on these campuses that such experiments need time to unfold and require new means of assessment. Consequently, these schools encounter all the problems normally associated with the evaluation of teaching and then some, although the additional difficulties emanate more from questions of educational philosophy than from the particular personnel policy.

Lack of Evidence and Support. As currently practiced, term contract systems do not foster the production of evidentiary documentation to defend and sustain nonrenewal decisions. Given the short-term nature of term contracts, the use of open files, and the opportunity for the judged to eventually evaluate the judges, there is little reason to believe that faculty will regularly offer critical commentaries about candidates for reappointment. To do so would be to engender hostility and to court retaliation. When dossiers contain primarily "sanitized" letters of reference and ambivalent evaluations, decision makers may be understandably chary about denying reappointment, especially where the institutional ethos emphasizes opportunities for growth and development. In some ways, then, contract systems may not suit fainthearted faculty and administrators. As a rule, when there are bullets to be bitten, administrators will be dining alone on a steady diet of reappointment decisions. Without much critical evidence or substantial faculty concurrence, even administrators determined to exercise quality control may be unable to say "no" to "just one more contract." If decision makers cannot say "no," it hardly matters how many opportunities a policy affords them to say so.

Allure of Incrementalism. The very nature of a renewal decision invites a decision to renew. Short-term appointments are short-term risks that most decision makers are inclined to take. Where there have been signs of incremental progress, why not see what another three to five years will bring, and another three to five years after that, and so on. Eventually, a series of short-term contracts evolve into a long-term commitment. If contracts permit mistakes to be easily undone, why not risk a mistake? Thus, at one of the schools we visited, a faculty member was reappointed on the premise that he would resign as soon as he obtained a position elsewhere. The purpose of the reappointment was to provide the faculty member with a legitimate base of operation to seek new employment. The faculty member never resigned, which led the provost to comment, "Now we're stuck with him for another three years. This would never happen under a tenure system. Tougher decisions are easier to get in a tenure system because of the finality of the decisions."

The same phenomenon occurs among middle managers at most colleges and universities. For the most part, administrators such as registrars, comptrollers, and counselors hold annual or short-term contracts. Despite the opportunity to make changes, data from several studies suggest that renewals are routine and longevity among office directors rather commonplace. In a study of collegiate middle managers, Scott (1978, p. 14) reports: "It is not uncommon when interviewing collegiate middle managers to find a director of an office who has served for twenty years or more in the same position, during which time his office's responsibilities have grown and expanded. . . . A variation of the 'Peter Principle' takes place: the person appointed head of a small service office stays at its head even while it grows in size and complexity; the required skills change but the same person remains director."

From the institutions and data we examined, we are persuaded that, whatever other virtues contract systems may offer, they will not—at least, as they are now operated—generate substantial or even modest turnover through nonrenewals. Indeed, as faculty members at Hampshire, Evergreen, UTPB, and similar schools accumulate more years of loyal service to the institution and as personal and professional relationships solidify, decisions to dismiss undoubtedly will be more difficult and even less common. At Hampshire, nonreappointments dropped from 14 percent at the conclusion of the first contract period to 6 percent at the conclusion of the second contract period. (Resignations increased from 5.6 percent to 17 percent.) If nonreappointments are scarce now, how much more scarce will such actions be when the decision concerns "seasoned veterans" who have given the institution "the best years of their lives"? Where will they go? What will they do, especially in an oversupplied market? We suspect that these journeymen will be allowed to stay. In an industry where employees are normally released or tenured after five or six years, the pressure will be enormous to follow suit, to renew contracts all but automatically after a similar "probationary period." If some of the pioneers at Hampshire, Evergreen, and UTPB are denied reappointment to a third or fourth contract, we will have been mistaken.

Effects on Innovation

A causal relationship, either positive or negative, between term contracts and innovation cannot be ascertained from the available data.

Hampshire, Evergreen, and, to a lesser extent, UTPB are educationally innovative institutions. Are they innovative *because of* term contracts, *despite* term contracts, or for reasons *unrelated to* term contracts? These three colleges posited and presumed that term contracts would promote experimentation. On the other hand, a popular academic axiom holds that a long-term commitment (namely, tenure), a long-range perspective, and a sense of security are prerequisites to the pursuit and implementation of new ideas—in other words, that permanence more than turnover stimulates innovation and experimentation. The proposition was well stated by the Harvard University Committee on Governance (1971, p. 17):

> Most of the major experimental changes in Harvard education—the "case system" at the law and business schools, the interdisciplinary programs such as Comparative Literature and American Civilization in the Graduate School of Arts and Sciences, and a long series of developments in the college, from the creation of History and Literature as an undergraduate interdisciplinary honors concentration to the formulation and launching of General Education—have derived from the thinking, the time, and the energies of *tenured* faculty members. May it not be fact that tenure—or, to use the crasser term, "job security,"—is one of the major stimuli to experimentation, providing a faculty member, as it does, the freedom to leave his standard arena of endeavor when he feels inspired to do so, without fear for the effect on his saleable professional reputation?

In an environment dramatically different from Harvard, Penina Glazer, the dean of the faculty at Hampshire in 1978, expressed a similar opinion, not as an endorsement of tenure but as an argument for ten-year contracts. Glazer suggested that "Innovation really rests on a core of stable, experienced, and semipermanent faculty."

Less favorably disposed to contracts or compromise, the Keast Commission concluded that "contract arrangements do not necessarily conduce to innovation" (AAUP/AAC Commission on Academic Tenure, 1973, p. 18). Nor, we would add, does tenure necessarily foster change. While we cannot with confidence assert much more than that, the commission apparently can. After suggesting that innovation at contract schools frequently represents gimmickry and faddism, the commission declared, "There is no evidence that *valuable* innovations in education are most likely to come from those whose positions in the institution are in jeopardy" (p. 18; emphasis added). More often, the commission noted, as the Harvard Committee had, that profound and enduring change results from the ideas and efforts of a core of permanent faculty.

We regard the commission's conclusions as flawed, for two reasons. First, the very data the commission cites on rates of renewal make plain that few faculty under contract are, in fact, in jeopardy. Second, the literature on turnover and innovation does not support a simplistic conclusion about the interrelationship of these phenomena. The data will support neither a positive nor a negative linear relationship, although the weight of evidence tends to support the notion that some turnover does foster innovation to a degree. In a review of studies of turnover, Price (1977, p. 106) concluded that "increases in turnover promote increases in innovation *up to a point*. When this point is reached, increases in turnover promote no additional increments in innovation. In other words, if there is a low or medium amount of turnover, innovation is the likely result. However, if turnover is high, innovation is not likely to result." Does turnover enhance organizational effectiveness? After examining the literature on that aspect of turnover, Price determined that "turnover generally has a basically negative impact on effectiveness" (p. 119).

The paradox may be, then, that some new blood promotes change, while too much new blood promotes chaos or at least hinders organizational effectiveness. How much is too much remains the question. Here Price's final words on the matter of innovation are instructive: "Systematic research, especially focusing on the differential result of degrees of turnover, is required to settle the issue" (p. 107). In short, after an exhaustive analysis of studies on turnover and change, Price cannot be definitive; nor can we; nor should the Keast Commission. Researchers and theoreticians do not yet know enough about the complex interrelationships between innovation and turnover or innovation and employment security for anyone to proclaim authoritatively that tenure will produce more change than term contracts or vice versa.

Effects on Faculty Morale and Performance

A causal relationship, either positive or negative, between term contracts and faculty morale or between term contracts and faculty performance cannot be ascertained from available data.

As with the relationship between term contracts and innovation, the interactions between term appointments and faculty morale or faculty performance are too complex and the data are too scanty to support definitive statements. On the matter of faculty morale, the Keast Commission determined that "Prolonged exposure to the uncertainties of contract renewal and all that goes with it seems likely to have damaging effects on faculty morale and performance. . . . The human costs of such an arrangement are incalculable" (AAUP/AAC Commission on Faculty Tenure, 1973, p. 17). As evidence, the commission cites unspecified "investigations" that document the anxiety inherent to probationary periods. Since term contracts are, by the commission's definition, endless probationary periods, logic dictates that the anxiety level will reach unbearable levels. Qualifiers such as "seems likely to" remove absoluteness from the commission's statement. Nevertheless, its comments and conclusions convey the impression that term contracts will have a catastrophic affect on faculty morale. We are reluctant to accept its conclusion or to make a comparably decisive statement. The state of faculty morale could be empirically tested if faculty members were asked to respond to a survey instrument such as the Institutional Functioning Inventory (IFI), which assesses the general climate, or "institutional esprit," on campus. IFI profiles from colleges with tenure and colleges with term contracts could be compared. Even then, however, causality would be difficult to demonstrate.

Insofar as impressions do count, faculty morale on campuses with term contracts seemed to us no better and no worse than morale at other new colleges with tenure systems. The faculty members we encountered at Hampshire, Evergreen, and UTPB did not appear to be distraught from the pains of "prolonged uncertainties." Perhaps these colleges are too new, or perhaps the faculty derive psychological comfort from the statistical probability of reappointment. Even at UTPB, where low morale and high anxiety were most evident, the central issues were mistrust and "a heavy-handed administration," and not term tenure. Furthermore, the most apprehensive faculty members we met over the course of our travels were junior faculty with little or no chance for tenure. Many of these faculty members would have welcomed an opportunity to serve under term contracts rather than confront unemployment or underemployment. In any case, we regard the commission's characterization of the psychological distress and demoralization caused by term contracts as hyperbolic and unsubstantiated. The faculties we observed on campuses without tenure were not "reduced to dependence and docility"—conditions that the commission believes endemic to term contracts. To the contrary, these faculties were vibrant, almost hyperactive, and critical, almost fiesty.

Beyond generalizations about the pall that term contracts cast, the commission intimates a negative correlation between term contracts and effective instruction: "It is not reasonable to believe that contract arrangements can be expected, in and of themselves, to produce better teaching or greater devotion to it" (p. 17). Of course, as the commission acknowledges, tenure "in and of itself" offers no guarantees either: "There will be good teachers as well as poor teachers under the contract system or any other system." Term contracts, however, may have an unusually inimical effect on teaching, the commission contends, to the degree that faculty with such tenuous appointments divert time, energy, and attention to the pursuit of new positions and professional status at the expense of students and institutional goals. (Curiously, as described in Chapter Six, the same argument—concerning the "mobility mindedness" of probationary faculty faced with the imposition of a tenure quota—surfaced at Colgate University. The problem hardly seems indigenous to contract systems.)

In our view, the commission makes too sharp a distinction between activities designed to enhance one's marketability and activities designed to enhance an institution. There may be more compatibility than conflict. Nothing quite seems to strengthen one's value on the home campus as much as a few offers to move elsewhere. More important, we found no evidence to sustain the commission's allegation. Instead, many faculty at Hampshire and Evergreen appeared to be excessively concerned with students, at the expense of scholarly research and professional development. Meanwhile, research universities struggle with policies and procedures to limit the activities of faculty overcommitted to clients and colleagues and unavailable to students.

Do faculty at colleges with contracts perform better than colleagues on campuses with tenure systems? Would the same individual do any better or worse under one policy or the other? Unlike the commission, we do not have ready answers. We are, in fact, reluctant even to intimate that faculty will perform better (or worse) under a contract than under tenure. We are prepared, however, to draw inferences and offer observations about the effect of contracts on certain circumstances *related* to performance:

Perspective. In the main, the faculty we interviewed at Hampshire, Evergreen, and UTPB focused on short-range plans to be well positioned for contract renewal. The question "What do I need to do to make the case for reappointment?" haunts the faculty member on a term contract, much as the question "What do I need to do to achieve tenure?" haunts the probationary faculty member, except that the latter obsession ends with a tenure decision after some six or seven years. With a few notable exceptions, there was little talk on campuses with term contracts about the long term or about individual development within the larger context of institutional development. In the view of the dean of the college, Hampshire can neither expect nor demand that faculty assume an institutional perspective: "Only a long-range commitment allows a 'call' on faculty at any time; only then is a faculty member's long-term development tied to the college's long-term development." A faculty task force at Hampshire offered a similar opinion: "Faculty reappointments are considered individually, each on its own merit. Concern for faculty rights and prerogatives weigh heavily in the deliberations. This, however, often makes it difficult to consider the particular reappointment either in comparative terms or in relation to overall college interests in program development or a particular definition of responsibilities."

Ironically, of course, administrators at other colleges and universities lament that, once tenured, faculty are "untouchable" and impervious to reason or persuasion. We are tempted to conclude that, irrespective of particular personnel policies, the very nature of the profession militates against "team play" and bureaucratic conformity. After all, most colleges and universities actively encourage open debate and vigorous dissent, even about institutional goals. Furthermore, most faculty members regard themselves as self-employed professionals within the harbor of an amorphous organization. Loyalties rest with a discipline and a profession more than with an institution. Neither a tenure system nor a term contract system inherently promotes greater harmony between individual agendas and long-range institutional goals. At Hampshire and Evergreen, the faculty unquestionably strive to be innovative, interdisciplinary, and student oriented—behaviors that conform to explicit institutional aims. Whether peer group or organizational pressure, without the carrot and stick of reappointment, would achieve the same results cannot be proved. At best, the "threat" of nonrenewal seems of marginal value, since few faculty are, in fact, ever denied reappointment.

Communication. At the very least, faculty growth contracts force professors to set goals, however modest or vague. Likewise, the mandate to extend or terminate contracts compels the college to consider and, ideally, to respond to these plans. Under the best of circumstances, such as at Hampshire, the formulation of growth contracts precipitates dialogues among faculty and between faculty and administrators; as a consequence, members of the campus community have some familiarity with one another's interests, activities, and ambitions. We believe that the preparation of growth contracts provides an opportunity, even an excuse, for deans and faculty members to hold conversations and reach agreements that might not otherwise occur. (Growth contracts and conventional tenure are not incompatible; see Coe College, Chapter Eight.)

Evaluation. Term contracts also promote more frequent communication about performance, a practice recommended by nearly all students of personnel administration. Whereas classical tenure policies invite drift and neglect after the tenure decision, term contracts demand periodic attention to performance evaluation. Although supervisors should, as a matter of course, communicate regularly with subordinates about performance, academic administrators, seldom trained to be "supervisors," may regard performance reviews as an unwelcome and uncomfortable chore to be avoided or summarily discharged. Term contracts compel performance reviews, however cursory or perfunctory. If practice makes perfect, the quality of the reviews should improve. Furthermore, if organizational theorists are correct about the positive relationship between performance and evaluation, the quality of the faculty's work should also improve.

Contrary to the Keast Commission, we uncovered no evidence that term contracts are detrimental to performance or decidedly inferior to tenure systems as a means to foster productive and effective faculty. On the other hand, we cannot affirm that faculty under term contracts will perform better than faculty under tenure systems, despite claims by advocates of term contracts that the threat of nonreappointment acts as a powerful incentive for faculty to improve. As far as we can determine, neither policy has any proven, consequential effects on faculty performance per se. Although many administrators, legislators, and trustees "know" otherwise, no research corroborates the "truism" that the productivity of faculty as scholars and the effectiveness of faculty as teachers decline after tenure (Blackburn, 1972). In any event, with or without the accoutrement of tenure, we would encourage faculty and administrators to establish goals, perhaps for a three- to five-year period, and to review performance regularly, since a periodic estimation of progress toward stated objectives contributes to a sense of achievement.

In that respect, growth contracts fall well within the boundaries of sound practice, although far short of a certain boon
(or detriment) to faculty effectiveness.

Effects on Academic Freedom

*Academic freedom can be and has been provided at col-
leges with term contract systems.*

Historically, the concepts of academic tenure and academic freedom have, almost as a matter of dogma, been inextricably linked. Academic freedom has three essential components: (1) the freedom to conduct and publish research, (2)
the freedom to teach and discuss appropriate subject matters
without introducing irrelevant issues, and (3) the freedom to
speak or write as a citizen without speaking on behalf of the
institution (unless authorized to do so). In order to obtain and
enjoy academic freedom, traditionalists assert, faculty must be
armed with the economic security and procedural protections
that only tenure can afford. Colleges with contract systems believe otherwise.

AAUP policy requires an internal appeal procedure with
the fullest measure of due process whenever a tenured faculty
member alleges that his dismissal violated the principles of academic freedom. Minimally, there would be a statement of reasons, service of notice, a hearing before a faculty committee,
right to counsel, a verbatim record, right to discovery, and right
to cross-examination. The burden of proof would rest with the
institution, and any actions by the president contrary to the
committee's recommendations would be accompanied by a
written statement of reasons to the faculty member and the
committee.

For probationary faculty, the matter becomes more prob-
lematic, as a simple syllogism demonstrates:

Academic freedom is essential to the practice of the profession.
Academic tenure is essential to the maintenance of academic freedom.

Therefore, untenured faculty cannot practice the profession.

To avoid that dilemma, the AAUP recommends that any probationary faculty member, persuaded that nonrenewal entailed a
violation of academic freedom, be afforded the opportunity to
make the case informally before a faculty committee. Should
informal methods fail to resolve the case, the faculty member
may utilize the same adjudicatory machinery available to tenured faculty, except that the burden of proof would fall on the
faculty member. If the grievant establishes a prima facie case,
then the institution must present evidence to justify the nonrenewal decision. In addition to that formal protection, tenure's
advocates purport that a secure, independent, and vigilant coterie of tenured faculty will not abide threats to or violations of
the academic freedom of untenured colleagues. Hence, as long
as some faculty are tenured, all faculty are protected.

Against the backdrop of AAUP policy, we can pose the
threshold question: Can academic freedom exist without academic tenure? If academic freedom translates as due process, we
believe that all the procedural protections afforded tenured faculty can be made available to faculty on term contracts. Were
term appointments and academic freedom inherently incompatible, the AAUP, by definition, could not fashion a policy to
protect probationary faculty against alleged violations, since
probationary faculty are faculty on term contracts.

At Hampshire and Evergreen, faculty members enjoy at
least as much protection as colleagues at institutions with conventional tenure systems. The rights and privileges of academic
freedom extend equally to all faculty without respect to rank or
tenure status. As the Evergreen *Handbook* proclaims: "We believe that the principles governing academic freedom and faculty responsibility at Evergreen must apply to all members of
the faculty and not just to senior members in some instances
and junior members in other instances." In addition, the protection against violations of academic freedom commences with
appointment at Hampshire and Evergreen; faculty need not fulfill a probationary period or achieve tenure to obtain a fuller
measure of protection. At UTPB, faculty are not accorded the

rights and privileges of tenure until appointed to term tenure. Substantively, the protections do not differ materially from standard AAUP policy. Indeed, both Hampshire and Evergreen explicitly subscribe to the principles embodied in the 1940 AAUP statement. Without tenured faculties, the procedures to ensure academic freedom do, of course, differ from the AAUP's prescriptions.

Hampshire originally established an external advisory council, the Council for Academic Freedom, as a "final arbiter to hear evidence and pass judgment on charges of alleged violations of academic freedom by the college." Comprised of scholars from other institutions, the council was to consider evidence presented by both parties and then render a final and binding determination. In the only case where a faculty member denied reappointment alleged a violation of academic freedom, the complaint never reached the council, since an internal appeals committee rejected the claim. Hampshire recently changed review procedures, in part to restrict the extent to which an appeal board could obligate the college to retain or compensate a successful plaintiff. Under the new system, academic freedom disputes not resolved by an intramural board may be appealed to a panel of faculty, three insiders and two outsiders selected from among a pool of four insiders and three outsiders. The outsiders are elected by the faculty senate from among nominations offered by the faculty at large. The appeals process includes all the elements of due process recommended by the AAUP. Decisions by the panel are reviewed by the board of trustees only when the award exceeds the complainant's salary or extends a contract for more than three years. The board, which may not hear new evidence or conduct an independent investigation, may revise the decision only if it finds that the decision "is not supported by substantial evidence . . . or is incorrect in the interpretation of the duties, privileges, and rights of the parties."

As we saw in the preceding chapter, Evergreen bears the burden of proof on nonreappointments, whether or not academic freedom is at issue. It, too, utilizes an appeal procedure that permits a neutral third party to render a binding decision.

Hampshire and Evergreen incontrovertibly dispel the no-

tion that academic freedom somehow cannot exist without academic tenure. Both colleges respect and protect academic freedom as well as institutions with conventional tenure policies do.
Neither college has even a slightly blemished record on the matter. Faculty have been free to teach, conduct research, and express opinions on issues from the Vietnam War to investments
in South Africa without any attempts by the institution to
exercise prior restraint or to impose sanctions after the fact.
While academic tenure certainly represents one time-honored
means to provide academic freedom, we must lay aside the unfounded notion that there are no other equally effective ways
to accomplish the same purpose. Despite all the ominous admonitions of tenure's defenders, most particularly the AAUP,
the fact remains that academic freedom can survive apart from
tenure and together with term contracts.

The Keast Commission properly notes that many institutions with term contracts do not have established appeal procedures to contest nonrenewals and thereby jeopardize academic
freedom. Most colleges without appeal procedures, however,
are within the public sector, where state statutes frequently provide recourse for dismissal. Moreover, where an employee's liberty or property interests are at stake, a state-supported school
must under the federal Constitution furnish due process anyway
(Edwards and Nordin, 1979; Kaplin, 1978). To suggest, therefore, as the Keast Commission does, that faculty at colleges
with term contracts lack adequate protection skews the argument and creates the mistaken impression that academic freedom and term contracts are mutually exclusive concepts. Academic freedom can be provided by policies linked to tenure, by
policies linked to term contracts, by negotiated agreements, or
by legislation. Institutions inclined to experiment with term contracts would be ill advised to forgo such a policy change solely on
the grounds that academic freedom could not be assured.

Effects on Time Commitments

Term contract systems predicated on faculty growth plans
are unlikely to be practicable at most colleges and universities.
Even though few faculty members at schools with term

contract systems are ever denied reappointment, the process still consumes a great deal of time, engages a good many people, and generates a substantial volume of material. Among Hampshire, Evergreen, and UTPB, none has a full-time faculty larger than 120. Yet even at these smaller schools, faculty and staff alike complain persistently about the effort required and the work load generated by the contract system. Faculty are overburdened as both referees and reviewers. "The cost to the system in time," observed a faculty member at Hampshire, "is almost not worth the price," a comment frequently echoed on all three campuses. Thus, among other reasons, Hampshire adopted ten-year contracts to reduce the number of decisions each year.

None of the persons we interviewed believed that the contract system, as practiced at these colleges, would work in a larger environment. And, indeed, among four-year colleges, only smaller schools have adopted the policy. Evergreen's first president reckoned the upper limit to be a full-time faculty of 150. While we cannot set a precise limit, that estimate seems reasonable. Reviewing and negotiating short-term contracts, especially growth contracts, can easily overload the system. Faculty work time can be extended or engulfed by obligations to write letters, review portfolios, and make recommendations. At the level of senior managers, where only one dean or provost serves irrespective of the number of faculty, the burdens can be even heavier if the reviews are to be comprehensive and considered.

Tenure decisions also require time, energy, and attention. Unlike tenure decisions, however, growth contracts involve an individually negotiated plan, and a similar decision about the same person recurs usually somewhere between every three to ten years. The process could consume a large university. If the University of Southern California, for example, placed everyone on five-year appointments, there would be, on the average, three hundred reviews a year, plus whatever searches voluntary attrition necessitated. At Penn State, the annual caseload could reach twenty-five contracts for a department head, seventy contracts for a dean, and up to five hundred contracts for the provost and the president. In some ways, term contracts make the bureaucratic burdens of tenure appear light.

The feasibility of growth contracts may also be limited by the special burdens the policy imposes on an institution to provide faculty with ample opportunities for professional growth and development. To be effective, growth contracts require an institutional commitment to professional development, both as a matter of philosophy and as a matter of practicality. In a damnation of the tenure system and an endorsement of term contracts as an alternative, Drucker (1977, p. 24), the renowned management consultant, suggests that academic institutions need to emulate "what is now standard practice in all other areas of employment in the knowledge industry"; that is, they need to provide opportunities for "systematic self-development of the professional in view of his or her own desires and abilities and in view of the needs and opportunities of the profession, employer, and market." In somewhat the same vein, Hampshire College's *Faculty Handbook* stresses the need for an adequate leave policy: "Hampshire has not adopted a tenure policy for its faculty for a number of reasons. It is expected that, eventually, many faculty will move on to other institutions. In order to make that possible, especially in today's shrinking market, faculty must have currency among their peers at other institutions. Such currency is rarely obtained by teaching experience and expertise, regardless of how innovative. That is a proven reality of the academic world. Given Hampshire's policy, the college has a special responsibility to faculty in this regard. . . . The college must provide faculty members with the time to pursue their own work, whatever that work may be. . . . That time is neither a right nor a privilege, it is a necessity." After two years, faculty are eligible for a semester's leave at full pay; after another two years, faculty are eligible for another leave, although no one may receive more than one full year of paid leave per ten years of employment. Approximately 20 percent of Hampshire's faculty are on sabbatical or unpaid leave in a given year. (Webster College, discussed in Chapter Five, adopted a generous sabbatical policy as an incentive for faculty to accept term appointments rather than tenure-track positions.)

Many colleges and universities may lack the philosophical

commitment or the fiscal and human resources to underwrite
generous sabbatical leave and faculty development programs for
all faculty. In the view of faculty at Evergreen and UTPB,
state-supported colleges, paid leaves are infrequent and faculty
development programs are inadequate. As a result, these faculties have pressured the administration to either provide greater
opportunities to remain current and marketable or to provide
greater economic security.

Effects on Faculty Recruitment

*No evidence suggests that term contract systems adverse-
ly affect efforts to recruit faculty.*

We cannot present any hard evidence that the policy hindered (or fostered) faculty recruitment efforts at the colleges
we studied. Each college reported that occasionally a prospective faculty member declined an offer of appointment partly because of the contract system; but each college also reported that
some faculty, occasionally tenured elsewhere, accepted appointments precisely because there was no tenure system. None of
the schools lacked candidates for faculty positions. From a review of faculty rosters, we can deduce that these colleges attracted well-trained instructors from a wide range of institutions
and at various stages of professional development, from recent
graduate students to senior professors. Would these faculty have
headed elsewhere under more favorable market conditions?
Would an even better or still wider range of candidates have applied had tenure or the prospects of tenure been available?
These questions have not been systematically investigated at the
institutions we visited. All the available evidence can be characterized as anecdotal, and all the anecdotes are furnished by fac
ulty and staff who have chosen to work under the contract system. The colleges, and therefore we, lack the data to assess the
impact of contract systems on faculty recruitment. On the basis
of conversations we had with faculty and staff on board, we
would speculate that the experimental and innovative nature of
the schools, more than the contract system per se, attracted faculty to these campuses and deterred others from applying. Far

fewer faculty seemed to be either attracted or repelled primarily on the basis of the contract system.

Effects on Retrenchment

Faculty contracts may facilitate layoffs or cutbacks should retrenchment be necessary.

When a contract ends, neither party normally bears any further obligations. The employer need not renew, the employee need not remain, and no one need offer any reasons to defend the action. Under such conditions, colleges can retrench with relatively greater ease than institutions with traditional tenure and retrenchment policies. Faculty can be released and programs discontinued through decisions not to renew appointments, a comparatively simple and efficient action when juxtaposed against procedures to remove tenured faculty. Term contracts, however, can be written to minimize or even negate that advantage, just as tenure policies can be written to maximize institutional flexibility with respect to retrenchment. Under either policy, the language can be broad and permissive or narrow and restrictive.

At Evergreen, the ability of the college "to pursue its goals as a learning community [shall] be considered the primary objective" to be achieved by cutback procedures. Before layoffs are ordered, the college will attempt reductions by natural attrition, reduced work loads, shared work, and elimination of visiting faculty. Should these "corrective measures prove inadequate," a state of "Extreme Financial Emergency" will be declared, and a faculty review panel will be elected to advise the deans and provost and to "review the qualifications of each member of the faculty, regardless of his or her remaining terms of appointment, with respect to the performance criteria articulated in the *Faculty Handbook* and decide who among the faculty are the most able to contribute to the academic mission of the college. On this basis, recommendations will be made to the president in order to accomplish the necessary reduction in the size of the faculty."

Evergreen's policy provides the latitude to make decisions on the basis of individual performance and programmatic needs.

We stress, however, that latitude derives from the layoff policy and not from the term contracts per se. Some colleges with term contracts have more conditional retrenchment policies. (Hampshire has none.) Conversely, colleges with tenure systems could enjoy equal flexibility with respect to layoffs, although most—as a reflex action, we suspect—embrace the more restrictive policies recommended by the AAUP.

The Keast Commission warns that administrators, exploiting the flexibility that contracts offer, may undertake arbitrary and capricious actions. We regard the commission's admonition as well-intentioned advice emanating from a critical view of term contracts and colleges with such a policy. Retrenchment on campuses with term contracts should be less whimsical, since the reappointment process generates an evaluative portfolio for each faculty member, so that layoff decisions can be based on relative performance and ability. The value of these records, however, will be substantially deflated to the extent that the assessments are uniformly praiseworthy.

Variations on a Theme

Although the conclusions we have drawn derive primarily from the experiences of three colleges, we did analyze the policies and practices of several other institutions with contract systems. When stripped of catchwords, the policies at these other campuses are fundamentally term appointments. Three variations of the general theme of term contracts deserve mention.

Although the Keast Commission reported that "all two-year colleges using contract systems . . . limit the initial contract and succeeding contracts to one year" (AAUP/AAC Commission on Academic Tenure, 1973, p. 11), multiyear contracts have since become quite common among community colleges. At Austin Community College (Texas), for example, faculty start with three one-year contracts. The college then issues a three-year contract to faculty deemed to be effective performers. Upon the satisfactory conclusion of that contract, the college issues five-year appointments. The Virginia Community College System has a very similar policy.

The same notion, that satisfactory performance warrants

an extended contract, has been implemented at Franklin Pierce College (New Hampshire) through *rolling contracts.* Faculty normally serve a "probationary period" no longer than seven years on annual or two-year contracts. Thereafter, the college issues a three-year contract, which continues automatically and indefinitely as long as the faculty member performs satisfactorily. Thus, a contract issued for Year One through Year Three would be extended through Year Four at the end of Year One and extended through Year Five at the end of Year Two—contingent, of course, on satisfactory performance. A faculty member evaluated as deficient at the end of the first year of a contract would have a year to improve. At the end of the second year, a satisfactory evaluation would prompt a new three-year contract from Year Three through Year Five. An unsatisfactory evaluation would mean that the third year of the first contract would be terminal. The Franklin Pierce policy has been incorporated into a union contract at the college.

Third, some colleges, like Goddard (in Plainfield, Vermont), have *variable-length contracts.* As the term suggests, the length of the contract may vary; at Goddard, it varies from one to five years. Criteria for determining the duration of the contract typically include years of service and quality of performance.

In sum, there are growth contracts, annual contracts, rolling contracts, variable-length contracts, term tenure, and no doubt a host of other mutations. However different the terminology may be, the several term contract policies are far more similar than different. We believe, therefore, that the conclusions and observations presented above would be equally applicable to the variations we did not study in detail.

Prognosis

Along with the practical limitations discussed earlier, term contracts suffer from a lack of prestige. Unless and until a research university or several prominent liberal arts colleges adopt the contract system to the exclusion of tenure, the policy will suffer a substantial measure of academic illegitimacy. Despite all the paeans to diversity, American colleges and universities, for better or worse, tend to follow the leaders. (The recent sweep to reform general education provides the latest illustration.) In general, research universities and eminent liberal arts colleges have a stronghold on the academy, and tenure has a stronghold on these institutions. The tendency to conform to directions set by elite institutions was not lost on James O'Toole, a professor of management at the University of Southern California, who renounced tenure eighteen months after he got it: "What do I hope to accomplish by this objection to the tenure system? Most optimistically, I would hope that a major university would set a precedent by announcing that it had abolished tenure" (O'Toole, 1979, p. 34). So far, none has; and we know of no university on the brink of such a decision.

No academic algebra should neatly or automatically equate the presence of a tenure system with excellence and distinction; there are many weak schools with strong tenure policies. Nevertheless, the presence of a tenure system does convey an aura of legitimacy and at least the appearance of an institution respectful of academic tradition. Conversely, the absence of tenure does not necessarily suggest an academically weak college or a politically weak faculty, although some administrators and professors elsewhere may harbor such suspicions. The absence of tenure does, however, convey an aura of illegitimacy, the semblance of a backstream, offbeat institution. At traditional colleges, faculty, staff, and trustees would not welcome that image or association.

With few exceptions, term contracts, to the exclusion of tenure, are likely to be limited to newer institutions that are by design experimental and outside the academic mainstream. That very fact, in turn, will further reduce the likelihood that other schools will adopt the policy, especially when—*unlike* Hampshire, Evergreen, and UTPB—the school must end a tenure system already in effect.

Were the advantages of term appointments, to the exclusion of tenure, fully exploited by colleges with such a policy, perhaps a few more institutions would overcome concerns about academic legitimacy and at least consider term contracts.

Few colleges, however, realize the principal benefit that term contracts promise: the opportunity to limit commitments to faculty and thereby to maintain the flexibility needed to change people and programs and upgrade quality. Term appointments offer an ever present option rarely exercised.

With too little evidence and in too many cases, the Keast Commission spoke too harshly of term contracts. We believe that the fears expressed by the commission were frequently overstated and occasionally misstated. Contracts are neither a curse, as the commission portrays them, nor a cure-all, as their advocates suggest. As a practical matter, the traditions of tenure and the resistance to term contracts are too strong to be overwhelmed by an alternative with uncertain advantages, clear drawbacks, and an illegitimate aura. Instead, colleges and universities concerned about or dissatisfied with conventional policies will probably consider first the less drastic modifications of classical tenure.

4.

Tenure
and Nontenure
Tracks

Under a typical term contract system, no faculty members are eligible for academic tenure; under a traditional tenure policy, no faculty members serve indefinitely on term appointments. Thus, term contract systems and academic tenure are generally regarded as mutually exclusive policies. A few colleges with established tenure systems have challenged that assumption with the addition of a so-called nontenure or extra-tenure track. Faculty members assigned to tenure-ineligible positions serve on term appointments that do not accrue toward fulfillment of the conventional probationary period. On these campuses, there are three categories of faculty: tenured, tenure eligible, and tenure ineligible.

Such efforts at peaceful coexistence between term contracts and academic tenure are not entirely unprecedented. By the early nineteenth century, Harvard manifested a "dual-track" system; professors were given "indefinite" or tenured appointments, whereas tutors, without any prospects for a permanent position, served on term contracts. Currently, tenure-ineligible appointments are commonly offered to accommodate scholars or artists-in-residence, to replace faculty members on leave, or to meet a temporary and often unexpected demand for specialized courses. These tenure-ineligible appointments meet specific, short-term needs. Some colleges have now extended the concept of tenure-ineligible appointments to include regular, full-time faculty members placed on a nontenure track with either fixed, renewable, or indefinite terms of employment. We report here on an imaginative non-tenure-track policy established at Webster College, a more typical policy enacted at Coe College, and a few variations adopted elsewhere.

Webster College

Founded in 1915 by the Sisters of Loretto, Webster College in suburban St. Louis was, like many other Catholic schools, profoundly affected by the ferment of the early 1960s as symbolized by Pope John XXIII and John F. Kennedy. Pope John encouraged a new openness toward other faiths, a reevaluation of the Church's mission in a secular society, and an examination of the roles and responsibilities to be assumed by clergy, nuns, and laity. Even people unaware of the internal debates sparked by the Pope's encyclicals could observe the external reforms as priests entered the political arena and nuns abandoned traditional garb. Kennedy's "New Frontier" was a temporal counterpart to the papal ecumenism. The President endeavored to reawaken America's sense of destiny and to renew the nation's commitment to the underprivileged at home and abroad. In these efforts, Kennedy delineated a special role for educators, a role exemplified by the Peace Corps and the coterie of Harvard professors in the executive branch of government.

Sister Jacqueline Grennan (now Wexler), the bright, energetic president of Webster College at the time, also achieved a degree of national prominence in the early 1960s. As a member of a national committee on education appointed by President Kennedy, Sister Grennan traveled often to Washington, D.C., and Cambridge, Massachusetts, and from time to time some committee members visited Webster. The presence of these educational and political leaders on campus and Sister "Jackie's" appearance on the cover of *Time* magazine excited the college's faculty and staff and kindled a sense of progress and momentum.

The college's optimism was reinforced by the addition to the faculty of some recent graduates from top-flight research universities. These newcomers contributed significantly to the college's academic programs and introduced a new perspective on faculty governance and personnel policies. Staffed and administered largely by the Sisters of Loretto, the college had historically functioned under the rules and regulations of the Order with little collegial participation. Moreover, the college did not have a tenure system, criteria for academic rank, a sabbatical leave program, or grievance procedures—policies the new faculty members deemed essential to the pursuit of excellence at Webster.

The press by lay faculty for shared governance and more traditional personnel policies coincided with a decision by the religious hierarchy to reexamine the Order's mission and the role of Webster College. This self-appraisal caused great turmoil and anguish among the nuns, shattered temporarily the college's sense of direction, and precipitated conflicts between religious and lay on the faculty as well as between newcomers and old-timers. In response to both internal and external pressures for change, the Sisters of Loretto in 1967 converted Webster College from a Catholic school for women into a secular, coeducational institution controlled by an independent board of trustees. The Sisters' decision restored, after several years of aimlessness, a sense of purpose and focus. Internal conflicts were moderated by a decision to treat lay and religious faculty as equals and by the establishment of formal as well as ad hoc committees to develop policies and procedures appropriate to the new Webster College. Another change encouraged the faculty and staff to complete the transformation of the college: in

mid-1969, Sister Jackie, who had earlier renounced her religious
vows, decided to marry, resigned the presidency, and moved
east to be president of Hunter College of the City University of
New York.

Leigh Gerdine, the first man to serve as president of Webster College, assumed office on January 1, 1970. As a first priority, Gerdine resolved to reduce the $2.5 million short-term debt
that threatened the college's survival. Toward that end, the president launched an aggressive development campaign to increase
revenues and closed the repertory theater to cut costs. A longtime supporter of the arts and the former chairman of the music
department and head of the symphony orchestra at Washington
University, Gerdine painfully recognized the need to close the
theater, which had been a significant cash drain on the college.

In office less than one month and immersed in the effort
to improve the college's finances, Gerdine next confronted a
faculty proposal for a tenure policy. The proposed policy recommended a five-year probationary period, interim evaluations,
peer review, an appeals procedure, a grandfather clause, and a
provision for sabbatical leaves. The last two provisions signified
that religious and lay faculty had resolved some earlier differences. The Sisters and older faculty had wanted a grandfather
clause to safeguard those persons issued "continuing appointments" by Jacqueline Grennan. "Continuing appointments" so
closely approximated tenure that the board of trustees, concerned about the number of long-term commitments, imposed a
33 percent limit on such appointments, a limit frequently referred to on campus as a tenure quota. Lay and younger faculty
had opposed a grandfather clause on grounds that no one on
"continuing appointment" had withstood the scrutiny of peer
review and that many of these individuals lacked appropriate
academic credentials. Sisters and older faculty once opposed a
sabbatical leave program as unnecessary and too expensive for
an institution committed essentially to undergraduate instruction. As a compromise, the two factions endorsed a sabbatical
leave program as a vehicle to upgrade the credentials of "grandfathered" faculty and to facilitate the research activities of
newer faculty.

President Gerdine viewed the proposal as standard fare, not tailored to meet Webster's particular circumstances. While appreciative of the faculty's desire for employment security and sensitive to the value that faculty attached to tenure as a symbol of academic respectability, Gerdine refused to approve the proposal. The college's financial position and revamped mission, the president reasoned, prohibited the long-term commitments that tenure entailed. Furthermore, Gerdine was not persuaded that a traditional tenure policy would actively contribute to faculty growth and development or help the college align rewards with risks and performance.

Over the next five months, faculty and administrators exchanged proposals and counterproposals for an academic personnel system. In May 1970, the parties finally reached agreement on a two-track system devised primarily by Gerdine. "Plan A" is a conventional tenure system with a stipulation that no more than one third of the faculty, inclusive of the ten or so individuals "grandfathered" by Sister Grennan, can hold tenure at any one time. "Plan B," now called the Faculty Development Leave (FDL) option, provides a generous sabbatical leave program for faculty members not on the tenure track. By the end of their second year of service at Webster, faculty members are required to choose either Plan A or Plan B, although policy permits shifts from one plan to the other as circumstances allow. (If and when the tenure ratio reaches 33 percent, Plan A will not be available as an option.) In the fifth year of the probationary period, faculty members on Plan A are reviewed for tenure. If granted tenure, faculty are eligible for a sabbatical leave of one semester at full pay or two semesters at half pay after the sixth year of service and every seven years thereafter. Appointed to annual contracts, Plan B faculty never encounter an "up-or-out" decision.

Faculty Development Leaves are granted to Plan B faculty as follows: after three years of service, one semester at half pay or a negotiated summer leave; or after four years of service, one semester at full pay or two semesters at half pay; or after five years of service, one semester and one summer at full pay. With the completion of each FDL, the cycle of eligibility starts anew.

Faculty Development Leaves are negotiated between the faculty member and the appropriate department chairman, advised by an ad hoc faculty committee. While the college affirms a desire to support FDLs, there are no assurances that leaves will be granted, nor are there any guarantees that the contracts of Plan B faculty members will be renewed. So far, the faculty at Webster have had no need to demand guarantees. Since the dual-track system began, no Plan B faculty member has ever been denied reappointment, and only one faculty member has been refused a Faculty Development Leave—and that decision was necessary to ensure that all three members of a department were not on leave simultaneously. (Under similar circumstances in other departments, some faculty members were persuaded to delay application for a leave.)

For a small college, only recently beset by financial difficulties, Webster has funded an extraordinary number of leaves over the past nine years—thirty-four FDLs and twenty-two sabbaticals. At any particular moment, 10-20 percent of the faculty may be on leave, and, as Gerdine likes to remind visitors, all these efforts of faculty development and enrichment have been accomplished without the support of foundations or other external sources of funds.

In the opinion of the president, "The system has been successfully implemented and successful." As evidence to that effect, Gerdine notes that (1) the faculty have developed new, accredited programs, especially at the graduate level, that have attracted so many students that graduate enrollments now outnumber undergraduates; (2) faculty have adjusted to a new clientele with no apparent difficulty—thanks to the FDL program, which helps professors "shift with the times"; (3) the college's long-term personnel commitments have been limited (the tenure ratio for 1979-80 was about 29 percent); (4) the college has recovered financially (the operating budget has been balanced, the repertory theater has been reopened, and enrollments are on the rise).

Gerdine does not deny that more Plan B faculty would like to be tenured, but he believes that most of them consider the FDL option an acceptable trade-off and a sufficiently attractive alternative to quell opposition to the tenure quota. Our conversations with members of the faculty largely confirmed Gerdine's observations. Most faculty members considered the FDL plan a "reasonable proposition under the circumstances." In fact, the entire art department decided to forgo the tenure track, since, as one member of the department commented, "artists need time to make art. Leaves provide that time. We are going to be a better faculty and a better department because we opted for FDLs." The only noticeable source of contention was an allegation by some faculty that the college's tenure level and one's chances for tenure were never easily ascertained from the administration. One professor claimed that the administration deliberately withheld or obfuscated such information in order to "use the uncertainty of tenure prospects to discourage some faculty and to encourage others to choose Plan A."

Whether consciously or not, Webster has been guided by a rudimentary principle of finance: Risk should be commensurate with reward. The greater the risk, the greater the reward. Thus, the perceived safety of a corporate bond and the dividend rate are, as a rule, directly related. Compensation plans for the armed services have long recognized the same principle through "combat pay." Although Webster does not pay Plan B faculty more than comparably qualified Plan A faculty, the FDL option clearly intends to provide a greater reward for faculty members disposed to a greater risk. In return for less employment security, Plan B faculty gain more frequent and more liberal leaves, a trade-off that the faculty on the whole has accepted. Under conventional tenure policy, risk and reward are inversely related. Insofar as tenured faculty generally enjoy more security and better pay than untenured colleagues, the operative principle would appear to be: The lesser the risk, the greater the reward.

Application of the risk/reward concept to academe has been urged by O'Toole (1979), who argued that tenure actually operates to depress academic salaries. Colleges and universities, in effect, discount professorial salaries by about 25 percent to offset the imputed value of tenure. In O'Toole's view, a faculty member would be better advised to tell the administration,

"Keep your tenure and pay me what I'm really worth." To date, no faculty has urged and no college has enacted O'Toole's recommendation. We would encourage colleges and universities to experiment with such a policy on a limited and optional basis, especially in disciplines where demand for personnel outstrips supply. In fields such as computer science, petroleum engineering, accounting, and economics, where alternative employment opportunities abound, tenure may be less important than compensation. To that degree, money more than security may be an effective magnet to draw scarce specialists to the campus.

Webster uses the lure of opportunity more than the lure of money, apparently with success. The college has been able to recruit and retain on B Plans faculty from first-rate graduate schools. While very few candidates for academic posts had advanced knowledge of the FDL option, nearly all responded favorably when the policy was presented. As the chances for tenure elsewhere decrease, more and more prospective faculty members may regard Webster's "extra touch" as an even more powerful attraction.

So far, so good. Like any personnel policy, however, Webster's "combat pay" system also has flaws. As we discovered with term contract systems generally, Plan B contracts are routinely renewed. The number of annual contracts renewed thus far totals several hundred. Indeed, we would hypothesize that the widespread acceptance of the policy may rest largely on the assumption that all Plan B contracts will be renewed. As practiced, Plan B faculty, like tenured colleagues elsewhere, may enjoy the best of both worlds: minimal risks through de facto employment security and greater rewards through FDLs. If and when some Plan B faculty members are terminated, for whatever reason, the popularity and durability of the policy will be tested.

As long as no Plan B faculty members are terminated and few elect to leave voluntarily, another potential problem will be averted. Plan B requires the college to commit substantial resources toward the professional development of faculty members without tenure. As a corollary, the college commits fewer resources to the nurturance of tenured professors, a population more likely to be permanent members of the faculty. Colleges and universities normally support the permanent faculty more generously, on the premise that the institution will reap the benefits of such investments over a longer period of time. Although data on turnover of Plan B faculty members were not available, the people we interviewed could recall only a few voluntary departures. In that case, the outflow of funds invested in Plan B faculty would probably be no greater than other colleges and universities suffer when tenured faculty leave voluntarily. To date, the matter of "misplaced" or "misspent" investments at Webster has not been at question, since so few faculty members (Plan A or B) have resigned. One could imagine, however, that the issue would rush to the fore if substantial numbers of Plan B faculty—current, visible, and mobile as a result of FDLs— were attracted elsewhere. Such a scenario seems improbable. We believe that for most Plan B faculty the FDLs represent, to borrow a phrase from industry, "golden handcuffs," an arrangement too agreeable to forsake.

In sum, Webster College has designed a non-tenure-track system that appears to serve the college's purposes well. The policy limits Webster's long-term commitments to academic personnel and programs. Plan B faculty regard the FDL option as a reasonable trade-off for the employment security that tenure provides. And, most important, both the faculty and the administration, with very few exceptions, believe that the FDL program contributes significantly to the maintenance of a vital and vibrant faculty.

Coe College

A select, liberal arts college in Cedar Rapids, Iowa, Coe College authorized a nontenure track in 1973 and concurrently adopted a formal evaluation process for tenured faculty. The faculty accepted these two changes in Coe's traditional tenure system as a compromise to forestall the imposition of a tenure quota by the board of trustees. (The origins of the compromise and the provisions of the evaluation system are discussed at length in Chapter Eight.) The establishment of a nontenure track was intended primarily to placate trustees concerned about the possibility of a totally tenured faculty. On the other hand, many faculty members fretted that a dual-track system unchecked could precipitate the erosion of academic tenure at Coe. In search of an acceptable middle ground, the faculty and President Leo Nussbaum agreed that tenure-ineligible slots would be restricted to no more than 10 percent of the full-time faculty positions.

The authority to designate a position as tenure ineligible rests with the dean of the college. The dean may assign positions to an extratenure track to accommodate temporary enrollment shifts, to enrich the curriculum periodically, or to explore student demand for a discipline or field not currently represented among the tenured or tenure-track faculty. Under certain conditions, the decision to classify a position as tenure ineligible may relate more to the tenure density of a department than to curricular considerations. In a heavily tenured department, the dean may designate a vacancy as tenure ineligible, so that, as the chairman of the mathematics department commented, "no one will be encouraged to think about tenure." In some completely tenured departments, such as chemistry, the dean has earmarked *an occupied position* as tenure ineligible. When the incumbent retires or resigns, the position must be reclassified as tenure ineligible to, as the dean stated, "alleviate the tenure crunch." The very possibility that a tenure-track position will be reclassified as tenure ineligible will, the administration hopes, be an effective disincentive for departments prone to advance everyone for tenure.

Coe's dual-track system has sparked relatively little controversy. Most faculty members prefer a limited number of nontenure-track positions to a policy that would have limited the number or percentage of tenured positions. One department maintained that the tenure-ineligible status of a vacancy hindered recruitment; and another department, insulted by the reclassification and convinced that the most qualified candidates would not apply, refused to recruit. No other department has taken such an extreme stance, perhaps because several faculty members first appointed to tenure-ineligible positions have been shifted to the tenure track after strong performances as teachers and scholars.

Fears that the tenure ratio would soar to unacceptable levels have thus far proved unfounded. The tenure density has fluctuated between 44 and 53 percent over the past five years; currently, 51 percent of the seventy-three full-time faculty members are tenured. On average, the college has denied tenure to 25-30 percent of the candidates considered for a permanent position.

Nontenure Tracks Elsewhere

While the profession lacks a precise census of nontenure tracks, several studies suggest that many colleges and universities permit tenure-ineligible appointments. A survey of such practices by the AAUP disclosed that "there has been a substantial increase in the extent to which institutions of higher education are staffed by 'non-tenure-track' teachers" (American Association of University Professors, 1978b, p. 267). Of 844 institutions polled by the College and University Personnel Association (1980, p. 28), 222 provided some "tenure-time credit," usually no more than three years, for service in tenure-ineligible positions. Although we can safely presume that colleges with a policy on "tenure-time credit" for tenure-ineligible personnel have a nontenure track of one sort or another, the survey does not reveal whether there are among the other 626 respondents some colleges with tenure-ineligible positions that do not accrue toward fulfillment of the probationary period. On the basis of the AAUP and CUPA surveys, a select review of faculty handbooks, and the doctoral research of DiBiase (1979), we conclude that extratenure tracks are quite commonplace.

The AAUP report identified three categories of tenure-incligible positions and presented anonymously several examples of each policy option. Drawing on several sources, we cite parenthetically for each AAUP classification a few institutions with such a policy:

1. Term contracts of one or more years *renewable indefinite-ly* (Colorado School of Mines, Pennsylvania State University, University of Wisconsin at Oshkosh).
2. Term contracts of one or more years *renewable for a limited number of years,* typically three and as many as seven (Hartwick College, Oklahoma State University, Rutgers University).
3. *Terminal appointments,* usually for two or three years, with no renewal possible under any circumstances, an option colorfully described by the AAUP as "folding chairs" (Temple University, University of Wisconsin System).

Among the many variations of non-tenure-track appointments, we would draw special attention to three. Aquinas College in Grand Rapids, Michigan, established an extratenure track in May 1979. Tenure-ineligible faculty members may serve indefinitely on three-year rolling contracts after a seven-year probationary period. Contingent on a satisfactory performance evaluation, the contracts are extended each year. "Either substandard performance or diminished need (for the services of tenure-ineligible faculty) would be reasons for shortening the contract to two years, then one, and then out, if the reasons were not removed" (Hruby, 1981, p. 26). The unique aspect of Aquinas's policy concerns the process the college has designed to determine which positions should be designated as tenure ineligible. As vacancies arise, the dean of the faculty determines whether a position should be placed on the tenure or the non-tenure track. The dean must then seek the approval of the faculty-dominated academic assembly and ultimately the approval of the board of trustees. Thus far, the dean has requested that ten of seventeen new appointments be classified as tenure ineligible, and in every case the academic assembly and the board of trustees has concurred.

For better or worse, the University of Wisconsin at Oshkosh has the most elaborate and detailed non-tenure-track policies, which add a plenitude of local "ordinances" to the numerous regulations applicable to all campuses of the university. At Oshkosh, any appointments in departments more than 70 percent tenured must be to "academic staff positions," a classification normally associated with administrative appointments. Academic staff may be offered fixed-term, one-year contracts renewable for six years with the option of five-year extensions thereafter. At any time, the academic staff member may be transferred to a tenure-track probationary appointment, with no more than five years of tenure-ineligible service credited toward fulfillment of the seven-year trial period. "Hence, a faculty member receiving an academic staff appointment could be given, for example, yearly contracts for six years followed by a five-year contract, a fixed-term terminal contract, or one-year contracts forever, or a combination of the three" (DiBiase, 1979, p. 87). An academic staff member on a temporary appointment could eventually achieve a position as a tenured faculty member; likewise, a probationary faculty member could on a "reverse transfer" be assigned to a tenure-ineligible position. In short, Oshkosh's policies permit almost every imaginable shift from one status to another. No policy could be more flexible—or more complicated.

Arguably a term contract system, the "dual-track" policy at the Colorado School of Mines provides elements of traditional tenure for certain senior faculty members and term appointments for faculty members at the lower academic ranks. After two years of satisfactory service as a professor or an associate professor, a faculty member attains a status defined in the *Faculty Handbook* as "de facto tenure." (The *Handbook* specifically states that the school does not grant de jure tenure as traditionally defined.) Faculty with de facto tenure may not be denied reappointment to an annual contract simply on the grounds that the administration believes a replacement might perform more effectively. Nonrenewal will be permitted only "for other good and sufficient reasons such as but not limited to failure to fulfill assigned responsibilities for teaching and research, failure to maintain satisfactory standards of professional performance, and failure to cooperate in achieving the goals of [one's] department and the school." Instructors and assistant professors are considered probationary personnel irrespective of their length of service. These faculty may be released for cause or, under the policy, to allow the school to hire someone "of apparent greater promise." Incidentally, one faculty member denied reappointment after eighteen consecutive years of service was denied any relief in a lawsuit that reached the Colorado Supreme Court. The Court declined "to hold that longevity of employment per se, without additional supportive facts, creates a protectable interest to the individual. . . . While plaintiff may have had a personal expectancy of continued employment, a subjective, unilateral expectancy does not constitute a constitutionally protected property interest" (*Laubach* v. *Bradley,* 527 P.2d 874 (1977); quoted by DiBiase, 1979, p. 104).

Advantages of Nontenure Tracks

A version of term appointments, nontenure tracks offer many of the same benefits and drawbacks as term contract systems. Yet nontenure tracks are much more prevalent—a reflection of certain strategic advantages and, to a lesser degree, certain substantive advantages that extratenure tracks promise.

Political Feasibility. Unlike a term contract system, a nontenure track neither replaces nor precludes traditional tenure. To substitute term contracts for an established tenure system would, at the very least, present formidable political and legal obstacles. By comparison, adoption of an extratenure track represents a most feasible alternative. While few faculties are likely to be enthralled by a nontenure track, resistance to the idea will almost certainly be less intense than opposition to the abolition of a classical tenure system. We do not mean to suggest that the administration or board of trustees at Webster, Coe, or any other college with a nontenure track proposed or preferred the elimination of conventional tenure practices. Rather, we mean only to observe that at mature institutions with firmly embedded tenure policies, a nontenure track constitutes a practical policy option and a politically acceptable compromise. Abandonment of tenure does not. (Unencumbered by entrenched traditions and prior commitments, new colleges such as Hampshire, Evergreen, and UTPB were relatively free to select academic tenure *or* term contracts as an employment policy for

faculty members.) Extratenure tracks stake a politically acceptable middle ground. From the perspective of trustees and ad
ministrators, the availability of tenure-ineligible positions lessens
the dangers and drawbacks of a tenure system; and from the
perspective of the faculty, the presence of a tenure system lessens the dangers and drawbacks of term appointments. In that
sense, the policies reinforce one another, so that theoretically a
college or university can exploit the advantages of term contracts and still retain the benefits of a tenure system. Thus, the
proposal generates some enthusiasm among administrators and
trustees haunted by the specter of a faculty entirely tenured; at
the same time, the preservation of a tenure system attenuates
the concerns and reduces the opposition of the faculty.

Not unexpectedly, therefore, tenure-ineligible appointments are very often made for political or administrative purposes rather than for curricular reasons. At Coe, for example,
many non-tenure-track appointments serve foremost to suppress
tenure levels and thereby to placate trustees. Other tenure-ineligible appointments intend to "punish" excessively tenured departments, a tactic we would not regard as an effective deter-
rent.

Freedom from Censure by AAUP. In 1978, an AAUP
committee on academic freedom and tenure considered the
matter of nontenure tracks. While generally sympathetic to the
use of tenure-ineligible positions as a means to provide specialized instruction or to meet distinctly temporary needs, the
AAUP condemned the creation of a nontenure track merely as a
mechanism to enhance institutional flexibility. As might be expected, the committee's report denounced the practice as inimical to academic freedom: "The protection of academic freedom
must take precedence over the claimed advantages of increased
flexibility. . . . The increase in flexibility which can be bought
by the creation of a second-class faculty status is neither so
great nor so immediate as first appears" (American Association
of University Professors, 1978b, p. 272). The committee also
objected to any policy that placed on a nontenure track faculty
members appointed to teach basic courses well within the traditional realm and standard fare of a college's curriculum:

"What is striking about the non-tenure-track arrangement . . . is that the appointments made under them are in subjects which can in no way be regarded as on probation" (p. 271). The AAUP recognizes that student demand for certain new courses and programs may be undetermined. In such cases, it recommends that the person *and the position* be placed on probation. Tenure-ineligible appointments should be confined to "special appointments clearly limited to a brief association with the institution, and reappointments of retired faculty members on special conditions" (p. 270). To comply with this regulation, a college or university would have to ensure "*both* that the appointment be clearly limited to a brief association with the institution *and* that the appointment be 'special.' . . . An appointment made to a candidate for a job in a subject central to an institution's educational program, which is not a job as a replacement for someone on leave, is not in the required sense special" (p. 271). Nonetheless, on many campuses, tenure-ineligible faculty teach composition, mathematics, foreign languages, history, and other core courses—practices that contravene the spirit of the AAUP's regulation. Confronted with a choice between increased flexibility and violation of AAUP policy, these colleges and universities evidently prefer the greater latitude a nontenure track purportedly offers.

Although the AAUP opposes the creation of nontenure tracks, the National Convention has yet to censure any institution for using tenure-ineligible appointments for purposes not approved by the association. In contrast, the AAUP zealously challenged and censured Bloomfield College and the Virginia Community College System when these institutions rescinded traditional tenure policies and introduced term contracts. Bloomfield's action was later overturned by a court of law (see Chapter Ten). If the AAUP should decide to censure rather than merely criticize institutions with a nontenure track, the practice may abate. In the meantime, however, the establishment of a nontenure track does not appear to invite censure by the AAUP, an important consideration on campuses where the views and actions of the AAUP carry status.

Enrichment. Unquestionably, extra-tenure-track positions

afford a college the opportunity to enrich its curriculum by appointing specialists on fixed-term contracts. In that way, a school may offer from time to time, without a long-term obligation, instruction in voice, winds, Vonnegut, disarmament, religious cults, or any other specialized or topical area. As mentioned, the AAUP commends the use of non-tenure-track appointments precisely for such purposes and benefits.

Flexibility. The principal substantive attractions of a nontenure track are, in fact, endemic to all term contracts; namely, the opportunity and flexibility to restrict financial and programmatic commitments. Unsure about student enrollments generally or the demand for particular course sequences, a college may resort to tenure-ineligible appointments for term contracts as a means to limit the institution's financial exposure or as a means to hedge any bets on a new or expanded curriculum. Were flexibility the sole or even the ultimate policy objective, the AAUP argues that tenure-*eligible* appointments could fulfill the purpose as effectively as a nontenure track. We agree only in part.

Academics generally believe that probationary appointments by definition entail far greater commitments and thereby constrain flexibility more than tenure-ineligible appointments. In fact, however, tenure policies can be and commonly are drawn so that obligations to probationary faculty members lapse as simply as contractual commitments to tenure-ineligible faculty members. The policy need only provide that probationary faculty serve on annual contracts without any rightful expectation of reappointment or tenure; that positions as well as people be on probation; and that no statement of reasons will be furnished upon nonrenewal.

To be sure, there may be some procedural differences. First, the lead time required to serve notice of nonrenewal may differ, a matter addressed shortly. Second, nonreappointment of a tenure-eligible faculty member may entail a more extensive peer review process. These are policy matters. Tenure-eligible and tenure-ineligible faculty *could* be afforded the same notice and subjected to the same review process. Indeed, the desire for equity and scrutiny may suggest that there should be uniform procedures. A more significant difference concerns the temporal dimension of the flexibility. Once probationary faculty achieve tenure, the institution assumes rather permanent and substantial obligations, which do constrain flexibility; in contrast, tenure-ineligible faculty may be continued indefinitely without any commitment beyond the current employment contract. Hence, tenure-eligible appointments provide time-sensitive flexibility, whereas tenure-ineligible appointments could offer endless latitude.

The reluctance on the part of many colleges and universities to appoint nearly all full-time faculty members to the tenure track may reflect both an overestimation of the contractual commitments to probationary faculty and a desire or need to preserve long-term maneuverability. In addition, senior professors and senior administrators alike probably view the non-reappointment of tenure-ineligible faculty as less painful to accomplish, since the psychological as well as the legal bonds between these individuals and the institution are not as strong as they are for tenure-eligible faculty.

Clarity and Certainty. Presented with forthright, explicit policy statements, recruits for tenure-ineligible positions should understand at the outset the nature of the appointment and the terms and conditions of employment. Since there will be no ambiguities, there should be no false expectations. Coe College requires that prospective appointees to tenure-ineligible positions "shall be notified in writing before they are appointed that they cannot expect their service at the college to lead to tenure."

In theory, then, a terminal or limited renewable appointment removes all the elements of uncertainty and thus some of the anxiety confronted by faculty on probationary appointments or on contracts renewable indefinitely. In practice, however, that rarely proves to be the case because most colleges with a non-tenure track allow tenure-ineligible faculty members to be transferred to the tenure stream. Exceptions to the rule are necessary to accommodate those cases where a faculty member originally assigned to a tenure-ineligible position emerges as a teacher/scholar far superior to probationary faculty. No college or university wants to lose a star performer, least of all by

virtue of a "technicality." Hence, most colleges with a nontenure track equivocate. The appointment of a faculty member to a
tenure-ineligible position at Coe, for example, "shall not prejudice the right of the college eventually to consider such an individual for tenure, should unforeseen changes in circumstances
make such considerations possible and advisable."

Once these "escape clauses" are applied, the presumed
advantages of clarity and certainty diminish. The shift of even
one faculty member from the nontenure to the tenure track
will ignite the hopes and expectations of nearly all other tenure-
ineligible faculty, especially to the extent that they consider
themselves to be as "exceptional" as the person transferred to a
probationary appointment. Even were exceptions not permitted,
the definitive nature of terminal and limited renewable appointments, where the limit has been reached, would not curtail anxiety. While advanced knowledge of a termination date may induce some faculty to seek employment opportunities elsewhere,
the certainty of nonrenewal does little to reduce the stress associated with an unsettled future.

As for faculty on indefinitely renewable contracts or limited renewable contracts where the limit has *not* been reached,
the strain would appear to be no less severe. Notice of nonreappointment may be served quite unexpectedly and quite abruptly, since on some campuses the university bears no obligation to
forewarn the tenure-ineligible faculty member of nonreappointment. The decision to renew or not to renew a contract may be
communicated to the faculty member as late as the registration
period of a semester. The obvious solution would be to provide
due notice. If advanced notice were linked to length of service,
some veteran faculty members on tenure-ineligible appointments could be entitled to earlier notice than some or even all
probationary faculty, a disparity that could be difficult to defend on a campus with traditional tenure policies. On the other
hand, failure to provide due notice to tenure-ineligible faculty,
particularly after several years of service, seems conspicuously
inequitable and needlessly insensitive. Thus, we recommend
that the AAUP's standards for notification of nonreappointment of probationary faculty apply to non-tenure-track faculty

as well: March 1 of the first year, December 15 of the second year, and at least twelve months' notice after more than two years of service.

Recommendations

When, if ever, should tenure-ineligible positions be authorized? We concur with the AAUP that the most obvious and appropriate circumstances are as short-term replacements, as special accommodations for retirees, and as special appointments for curricular enrichment. To the AAUP's list, we would add appointments where the candidate lacks and appears to be unlikely to acquire soon the minimum academic credentials necessary to qualify for tenure; full-time appointments to research institutes, programs, and centers wholly or largely supported on "soft" money; and temporary appointments to fill a sudden vacancy where a comprehensive search cannot be conducted quickly enough to meet the immediate need. Any of these circumstances may reasonably justify the employment of tenure-ineligible faculty members.

The more troublesome question concerns the use of tenure-ineligible faculty to staff "regular" courses and programs. To be candid, we are ambivalent about such a practice. On the one hand, we agree with the AAUP that, where doubts exist about the direction of a program or the demand for certain courses, the new faculty member and the position should be placed on probation. Over a five- to seven-year probationary period, the future of a program and the manpower requirements may be clarified. If the person proves unqualified or the position proves unwarranted, or both, then the faculty member should be terminated. In the interim trial period, however, the faculty member operates within the mainstream of the academic community and derives the considerable benefits of that status. Too often, tenure-ineligible faculty suffer as third-class citizens disenfranchised from collegiate and departmental governance, undersupported for research and faculty development, overlooked for peer review and guidance, and, perhaps worst, distanced from colleagues. As one senior professor responded to the AAUP survey on non-tenure-track faculty, "No one likes to make friends with a dying person" (1978b, p. 270). In other words, faculty and administrators are reluctant to invest emotionally or financially in a potential transient. In kind, the tenure-ineligible faculty member may choose to be equally detached and disengaged from the affairs of the university and, understandably, somewhat less devoted to students' needs outside the classroom. All these reasons argue for tenure-track positions.

On the other hand, there may be occasions where the doubts are long term and far ranging. Five or six years ago, for example, a liberal arts college, in response to student enrollments, may have added another historian to the tenure track. Now, on the eve of the candidate's tenure decision, student demand has waned slightly yet perceptibly, and the long-range prospects for enrollments at the college generally and in history more specifically appear to be most uncertain. No one disputes the need for some historians; the question is "How many historians?" Under these circumstances, should the college tenure the faculty member and activate program reduction and faculty retrenchment policies as necessary, or should the college waive the "up-or-out" rule and thereby defer the decision? (This second option is discussed in Chapter Five.) Alternatively, the college could deny the candidate tenure and appoint a tenure-ineligible faculty member as a replacement until the situation stabilizes. Such an option has obvious appeal, particularly given the overabundance of historians and the cumbersome procedures and contentious nature of retrenchment decisions. On a larger scale, the dilemma could be college wide rather than department specific, and financial as much as programmatic. Again, the choices are (1) to make tenure-ineligible appointments to enhance flexibility, to guard against overcapacity, and to preserve liquidity or (2) to tenure faculty and, as circumstances require, invoke the policies and procedures of financial exigency. In both examples, we know which courses of action would be easier. But which would be better?

Rather than flatly recommend or condemn non-tenure-track appointments for "regular" courses and programs, we offer a certain preferred sequence of actions. First, all colleges and

universities should, to the extent that human and fiscal resources permit, develop long-range strategic plans that assess the
college's opportunities and constraints. Such efforts, undertaken by all too few institutions, should help the academic administration construct a faculty consonant with the college's
missions and markets (see Chapter Ten). Armed with a strategic
plan, the administration should be emboldened to take *calculated* risks on tenure-eligible appointments. As the trial periods
of tenure-track faculty proceed, the plan will be revised, updated, and sharpened; and the academic administration will furnish more current and more definitive prognoses to probationary faculty members.

　　Aquinas has attempted valiantly to define, in essence, a
core faculty, an irreducible minimum necessary to offer the
bedrock programs of the college. Based on that determination,
as well as economic and demographic considerations, the academic assembly decides the tenure-track status of each vacancy
on a case-by-case basis. While Aquinas has at least started down
the path to a systematic assessment of manpower needs, other
colleges with nontenure tracks seem to authorize tenure-ineligible positions for curricular (as opposed to political) reasons in a
more serendipitous or at least a less studied fashion. The decisions appear to derive more from intuition than information,
more from an ill-defined sense of "the difficult years ahead"
than from a careful estimation of that college's future.

　　At the same time that a college develops a strategic plan,
the administration, in consultation with the faculty, should
make certain that policies concerned with commitments to probationary faculty are clearly and narrowly drawn and that policies germane to program reduction, program discontinuation,
and financial distress are equally lucid and phrased so as to
allow management ample discretion and latitude (see Chapter
Ten). If colleges, to the benefit of the faculty, agree to assume
certain risks with appointments to the tenure track and indeed
to the tenured ranks, then the faculty must recognize and, ideally, appreciate that the college needs an "insurance policy" to
cover those risks. Workable, sensible, and adaptable procedures
for staff reduction constitute that "insurance policy."

At colleges with strategic plans and effective policies, the need for tenure-ineligible appointments to staff traditional assignments would, we believe, be occasional and exceptional. In the absence of severe market dislocations, financial exigency, curricular overhaul, or a volatile environment, extra-tenure-track appointments to handle conventional courses may be little more than an acknowledgment of inadequate planning or an excuse to avoid the difficult decisions forced by tenure policies.

In any event, when such tenure-ineligible positions are deemed genuinely necessary, we recommend the following policy provisions:

1. Any appointments should be either terminal or else renewable for up to six years. Appointments with fixed terms provide certainty, encourage faculty to seek early employment opportunities elsewhere, prevent casual and even careless reappointments year after year, and protect the faculty against indefinitely renewable appointments as a device to circumvent the tenure system. (One large research university has seventy-eight tenure-ineligible instructors with nine or more years of service.)

2. Notice of nonrenewal should conform to the AAUP guidelines for probationary faculty members.

3. Transfer to the tenure track should not be permitted. Such a stipulation will preserve the distinction between tenure-eligible and tenure-ineligible appointments, minimize false expectations, and discourage offhand use of the nontenure track.

4. Promotion in rank should be permitted if a tenure-ineligible faculty member satisfies the prescribed criteria and standards for "regular" faculty.

5. As a matter of equity, salaries and benefits for tenure-ineligible faculty should be comparable to those for similarly situated faculty on the tenure track, as long as their assignments and responsibilities do not differ markedly. The AAUP survey discovered that non-tenure-track appointees are paid less than "regular" faculty at some institutions and comparably well at others. Likewise, some institutions provide merit pay increases automatically on renewal, while other colleges advise tenure-ineligible faculty that pay increases may be given on renewal

but should not be expected. Fringe benefits were, on the whole, "comparable" (American Association of University Professors, 1978b, p. 269).

6. Performance appraisals, comparable to the assessment of tenure-track candidates, should be conducted annually. Properly executed, such appraisals should benefit both the faculty member and the institution.

7. Except where personnel decisions are at issue, tenure-ineligible faculty should be encouraged to participate in faculty governance and departmental deliberations. Similarly, non-tenure-track faculty should not, as a matter of policy, be excluded from faculty development activities or research funds.

Taken together, these policies will, we believe, curtail potential abuses of non-tenure-track faculty and also curtail the creation of tenure-ineligible positions—both laudable objectives.

5.

Extended
Probationary Periods
and Suspension
of "Up-or-Out" Rule

Some managers subscribe to the principle "Never decide today what can be decided tomorrow." The additional time, whether a day or a year, provides an opportunity to ruminate about the decision, to monitor related events, and to accumulate more information. Where difficult decisions are at issue, dilatory tactics also postpone the anguish. Persuaded of the advantages of delay, some colleges and universities have elected to defer tenure decisions, either through an extension of the probationary period or through the abolition of the "up-or-out" rule. We analyze here both these modifications of traditional tenure policies.

Extended Probationary Periods

In 1716, Harvard instituted three-year appointments for tutors; forty-four years later, it set an eight-year limit on the

91

length of time a tutor could serve at that rank. The regulation was, according to Metzger (1973, p. 119), intended to prevent reappointments "out of neglect or sympathy" and "to defeat the impulsions of kindness" which can influence the evaluation of personnel. In the early eighteenth century, the university also started to offer endowed professorships without limit of time. By 1820, there were, in essence, temporary tutors and permanent professors, the distant forerunners of probationary and tenured faculty. The more elaborate rank structure, coupled with the temporal limitations on appointments, enabled the university to promote faculty or to deny reappointment—to "up" or to "out." In fact, however, Harvard sometimes promoted but rarely discontinued term faculty: "[It] allowed the up but did not enforce the out. The effect was to create a two-track system, in which the nonpromoted teacher, reappointed time and again, kept pace in compiling years of service with his higher-ranking colleagues. The virtue of a two-track system was that it did not necessarily fling anyone off the road. But, unlike the single track that led to an inescapable fork, it offered the nonpromoted teacher no surcease from the pain of temporariness, and no certainty as to when, if ever, he would gain relief" (Metzger, 1973, p. 122). In 1914, the newly formed American Association of University Professors decided that one track, with a finite period of probation, was far better than two. The association endorsed a ten-year probationary period for all faculty at all collegiate institutions. In 1940, the AAUP reduced the recommended trial period to seven years.

Most academicians accept as sacrosanct the seven-year limit endorsed by the AAUP; 62 percent of the colleges and universities surveyed by the Keast Commission in 1972 reported maximum probationary periods of less than seven years. Within the public sector, 45 percent of the universities, 42 percent of the four-year colleges, and 80 percent of the two-year colleges had probationary periods of five years or less. Among private institutions, the comparable data were 16, 30, and 53 percent. A more recent poll by the American Council on Education (Atelsek and Gomberg, 1980, p. 16) disclosed that the gap between the public and private sectors had narrowed and that the duration of the average probationary period had lengthened. For the academic year 1978-79, the average probationary periods were 5.7 years at public universities, 6.1 years at private universities, 5.3 years at public four-year colleges, and 5.8 years at private four-year colleges. The longer probationary periods probably reflect a response to the onset of a steady-state era and a concomitant desire to slow the rapid march of faculty members toward the tenure decision. On some campuses, the decision to prolong the probationary period may also reflect a desire to observe and evaluate a faculty member's performance over a longer time frame. Whatever the particular mix of motives, most institutions, especially private schools, surveyed by the ACE expected the probationary period to lengthen slightly over the next five years. And while the average probationary period seems likely to remain well within the seven-year standard prescribed by the AAUP, some colleges and universities of considerable repute—Columbia, Princeton, Vassar, and the Harvard Business School, to name a few—have already exceeded that limit by as many as four years. We examine here the extended probationary period of the University of Rochester and then describe briefly the policies of the University of Georgia and the University of Tulsa.

University of Rochester. Concerned that each tenure appointment "commits about a million dollars, makes a substantial contribution to the character and quality of a department (especially a small department), and shapes the future university to a nonnegligible degree," President Robert L. Sproull in October 1970 issued new procedures for tenure decisions at the University of Rochester. As one academic administrator recalled, the regulations were intended to minimize the possibility that an unworthy candidate would earn tenure or that a potential Nobel Prize winner would be denied tenure. To add more rigor and scrutiny to the review process, the president ordered that an ad hoc advisory committee be established for each candidate advanced for tenure by a department. The ad hoc committees would normally be composed of "no more than one member from the candidate's department, at least one member from a college (within the same 'division' as the candidate) other than that of the candidate, and whenever possible at least one member from another 'division' of the university. . . . In the case of a particularly strong department, it might be possible to have one member from outside the university." The divisions at Rochester are (1) Humanities; (2) Biological Sciences and Medicine; (3) Physical Sciences, Mathematics, Engineering and Applied Sciences; and (4) Social Sciences, History, Business, and Education. Although the president appoints the committee and meets at least once with its members, the committee reports directly to the appropriate dean. (Unless the committee requests otherwise, its composition would not ordinarily be revealed to the department chairman or the candidate.) If the dean recommends tenure, the committee's unsigned report must accompany the recommendation. Where the committee recommends tenure and the dean does not, the policy advises that the dean "probably should forward both his and the committee's analysis to the president." This procedure was not required, Sproull's letter continued, "but it would be good practice unless the dean could convince the committee that new information or arguments vitiated the committee's report." The president's announcement of the new procedures ended with a reminder that these were "*minimum* procedures for *review*" and could be intensified and broadened by the dean and department chairmen.

Not unexpectedly, Sproull's pronouncement triggered a flurry of discussion and activity. In the spring of 1971, the Academic Council* established a committee to explore promotion and tenure policies and practices. Some ten months later, the council considered the committee's report and shortly thereafter released the document to the faculty. The report "eschewed generalized debate about tenure as not fruitful" and focused instead on strategies and policies to improve the current

---

*The Academic Council is a large advisory body reporting to the president. Members serve by virtue of their office (academic deans, associate academic deans, all former chairmen of the steering committees of the various faculties, and others). The council reviews long-term policy issues, often with the help of specially appointed task forces. Approved policy changes are submitted to the president, who forwards them to the steering committee of the University Senate.

system. The principal objectives were to provide greater staffing flexibility and to improve the university's ability to recruit outstanding young faculty members. These goals were, at once, both important and difficult to achieve as the rapid growth of the last ten to fifteen years ended and a steady state dawned. The committee realized that, as long as the faculty expanded, "a substantial fraction" of the faculty members on probation could be promoted to tenure without danger to the overall balance between tenured and untenured faculty. On the other hand, the report acknowledged, "When the growth disappears, . . . either the fraction of young tenured faculty who ultimately get tenure must be drastically reduced or the fraction of the faculty on tenure will rise significantly." As an example of the prospective dilemma, the committee estimated that the College of Arts and Sciences could anticipate only ten retirements between 1972 and 1978, while as many as ninety-eight assistant professors might reach the tenure decision over that six-year period. In the absence of growth, the committee could identify only four possibilities: "Either (1) a much smaller fraction of the young faculty can be offered tenure, or (2) the fraction of faculty with tenure must be allowed to rise substantially, or (3) the tenure regulations must be changed, or (4) some means must be found for providing more openings in the tenure ranks, or some combination of these four." "Whatever is done," the committee acknowledged, "it seems likely that tenure prospects for new Ph.D.s during the next decade are going to be much dimmer than has been true in the past."

Faced with these choices and prospects, the committee recommended that the university adopt an eleven-year probationary period and simultaneously sever the bond between promotion to associate professor and promotion to tenure. The eleven-year probationary period would generally be comprised of term contracts for four, three, and four years. To guard against routine renewals for the entire eleven-year span, the committee proposed that "the standards for review before reappointment and for appointment beyond seven years shall not be lower than those currently used." Furthermore, reappointment after seven years as an assistant professor would be contingent on promotion to associate professor. A longer probationary period would presumably afford the university "a better basis" to determine with greater confidence a faculty member's "promise of excellence." At best, the committee noted, a seven-year timetable requires a tenure decision in the sixth year; and such a decision would have to be based on a faculty member's performance record over the first five years, a period devoted largely to course preparation. As a result, the future potential of tenure candidates "must often be inferred from one or two articles, a very unsatisfactory sample from which to generalize." The longer probationary period was also considered advantageous to faculty members for at least two reasons:

> (1) In the short run, there will be a few more vacancies due to retirements, resignations, and so forth, which can be filled out of the present stock of assistant professors, who are able to stay on but would otherwise be forced out; (2) in the longer run, extending the length of time to the up-or-out decision has the effect of reducing the input of assistant professors each year. When the annual flow into the assistant professor rank declines, a larger fraction of those who come here can eventually be granted tenure. In other words, a six-year period to the up-or-out decision means more turnover of assistant professors than a ten-year period. With the former plan, we hire more new assistant professors each year and grant tenure to a smaller fraction. The committee believes that lengthening the period of probation will make the University of Rochester more attractive to young faculty—that on balance they will prefer the higher probability of being granted tenure to having tenure for a longer portion of their academic career.

Similarly, the committee believed that prospective faculty would be enticed by a policy that permitted promotions to associate professor without any attendant requirements that the candidate stand for promotion to tenure.

Between March and May 1972, the report was widely discussed by department chairmen, the Academic Council, the various college faculties, the University Senate, the University Committee on Tenure and Privileges, and the Cabinet of Deans. Finally, on September 22, the executive committee of the board of trustees approved a new statement on "Lengths of Appointments at Faculty Ranks." The new policy distinguished between "unlimited" and "limited" tenure. Unlimited tenure confers all the rights and privileges traditionally associated with classical tenure; limited tenure at Rochester, like term tenure at the University of Texas at Permian Basin, confers the same rights and privileges, inclusive of academic freedom, except for a fixed period of time. Under the new policy, appointments may be made as follows:

Rank	Contract Length	Years of Service at Rank
Instructor	1 or 2 years	Normally 3, maximum 5
Assistant professor	Up to 4 years	Maximum 7
Associate professor with limited tenure	Up to 5 years	Maximum 5

The maximum combined service as an assistant professor and an associate professor with limited tenure may not exceed eleven years. Associate professors may be and professors must be appointed to positions with unlimited tenure, although external appointments of a professor may be without tenure for up to five years. At that time, the professor must be tenured or terminated.

The board of trustees substantially incorporated the recommendations of the Academic Council's Committee on Tenure. The new policy extended the probationary period to eleven years and loosened the tie between promotion to tenure and promotion to associate professor. Rochester loosened more then severed the bond between tenure and promotion, insofar as unlimited or traditional tenure and an associate professorship were still linked. Now, however, there was another option: associate professor with limited tenure. In a statement on review procedures, disseminated to the faculty in January 1973, President Sproull and Chancellor W. Allen Wallis disclosed their intention to separate further the promotion and tenure decisions. Over time, the normal process would be to evaluate a faculty member for tenure well after promotion to associate professor; for the two decisions differed significantly. The joint memorandum noted: "Promotion is many things: it is a signal of encouragement, a vote of confidence in future performance, and an acknowledgment of current teaching and scholarly performance. It should not be used to retain a person who has little prospect of eventual tenure. In both nomination and review, the criteria and use of indicators should, in fact, be the same as for tenure decisions; the threshold of quality should be as high as for tenure, but of course one's confidence that the candidate will exceed that threshold need not be as great."

Although not directly related to the extended probationary period, the ad hoc committee structure devised by Sproull deserves a final word, since the new procedure was cleverly designed to serve a larger purpose than more meticulous reviews of candidates for tenure. Especially in the first years of operation, the committee usually and deliberately consisted of the chairman of one of the weaker departments and two well-respected, quality-minded faculty members. Exposed to the thoughtful and thorough approach to evaluation taken by the faculty members, many department chairmen soon recognized the need to construct better dossiers and more persuasive cases, as well as to exercise more scrutiny at the department level. The result, in short order, was a noticeable improvement in the quality of the documentation forwarded by the chairmen and, some administrators have argued, a like improvement in the degree of selectivity demonstrated by the chairmen.

Georgia and Tulsa. Unlike term contracts, there are not that many variations on the basic theme of an extended probationary period. The University System of Georgia, however, added a new wrinkle, and the University of Tulsa added more years.

After two years of study by a committee of regents and a

committee of faculty, the University System of Georgia in 1975 also adopted an eleven-year probationary period. (The university system includes all state-supported two- and four-year colleges as well as the University of Georgia, Georgia Tech, and Georgia State.) The minimum probationary period was set at five years, with up to three years' credit for prior service. The maximum trial period for faculty at the rank of assistant professor or above was fixed at seven years, with the possibility of a terminal contract for the eighth year. Inclusive of service as a lecturer or an instructor, the probationary period could extend to ten years plus a terminal, one-year contract. The new wrinkle at Georgia was a proviso that the names of untenured faculty members continued beyond the seventh year and the "justification for such retention" be made a matter of record "available for public inspection." The requirement of public disclosure was designed supposedly to inhibit routine extensions and to encourage administrators to develop defensible rationales for exceptional cases that warranted a longer trial period.

One year after Georgia acted, Tulsa leapfrogged to a possible thirteen-year probationary period. With one year's notice added for all terminations, the new policy allows a thirteen-year trial period under these conditions:

- No one may serve as an assistant professor for more than six years.
- No one may serve as an associate professor without tenure for more than six years.
- No one at the rank of assistant professor or associate professor without tenure may serve at Tulsa for more than twelve years, inclusive of service as an instructor.
- No one may serve at the rank of professor without tenure for more than six years.

As a result of these stipulations, a faculty member with twelve years of combined service as an instructor and assistant professor must be terminated or promoted to associate professor on "continuing appointment," Tulsa's euphemism for tenure. A faculty member with six years' service as an assistant professor but less than twelve years of combined service must be terminated or promoted to associate professor on "term appointment." An associate professor on term appointment must be tenured or terminated after six years at that rank or after twelve years of combined service. There are, then, a number of paths that lead to a thirteen-year probationary period, perhaps the longest trial period among American colleges and universities.

Suspension of "Up-or-Out" Rule

Whereas extended probationary periods postpone tenure decisions for a finite amount of time, abolition of the "up-or-out" rule allows an institution to defer the decision indefinitely. More commonly, however, a "tenure-like" performance review and decision occur during the next-to-last year of the prescribed probationary period. At that time, faculty members are either awarded tenure, declared tenurable, or denied tenure and issued a terminal contract. Tenurable faculty members are persons qualified for tenure who would, in fact, be awarded tenure if a permanent position, or a "tenure slot," were available. Such slots are typically limited by a tenure quota. Tenurable faculty may remain at the institution on multiyear contracts and await a vacancy in the tenured ranks. In theory, a tenurable faculty member could be terminated at the conclusion of a term contract; in practice, that does not appear to happen. The relaxation of the "up-or-out" proviso thereby offsets the constraints of a tenure quota, a circumstance that would prompt most observers to ask why a college or university would adopt one policy to neutralize another policy. Among the institutions without an "up-or-out" rule and with a tenure quota, we examine closely Union College and consider similar policies at Hartwick College and Albion College.

Union College. If not the first college to abandon the "up-or-out" rule, Union College (in Schenectady, New York) has certainly been the most celebrated. Such a "radical departure" by such a traditional and respected liberal arts college was sure to attract attention. Additional publicity was self-generated by an essay and speech by Willard Enteman (1973, 1974), then

provost of the college and architect of the policy, and to a lesser
extent by doctoral research on the matter by a college staff
member (Wolf, 1980).

The roots of the policy change were grounded in the
rapid expansion of the college in the 1960s and the concurrent
infusion of better-trained, better-credentialed faculty members.
As the rate of enrollment increases decelerated and costs soared,
these new faculty members neared the tenure decision. Although
the college was only 42 percent tenured in 1970, President Har-
old Martin feared that the tenure ratio could rise briskly—to 80
or even 90 percent. In addition, recent deficits aroused concerns
among both the faculty and the administration about the col
lege's stability and the potential erosion of their economic security. Martin reviewed the prognosis with the board of trustees,
and the board decided to (1) grant modest salary increments,
(2) appoint all new faculty to one-year contracts, and (3) impose a tenure limit of 60 percent. Together, these measures
would reduce long-term financial and programmatic commitments at a time of uncertainty and austerity.

Because the faculty had not been fully consulted about
these decisions, the results were predictable: a storm of protest
and months of after-the-fact discussions between the faculty
and the provost. Enteman realized quickly that the central issue
was the nonnegotiable position of the president and the board
on the 60 percent tenure quota. As conversations between the
provost and the faculty continued, the board decided to rescind
the requirement that all new contracts be limited to one year.
Although the requirement was originally intended to restrict
long-term commitments to the foreign language programs, early
experiences suggested that—in the interest of equity—either all
new contracts or none should be confined to one year. Since annual appointments were neither feasible nor desirable in many
disciplines, the board revoked the policy, and the faculty's attention fastened on the tenure quota and a search for alternatives.

The notion of multiyear contracts for everyone was rejected as too traumatic a change and too dangerous an attack on
the foundations of academic freedom. An extended probation-

ary period, perhaps as long as fourteen years, was also discarded
as too injurious to academic freedom and too lengthy a period
for untenured colleagues to endure the stress and suspense of
probationary status. Although a few faculty members considered unionization an appropriate response to the board's alleg-
edly arbitrary action, the proposal attracted little enthusiasm.
Other professors experimented briefly with models of lavishly
supported "superstars" on temporary appointments, but the
president swiftly communicated to the faculty that such an alternative was unacceptable. As the deliberations proceeded,
Enteman identified the "up-or-out" rule as the critical obstacle
to resolution of the fundamental problem. Prodded and persuaded by the provost, the faculty, little by little, reached the
same conclusion.

Enteman's conceptual breakthrough led to an inventive,
three-part policy: (1) a 60 percent college-wide tenure quota,
(2) abolition of the "up-or-out" rule, (3) a *minimum* tenure
quota of 33 percent. The third provision represented a unique,
shrewd, and necessary strategem devised by Enteman to alleviate widespread concern among the faculty that an end to the
"up-or-out" rule could be the precursor to tenure's demise at
Union. If the tenure level for any three-year period were ever to
average less than the prescribed minimum, all tenurable faculty
beyond the seventh year of service would automatically be tenured. Seventy-five percent of the faculty endorsed the new policies, which were then approved by the board of trustees in June
1973.

The procedures for implementation established two separate committees, one to review positions and the other to review candidates. The Consultation (or "position") Committee,
which reports to the president, numbers two senior administrators and seven faculty members (usually tenured): the vice-
president for academic affairs; the dean of graduate studies and
continuing education; and the chairmen of the Planning and Priorities Committee, the Academic Affairs Committee, the Faculty Review Board, and the four college divisions: Humanities,
Social Sciences, Science, and Engineering. Without reference to
the qualifications of any candidates for tenure, the committee

estimates faculty manpower requirements and assigns tenure
slots for all programs and departments within the constraints of
the 60 percent limit on tenured appointments. Updated annually, these four-year forecasts are reviewed and acted on by the
board of trustees. After approval by the board, the projections
are distributed to the faculty at large. College policy requires
that "every decision . . . to recommend to the president any additional tenured appointment to the faculty shall be consistent
with the estimate set forth in the resolution then most recently
adopted by the board of trustees."

The Faculty Review Board (or "person" committee)—
comprised of five senior faculty members, the vice president for
academic affairs, and the dean of graduate studies—bears responsibility for the evaluation of tenure candidates. (The committee also includes three untenured faculty members without
vote on tenure decisions.) If a candidate has been advanced for
consideration by the department and such consideration has
been approved by the dean of the faculty, the president constitutes a special ad hoc committee to review in depth the candidate's qualifications. Normally a four-person committee with
only one member from the candidate's department and only
one member from the candidate's division, the committee may
add an "outside professional" to the group. The ad hoc committee submits a report to and meets with the Review Board, which
supposedly assesses each candidate exclusively on grounds of
merit, without any regard for the numerical limits projected by
the "position" committee. Although the Review Board has
knowledge of the number of vacancies in the tenured ranks,
that information, a senior staff member assured us, "has no
bearing" on any decisions about "tenurability." The recommendations of the Review Board and the reports of the ad hoc committees are forwarded to the president. After considering the
advice of the various committees and the recommendations of
the senior officers, the board of trustees ultimately decides each
case. Faculty members deemed unfit for tenure are issued a terminal contract. Qualified candidates are granted tenure *as long
as* a tenure slot exists, as determined by the Consultation Committee. In departments without any available tenured positions,

a faculty member otherwise qualified for tenure receives a three-to five-year contract renewable indefinitely. These persons constitute the tenurable faculty. In instances where there are two or more faculty members worthy of tenure in a department with only one open slot, the Review Board must establish a priority list.

   To move from tenurable to tenured status, the faculty member must be reviewed again by the Review Board and compared with all candidates currently eligible for tenure. That stipulation, Enteman claimed, ensures that tenurable faculty members are measured against contemporary competition and not the standards of the past. Conceivably, then, a person once declared tenurable could subsequently be "bumped" by a newer, stronger candidate for tenure. The bypassed faculty member may continue on term contracts unless the individual was now determined to be untenurable. In that case, the person would receive a two-year terminal contract or one year's notice plus the financial equivalent of one year's service. All tenurable faculty members must be evaluated for "tenurability" at least once every six years.

   About 52 percent of Union's faculty currently hold tenure. Although one might expect, therefore, that some of the nineteen tenurable faculty members will be awarded tenure, these persons are affiliated with departments that are more than 60 percent tenured. As Dwight Wolf, assistant to the president, explained to us in January 1981, the college-wide quota applies to each department as well. That appears to represent a shift in policy effected too recently for analysis here.

   Hartwick and Albion. A once unthinkable departure from a well-established precedent sometimes seems more sensible after the stranglehold of that tradition has been shattered elsewhere. And so the "reformation" started at Union spread. In October 1974, Hartwick College, located only seventy-five miles from Union, initiated renewable four-year contracts for faculty members determined to be qualified for tenure in a department with a tenure ratio greater than 75 percent. The policy further provided that "special consideration may be given in departments in which there are tenured persons who are within five years of retirement."

Situated about eighty miles south of Lansing, Michigan, Albion College also decided in 1974 to waive a mandatory "up-or-out" decision so that talented candidates for tenure could be retained rather than released for reasons of short-term or long-term financial and programmatic considerations. As reported by the college's newsletter, the faculty voted on four proposals:

1. Suspension of the "up-or-out" proviso.
2. Elimination of all departmental and collegiate tenure quotas.
3. Maintenance of both the 75 percent tenure quota and the "up-or-out" rule.
4. None of the above.

The first option, supported by the administration, garnered fifty-eight votes, while the second proposal, advocated by the local AAUP, attracted twenty-eight votes. Support for the third and fourth options totaled five votes. As ultimately approved by the board of trustees, the policy permits renewable two-year contracts for candidates approved for tenure where no permanent positions are available. As vacancies occur within the tenured ranks, these faculty shall normally assume any such positions. President Bernard Lomas praised the policy as a device to "draw a balance between the need to protect the principles of academic freedom through tenure, to meet the college's need for future flexibility, and to preserve the legitimate expectations and hopes of nontenured faculty members." The president did not address a common perception on campus that administrative support for the new policy was primarily motivated by a desire to thwart the formation of a faculty union. In the first year of the new policy, five faculty members were tenured, three tenurable faculty members were issued two-year contracts, and two candidates were terminated. (We have been unable to secure more recent and complete data from the College.)

Strengths and Weaknesses of Dilatory Policies

Extended Probationary Periods. In rare instances, a college, or more often a university, may offer a faculty member "instant tenure," an appointment to a permanent position without any probationary period. Generally, such offers are tendered only to eminent professors who are already tenured at another institution. With these special cases excepted, most academicians agree that some probationary period should precede the award of tenure. Disputes and disagreements center on how long a courtship should precede the establishment of a permanent relationship.

In the opinion of the Keast Commission, "The probationary period should be long enough to permit careful consideration of the faculty member's qualifications. But it should not be so long as to postpone unduly the faculty member's enjoyment of the full benefits of permanent status, keeping him in jeopardy of termination into middle life. And it should not be so long as to erode the tenure principle by greatly increasing the numbers who do not have its protection" (AAUP/AAC Commission on Academic Tenure, 1973, p. 58). These views translated into a recommendation that the probationary period be no less than five years and no more than seven. Jordan Kurland, associate general secretary of the AAUP, supports the commission's position. He explained to us that the association had not censured violators of the seven-year standard because those institutions were "major research universities where due process and academic freedom were not at issue." The AAUP's stance, Kurland cautioned, might be quite different at some two- and four-year colleges where the traditions of faculty governance, due process, and academic freedom were not as deeply embedded. Contrary to the Keast Commission's conclusion, Kurland also maintained that colleges concerned primarily with undergraduate instruction could probably evaluate a faculty member's performance in less than seven years. The commission had contended that teaching was perhaps more difficult to evaluate than research; therefore, undergraduate institutions required as much or more time to assess a faculty member's performance.

The value of a probationary period probably depends far less on length and far more on whether the faculty and staff properly exploit the trial period. If over the course of a probationary period, whatever its duration, a faculty member under-

goes the same experience every year, then probationary periods
are likely to be unfulfilling as well as unrevealing. Assignments
for untenured faculty members should be deliberately and
thoughtfully constructed so as to provide candidates maximum
opportunities for improvement and to provide decision makers
maximum opportunities for assessment. Where there are questions about a faculty member's abilities or talents in a particular
area, the probationary period should be consciously used to resolve those doubts. If an untenured faculty member demonstrates promise as a teacher but produces little as a researcher
(and if both talents are important), then the department chairman or dean should offer that person an assignment more conducive to research. If the individual does not produce under
favorable circumstances, then there is little reason to believe that
a prolific researcher will soon or eventually emerge under more
normal circumstances. The division of labor should not, of course,
be so skewed as to present a wholly artificial work environment.
Instead, the probationary period should allow the faculty member from time to time to devote special attention to certain critical areas of responsibility. Why offer the tenure candidate the
same assignment year after year and use intuition and guesswork
to determine whether the individual will ever produce as a scholar? Why not, instead, use the probationary period to test the
proposition? Some may claim that inequities will result—that
among untenured faculty prolific researchers, for example, would
be afforded less time than unproductive scholars to conduct research. Perhaps, although the researcher might be afforded a
similar advantage to improve as a classroom teacher. Policy
could stipulate, moreover, that all parties borrow against future
assignments, with severe imbalances corrected over time.

The key considerations are to articulate criteria and standards for tenure, to devise assignments and opportunities that
enable the faculty member to demonstrate merit, and to design
evaluation procedures that enable peers and supervisors to assess
the candidate's qualifications (see Chapter Eight). Were these
criteria applied, one would expect probationary periods on a
particular campus to be more varied than uniform. To presume
that all faculty need the same number of years to bloom or wilt

understates the intellectual, developmental, and disciplinary differences among untenured faculty. (For data on the relationship between creative productivity and age, see Berenson, 1966; Dennis, 1966.) We doubt, therefore, that any "magic number" fits all institutions, all colleges within a university, or all faculty members within a college. At a well-managed institution, we would expect both positive and negative decisions to be scattered across a distribution curve and not congregated at the next-to-last year of the probationary period. Some exceptionally talented candidates will manifest evident fitness for tenure after only a few years; and, similarly, some decidedly deficient candidates will manifest evident unfitness for tenure after an equally brief period. In these instances, early tenure and early termination, respectively, may be warranted. For all the other more questionable cases, the probationary period should continue until the opportunity costs associated with a prolonged probationary period offset the marginal value of any additional data that may be accumulated to inform the tenure decision. Most four-year colleges and universities believe the crossover occurs around the sixth year. With limited exceptions noted later, we tend to agree. Whatever the maximum length of the probationary period, we would urge all academic administrators to ask as the trial period proceeds, "What more do we seek to learn, and how can we best secure that information?" The answers to these questions should be shared with the candidate. Ideally, all ambiguities should be resolved by the conclusion of the probationary period. More often, however, questions linger and doubts persist. When in doubt, weed out. While a rigorously selective university may occasionally terminate a latent genius, such rare mistakes seem far preferable to a system that tenures everyone so as to overlook no one.

As we turn from a general approach to probationary periods to the special advantages and disadvantages of extended trial periods, we recall the gaps between the promise and the performance of term contracts. Term contracts, in theory, provide regular occasions to exercise discretion, although few colleges capitalize on that opportunity. Likewise, lengthy probationary periods present a chance to collect "longitudinal data" over an extended observation period; yet we have no evidence to suggest that Rochester, Georgia, or Tulsa significantly alters faculty assignments or evaluation procedures to exploit that opportunity. With the important exception of temporal limitations on rank, the nature of an eleven- (or a thirteen-) year probationary period and, more particularly, the nature of the seventh through eleventh years do not appear to differ markedly from briefer trial periods at other universities. The extra years appear to be more of the same. Faculty assignments and evaluation procedures after the seventh year do not seem to be specifically designed to resolve unanswered questions about a faculty member's potential. In fact, the public disclosures required at Georgia to retain a faculty member beyond the seventh year are more likely to produce bland evaluations than detailed statements of deficiencies and performance objectives.

Much as a longer probationary period theoretically allows an institution to gather more data and render a more enlightened decision about a candidate, the additional time should permit the administration to improve its understanding of institutional trends and needs and then to match priorities and personnel. Of course, an institution long on probationary periods and short on astute planners will drift and err regardless of the duration of the trial period. An institution attentive to the long term should, as a rule, be able to avoid from the outset probationary appointments incompatible with program priorities.

An extended probationary period does, however, promise both the faculty member and the college or university a significant "passive" advantage that may be realized without *any* administrative acumen or action. From the perspective of an untenured faculty member, especially one with limited options, an extended probationary period (or suspension of the "up-or-out" rule) may be preferable to the alternatives of relocation, underemployment, or unemployment. Perhaps more significantly, an extended probationary period enhances the mathematical probability of tenure. The relationship between the length of the probationary period and the probability of tenure had been expressed by Luecke (1974, p. 279) as $c = py$, where c represents the probability of promotion to tenure, p represents the percentage of untenured faculty tenured each year, and y represents the *average* number of years faculty serve on probation. As-sume, for example, that 5 percent of the untenured faculty at a university achieve tenure each year and that the probationary period averages six years. Then, in accordance with the $c = py$ formula: $x = (.05)(6)$. Under those conditions, x equals .3; that is, the chances are three in ten that a faculty member will ulti-mately attain tenure at that university. If we change the average probationary period to nine years, then $x = (.05)(9)$. Now x equals .45; that is, faculty enjoy almost a 50 percent chance of tenure as a result of the extension of the average probationary period from six to nine years. In short, the longer an untenured faculty member remains at an institution, the more likely math-ematically that the person will eventually be among the fraction promoted to tenure.

An extended probationary period can slow the rate at which faculty members become eligible for tenure. And because a longer probationary period increases a cohort's probability of tenure, the college's tenure ratio can be lowered while a candi-date's chances for tenure are not. A formula developed by the AAUP illustrates the interrelationships (American Association of University Professors, 1973b, p. 201):

T = percent of total faculty tenured
r = annual rate of attrition from tenured ranks
p = annual rate of promotion to tenure among *all* un-tenured faculty
a = percent of departing tenured faculty replaced by untenured faculty
P_c = probability of promotion to tenure within a given faculty cohort
t = average number of years faculty ultimately tenured serve on probation

For the formula

$$\frac{1-T}{T} = \frac{art}{P_c}$$

we substitute the following values:

$$\frac{1 - .65}{.65} = \frac{1.0 \times .02 \times 6}{x}$$

In other words, what must the cohort probability be to maintain a tenure ratio no greater than 65 percent with a 2 percent attrition from the tenured ranks and a six-year probationary period? In the equation above, x equals .222; or, stated another way, since

$$p = \frac{P_c}{t}$$

about 3.7 percent of the untenured faculty will be tenured each year. If the college seeks to maintain a tenure ratio below 55 percent and at least a two in ten probability of tenure for probationary faculty, the college could establish a nine-year average trial period:

$$\frac{1 - .55}{.55} = \frac{1.0 \times .02 \times 9}{x}$$

Here x equals .220. Over a nine-year probationary period, fewer faculty will be promoted each year—2.4 percent versus 3.7 percent—but each faculty member will be eligible for tenure for three more years. Hence, a nine-year probationary period and a 55 percent tenure limit yield the same cohort probability as a 65 percent tenure limit and a six-year probationary period. The college thus has a trade-off to consider.*

The straitened circumstances of the 1980s and 1990s may induce both faculty and administrators to support any reasonable policy that increases the probability of tenure and decreases the maximum tenure ratio. While an extended probationary period may improve a cohort's probability of tenure, the same policy may, as the Keast Commission alleged, also in-

---

*The reliance by the AAUP on the average probationary period for faculty ultimately tenured, as opposed to the average for all untenured faculty, leads to distortions, since faculty eventually tenured probably experience a somewhat longer probationary period and the longer the average probationary period, the lower the annual rate of promotion need be to achieve a particular cohort probability.

crease cohort anxiety as the period of uncertainty lengthens and
the tensions mount. Since we were not afforded an opportunity
to interview faculty beyond the seventh year of probationary
service, we cannot comment firsthand about the prevalence or
intensity of any anxieties these faculty numbers may have experienced. We are not at all certain, however, that a linear relationship exists between the length of a probationary period and
the degree of anxiety. Among colleagues beyond the seventh
year of probation at the Harvard Business School, Chait did not
observe any unusual strain or acute distress, despite the keen
competition for a limited number of tenure slots. Perhaps these
probationary faculty members were comforted by the knowledge that candidates denied tenure there seldom suffer a fate
worse than "banishment" to another fine university or to a
lucrative corporate position.

For most faculty members denied tenure, the options are
not likely to be as many or as pleasant. Indeed, faculty denied
tenure at quite ordinary institutions after a particularly lengthy
probationary period may be especially disadvantaged. Prospective employers may conclude, rightly or wrongly, that anyone
deemed unsuitable for tenure after an eleven- or thirteen-year
trial period at an uncelebrated or even average institution represents a poor risk. In that sense, the faculty member denied tenure after only five or six years may bear a less harmful stigma.

While we can only speculate about the effects of a prolonged probationary period on faculty anxiety or career mobility, the data available from Rochester speak more directly to
the concern that extended probationary periods will invite contract renewals until the trial period nears completion and that
separation will then prove to be difficult or impossible. From
1974-75 through 1979-80, twenty-five faculty members at
Rochester were promoted to associate professor with limited
tenure and fourteen were denied. While a definitive conclusion
would be premature, early results suggest that promotion to
associate professor with limited tenure has hardly been automatic. Over the same period, sixteen faculty members were denied unlimited tenure, four after more than seven years—evidence that continuation beyond the seventh year has not been

commonplace or tantamount to a position of unlimited tenure. Rochester's ability to resist routine reappointments for all faculty through the tenth year can be attributed in part to a tradition of excellence and in part to the limits on time in rank—a policy that requires positive action and a comprehensive review to renew a contract after the seventh year. The University of Georgia System and the University of Tulsa also restrict the length of time faculty members on probation may continue toward the tenure decision without attainment of a promotion.

Distinguished research universities are probably best positioned to maximize the advantages and skirt the pitfalls of long probationary periods. Already imbued with a commitment to excellence and already acclimated to rigorous and comprehensive reviews, first-rate universities are less prone to continue mediocre or ineffective faculty members for the entire duration of an extended probationary period. Furthermore, these schools, more than others, command the resources and flexibility to provide varied assignments and special opportunities to faculty members of apparent promise, so as to gauge more completely the candidates' capabilities and potential. Unless the requisite traditions of excellence and selectivity and the necessary financial resources are present or unless the paramount objective is to improve a cohort's probability for tenure, we question whether most colleges and universities would benefit from a probationary period much longer than seven or eight years. A more prudent course of action would be to use purposefully and more effectively a five- to eight-year trial period.

The separation of promotion and tenure decisions, as adopted by the University of Rochester, represents, we believe, a more broadly applicable and sound practice. We can see no reason for inextricably linking promotion to associate professor with attainment of tenure. After a few years, an assistant professor may well deserve the economic and symbolic rewards a promotion conveys but may not yet have established a "track record" that warrants tenure. Promotion to associate professor provides an appropriate way to recognize competence without a simultaneous commitment to permanence. On the other hand, we would link tenure and promotion to professor, which (we trust) signifies that the faculty member meets the university's utmost standards. Surely the academic standard-bearers and presumed leaders of a department or school merit tenure. We are hard pressed to imagine a circumstance, save some external appointments to a professorship, where a faculty member would be sufficiently superior to deserve promotion to professor yet not so superior as to deserve tenure. At the other extreme, we question the logic of awarding tenure to an instructor. At the very least, someone qualified for tenure should, in our view, also be qualified for a position as assistant professor. (At Harvard University, promotion to professor and promotion to tenure are one and the same; assistant and associate professors are ineligible for tenure.)

Suspension of "Up-or-Out" Rule. The University of Rochester wanted to enhance selectivity through more comprehensive and more conclusive evaluations of tenure candidates. The university thus added a finite amount of time to the probationary period. The objectives at Union College were quite different. The college wanted to retain certain faculty members who were about to be terminated at the end of a seven-year probationary period solely because of the constraints of a tenure quota. There was, in effect, no more room at the inn, at least not within the tenured quarters. Hence, the college created a new class of academic citizens—tenurable faculty—and provided these individuals with an essentially infinite amount of time beyond the probationary period. In this manner, Union, as well as Albion and Hartwick, accomplished indirectly what could not have been accomplished directly under college bylaws. The schools successfully circumvented the numerical limits imposed on the tenured ranks.

If one defines "success" as the achievement of an objective, the policy must be considered successful. In the eight years since elimination of the "up-or-out" rule at Union, four faculty members have moved from tenurable to tenured status and nineteen faculty members are currently tenurable. Of the nineteen, five are under a second four-year contract. No one declared tenurable has ever subsequently been declared untenurable, and no one ever expects such a declaration. As President

Thomas Bonner admitted, tenurable faculty could anticipate tenure except in the improbable case of a "negative review." Unlike the limited tenure faculty at Rochester or the untenured faculty beyond the seventh year at Princeton, Columbia, and the Harvard Business School, tenurable faculty are, we believe, a rose by another name. For all intents and purposes, the campus community regards tenurable faculty as tenured faculty, and indeed the former appear to be every bit as secure as the latter. As one dean observed about tenurable faculty, "They raise as much hell as the tenured faculty."

The policy appears to have satisfied all parties to the original debate at Union. The administration has been able to retain valued faculty members, and these twenty-three persons have been able to remain at the college rather than seek employment opportunities elsewhere at an especially inauspicious time. And, as reported by senior administrators, the board of trustees seemed heartened by the fact that the tenure level, at least the "pure" tenure level, remained comfortably below the prescribed upper limit. Only the AAUP was not enamored of the new policy. It did not censure Union; however, shortly after the college had discarded the "up-or-out" mandate, an AAUP committee charged with safeguarding academic freedom condemned the violation of AAUP standards:

> [We find] wholly inimical to the principles of academic freedom which tenure serves . . . the policy adopted at a few institutions of withholding tenure from admittedly qualified candidates who have completed the maximum probationary period but retaining them in a kind of holding pattern, perpetually more vulnerable than their tenured colleagues to termination, unless and until the [tenure] quota eases for them and they too are granted tenure. Assuming they have fully earned an entitlement to tenure, there can be no justification for continuing them in a less favorable and more vulnerable status than their tenured colleagues [American Association of University Professors, 1973a, p. 429].

Since we do not believe that tenure is a prerequisite to academic freedom and since the tenurable faculty at Union College appear to suffer no deprivation of liberty or license, we do not endorse the AAUP's broadside.

For different reasons, however, we too do not commend "holding patterns" to other colleges and universities. As practiced at Union and elsewhere, the abolition of the "up-or-out" provision and the creation of a tenurable status must, we believe, be regarded essentially as a cosmetic change and a deceptive "solution" to the problems posed by a tenure quota. The policy creates an illusion, although perhaps a politically expedient one, that masks a more accurate estimation of the college's tenure density. When tenurable faculty are added to the tenured ranks, the tenure ratio at Union for 1980-81 rises from 52 percent to 64 percent.

While we are dubious about the purported advantages associated with suspension of the "up-or-out" rule, we have no doubts about the value of manpower forecasts. All colleges and universities would be well advised to estimate the fiscal and human resource requirements of each department and school over at least a four- or five-year horizon. In Chapters Seven and Ten, we discuss more broadly the need to consider institutional priorities as a criterion for tenure and the need to plan. Here we are concerned more narrowly with the approach adopted at Union.

Union College—quite properly, we believe—elected to separate forecasts about manpower needs and tenure densities from deliberations about a candidate's qualifications for tenure. (The endeavors probably require quite different skills.) Enteman asserted that these independent perspectives produced better personnel decisions, because the Review Board was able to concentrate solely and intently on the candidate's merit, without the distraction of questions related to institutional considerations. We are not as certain that the issues can or should be altogether divorced for specific tenure decisions. Can a "person" committee informed about the availability of tenure slots truly disregard that information as candidates are reviewed? With the knowledge, for example, that Department X has no tenure posi-

tion available, would not some committee members afford a
candidate the benefit of the doubt inasmuch as a positive decision would lead only to a tenurable and not a tenured appointment? Likewise, can a position committee allocate tenure slots
with objectivity when at a small college, such as Union, the
members of the committee can readily discern the implications
for individuals of decisions about positions. In that sense, the
assignment of a tenured position to a department can be equivalent to the conferment of tenure to a particular person. And
even were we to assume that each committee could adopt a uni-
dimensional perspective, the question remains whether or not
that would be desirable. We recommend instead that individual
merit and institutional needs be placed on a balance scale of
sorts. The ideal candidate, of course, would be exceptionally
qualified for tenure in an essential program. Are there not, however, occasions when an individual who has rare ability but is
only modestly matched to the college's priorities should be tenured? Conversely, there are undoubtedly occasions when a person affiliated with a moribund department should be denied
tenure despite that candidate's acceptable qualifications. For
these reasons, we believe that considerations of individual merit
and institutional needs should never be quite as partitioned as
some purists might propose.

The opportune moment for position control arises not a
year or a day before a tenure decision. With an effective long-
range plan, a committee or a senior academic officer should be
positioned to forewarn a department long before then about
the eligibility of a *position* for tenure. At the least, a position
committee or a provost should be able to reach a decision about
the viability of the position by the midpoint of the incumbent's
probationary period. Thereafter, the candidate could safely assume that, in the absence of any abrupt and unforeseeable
changes in the college's condition, tenure will be a matter of
merit. Optimally, the position decision should be rendered at
the time a department seeks authorization to fill a vacancy. As a
slightly different alternative, Dartmouth and Princeton assign
departments, based on estimates of turnover and need, a certain
number of tenure slots for about a ten-year period. Within those

guidelines and the limits of the probationary period, the department then decides which candidates to recommend for tenure
and when.

In conclusion, the circumstances that impelled Union to
embrace a transparent subterfuge are understandable. The provost and the faculty wanted to retain a bright cadre of new faculty, and the prospects of "massive retirements" allayed Enteman's worries about a temporary bulge in the tenure ratio in the
event that these newcomers gained permanent status. The board
of trustees and the president, however, were resolutely wedded
to a 60 percent tenure limit. In consultation with the faculty,
Enteman followed the path of least resistance to a policy that
would permit the college to retain able faculty about to be sacri-
ficed on the altar of a tenure quota. The path led to the won-
derland of tenurable status, where new labels seemed to "solve"
a stubborn problem.

We have some admiration for Enteman's ingenuity and re-
sourcefulness. Under the circumstances, suspension of the "up-
or-out" rule may have been the only avenue of escape from the
dilemma the provost and the faculty encountered. Unless faced
with very similar circumstances, colleges and universities with
traditional tenure systems would, we believe, be better advised
on balance to retain the "up-or-out" provision. To the extent
that relaxation of the "up-or-out" rule contributes to a relaxation of standards, a college that so modifies traditional tenure
practices would be disserved. Perhaps the most charitable and
most accurate interpretation of the policy decisions at Union
College particularly and at Albion and Hartwick more generally
would be to view these actions as representative of the artful
machinations frequently spawned and necessitated by the imposition of tenure quotas.

6.

Tenure
Quotas

Quotas are commonly advanced as a solution to a problem. To control the influx of people and products from foreign lands, the American government periodically places limits on immigration and the importation of select manufactures. The more severely the import threatens American society or industry, the greater the clamor for controls. At one time or another, the United States has established restrictions on "imports" as different as European nationals, Japanese televisions, and Italian shoes. Quotas are not unknown to universities either. Some campuses, for instance, once imposed insidious quotas on the admission of students from certain ethnic and religious groups. Today there are quotas on the number of athletic scholarships a university may offer and on the number of campus visits a prospective student/athlete may accept. There are also tenure quotas, hardly a new phenomenon.

Although most faculty and administrators regard tenure quotas as a relatively "newfangled . . . restriction on faculty advancement," the same policy was, as the Keast Commission noted, commonplace on American campuses prior to World War II, another period of stabilized enrollments (AAUP/AAC Commission on Academic Tenure, 1973, p. 49). During the late 1950s and 1960s, the practice was abandoned as college and university faculties expanded rapidly. As the tenure ranks swelled on many campuses in the late 1960s and early 1970s, administrators and trustees first wondered and then worried whether the trend toward a "tenured-in" faculty could be slowed, halted, or even reversed. With voluntary turnover among faculty diminished by limited opportunities, any solution would have to ensure that fewer faculty earned tenure. Unsure that the normal tenure review process would produce sufficient selectivity, some administrators and trustees, as well as some faculty members, preferred the establishment of a tenure quota—a more drastic and emphatic, though not unprecedented, measure that imposes an upper limit on the percentage of faculty who may hold tenure at any one time. Thus, between 1972 and 1974, the proportion of colleges with an upper limit on tenure levels increased from 5.9 percent to 9.3 percent, a 58 percent rise. Of the three hundred or so institutions with tenure quotas or guidelines, we report briefly here on three cases: Colgate University, the City University of New York, and the New Jersey State Colleges.

Colgate University*

Colgate University first implemented a tenure quota in January 1969, when President Vincent Barnett recommended and the board of trustees approved a motion to adopt "a general guideline that no more than 55 percent of the academic faculty, excluding physical education and library, may be on tenure at any given time." At the time, 52 percent of the faculty

*This section is based in part on a more detailed case study by Emenhiser and Chait (1976).

held tenure. The board simultaneously adopted a guideline for faculty distribution by rank: professors, 33 percent; associate professors, 22 percent; assistant professors, 25 percent; and instructors, 20 percent. The actual percentages at the time were 31, 22, 25, and 22, respectively. Since Barnett's retirement was imminent, some faculty viewed the guidelines as a "parting shot"; others regarded the president's action as a "legacy" to preserve excellence at Colgate.

Barnett had urged adoption of the guidelines primarily for two reasons. Above all else, the president regarded a tenure quota as a means to compel selectivity and thereby safeguard quality. The limit on tenure would force not so much choices *between* the qualified and the unqualified but choices *among* the qualified, so that the most qualified could be selected. In that way, the overall caliber of Colgate's faculty would be continually upgraded. Second, the tenure and rank guidelines would enable the university to offer competitive salaries. A tenure quota would ensure a certain percentage of untenured faculty, presumably at lower academic ranks and at lower salaries. The rank guidelines would prevent automatic passage by tenured and untenured faculty alike from one rank to the next, a "rank inflation" based on little more than length of service. With the faculty somewhat evenly distributed among the various ranks, the money "saved" could be redirected to provide the competitive salaries necessary to retain the university's most distinguished senior members.

Aside from some minor criticisms about the lack of prior consultation between the president and the faculty and the effect of the guidelines on morale, no one, certainly not the faculty, paid much attention to the guidelines until more than two years had passed and the 55 percent limit had been exceeded. In the fall of 1971, Dean Frank Wallin advised the faculty that the tenure level had reached 60.8 percent and that, on average, each year for the next five years, eight faculty members would be eligible for tenure while only three would retire. To remain close to the board's guidelines under those conditions would require the university to render no more than three favorable tenure decisions a year.

Wallin's report triggered a series of discussions and debates over the next seventeen months about tenure quotas and alternatives that might obviate the need for a quota or blunt the impact of the guidelines. There was no shortage of suggestions. Some faculty members urged greater emphasis on early retirement as a means to accelerate turnover. Others recommended that the university add more students to generate more positions and thereby reduce the tenure ratio. One option that attracted sustained attention was a plan to offer new faculty annual contracts limited to three renewals, although a rigorous third-year review would permit exceptional candidates to continue another three years and then be considered for tenure. Proponents of the plan contended that a comprehensive third-year review would increase selectivity and, in effect, allow the university to accept rather than reject candidates for tenure.

Gradually, the discussion shifted from the somewhat remote possibility of alternative policies to more practical concerns about the guidelines. While nearly every faculty member voiced an opinion on the guidelines, the many criticisms can be reduced to variations on five themes.

1. Application of the guidelines to faculty appointed prior to the introduction of "numerical considerations" would constitute an unconscionable breach of faith. Some faculty with multiple offers selected Colgate partly because of the brighter prospects for promotion from within to the tenured and senior ranks.
2. The guidelines will intensify anxiety as well as foster ruthless competition and ignominious comparisons among untenured colleagues.
3. The guidelines should not be applied until the university clearly defines the substantive criteria for tenure decisions.
4. Untenured faculty will be dispirited by the knowledge that mathematical considerations may preclude tenure irrespective of one's accomplishments as a probationary faculty member.
5. Without a reasonable prospect for tenure, probationary faculty will emphasize activities designed to gain national rec-

ognition rather than concentrate on activities valued locally, such as general education, university governance, classroom instruction, and supervision of independent studies.

On the basis of these objections, the AAUP chapter on campus recommended that the guidelines be indefinitely suspended and that the retention of untenured faculty now at Colgate be determined solely on the basis of excellence, "independent of questions relating to administrative needs and purposes." Doubtful that the board of trustees would rescind the guidelines and more openly sympathetic to the need for quality control, the Faculty Affairs Committee resolved that the guidelines should be changed from 55 to 65 percent. A 65 percent guideline, the committee reasoned, would not victimize faculty appointed prior to adoption of the regulation. At the same time, the new guideline would still compel selectivity and ensure ample opportunities to appoint new faculty. Furthermore, the committee believed that the board would be more amenable to an upward revision of the 55 percent limit than to elimination or suspension of the guidelines. At a special session in April 1972, the faculty accepted and forwarded the committee's recommendation to the board of trustees' Faculty Affairs Committee.

Over the next nine months, the committee discussed the guidelines on several occasions with members of the faculty. By January 1973, the trustee committee had failed to reach consensus or closure on the matter. With the tenure level then at 62 percent, Thomas Bartlett, Barnett's successor, strongly recommended that the guideline be raised to 65 percent and reviewed five years thereafter. A divided board finally coalesced around an amended proposal to accept a 65 percent limit for three years with an "automatic return" to 55 percent "as soon as practicable." (Unless the base were enlarged, a return to 55 percent would require three retirements and only two tenure appointments each year until 1991.) The motion passed with one dissenting vote.

In 1974, John Morris, director of the Division of University Studies and a longtime member of the Colgate faculty, succeeded Frank Wallin as dean and provost when Wallin assumed the presidency of Earlham College. As a member of the Dean's Advisory Council (a council of all department heads), Morris had observed firsthand the anxieties and tensions that the tenure guidelines had produced among the faculty. Morris decided, therefore, to deemphasize numbers and stress quality. When the Advisory Council convened to consider the tenure docket, the provost requested that the deliberations focus on each candidate's qualifications for tenure without reference to the quota. To alleviate concerns among the faculty that the guidelines would nevertheless dominate discussions and decisions, Morris invited three faculty "watchdogs" to attend the committee's meetings as observers.

The provost's emphasis on quality resurrected a theme that had pervaded the entire debate about tenure guidelines: the need for explicit criteria to govern tenure decisions. At Morris's request, a faculty committee developed a "Statement of Criteria for Reappointment, Promotion, and Tenure" and presented the document to the faculty for consideration in late May 1975. At a meeting attended by 40 percent of the faculty, the vote on the proposed criteria was precisely even. While the president could have cast a ballot to break the deadlock, Bartlett elected to return the statement to committee for further study, since too few faculty had participated in too vital a decision to be determined by a "tie breaker." Eight months later, the faculty reconsidered the proposal, only slightly revised. "Guidelines" replaced "criteria" in the title, and "highly selective" replaced "competitive" in the preamble as a characterization of the nature of personnel decisions. By a vote of 38-10-6, which once again represented substantially less than half of the faculty, the proposal passed. Apparently the statement simply codified convention, for otherwise a much larger turnout could have been expected.

At the conclusion of the 1977-78 academic year, the Faculty Affairs Committee reported on the operation of the tenure guidelines and recommended that the guidelines be amended to establish 55-65 percent as an acceptable, "flexible, long-term" range.

If a trend develops which suggests that we are making tenure decisions which would take us below 55 percent, this shall be taken as an indication that personnel policies are in need of review. Continued tenure decisions which yield fewer than 55 percent of the faculty on tenure should raise questions about the future leadership of departments and the university and about the quality of the applicant pool, our hiring practices, the possible need for senior level appointments, and the effect on junior faculty morale. Similarly, a trend which would take us beyond 65 percent shall also indicate the need for a review of personnel policies and an examination of the impact of such a trend on departments, the university, faculty quality, and faculty salaries. Both such situations would require us to differentiate between short-run aberrations due to the age structure of the faculty and changes in the retirement age, and longer-run implications. Initial investigations shall be conducted by the Dean's Advisory Council and the Faculty Committee on Promotion and Tenure, with results passed on to the Faculty Affairs Committee.

On a second matter of concern to the faculty, the committee recommended that tenure decisions be based on individual merit and that institutional factors, such as program needs and tenure levels, be considered well before the tenure decision, ideally at the time of appointment and certainly as part of the comprehensive third-year review. These recommendations were subsequently approved by the faculty and the board of trustees.

Between 1972-73 and 1977-78—as the result of seventeen retirements and resignations, one death, and, most significantly, the denial of tenure to twenty-eight of forty-six candidates—the tenure ratio at Colgate dropped from 62 percent to 58 percent. Over the next two years, however, twelve of fourteen faculty earned tenure, only four faculty members departed, and, as a result, the tenure level returned to nearly 62 percent. While Colgate remains within the 55-65 percent range prescribed by the newest guidelines, the upper limit could be tested soon. Whether the administration would advance candidates for tenure where the 65 percent limit would be surpassed and whether the board would accept those recommendations remain to be seen.

City University of New York (CUNY)

With a mix of pride and anguish, Robert Kibbee, chancellor of the City University of New York, once remarked, "There's no story about CUNY that isn't true." The unusual yet undisputed story of the university's efforts to establish a tenure quota seems to substantiate Kibbee's contention. Twice the university attempted to impose a tenure quota, and twice the university failed. An arbitrator nullified the first quota, and the faculty union overturned the second.

The first endeavor began in the fall of 1970. After a series of discussions with the CUNY college presidents and various board members, Chancellor Albert Bowker discerned a consensus. In a letter to the presidents dated October 7, 1970, Bowker noted general agreement on the need to award tenure more selectively. (The norm had been to award tenure rather freely and promotions rather sparingly.) The chancellor reminded the campus presidents of several policy decisions reached the previous spring: newly appointed faculty should have at least a 50 percent chance at tenure; no department should have a full-time faculty more than 75 percent tenured; and special justification would be required for any tenure recommendations that would violate these policies. As the contents of Bowker's letter became known, the faculty denounced the "capricious" imposition of "arbitrary quotas" and complained about the unwarranted intrusion of the central administration into the tenure review process. Trying to quiet this uproar, Bowker wrote Belle Zeller, president of the faculty union, denying any intention to remove the decision-making process from the local campuses and defending a new procedure requiring faculty review committees to rank-order candidates recommended for tenure.

Later that fall, President Kurt Schmeller of Queensborough Community College recommended tenure for fifty-nine of sixty-one eligible candidates. Schmeller communicated to the chancellor that the Faculty Review Committee had refused to rank-order the candidates and that, were all fifty-nine recommendations approved, the college's tenure level would reach 51 percent. The Board of Higher Education's Committee on the City University of New York promptly asked to meet with Schmeller. On the basis of that session, Schmeller was convinced that the only available options were to trim the number of positive recommendations or run the risk that the board would reject the entire complement of candidates from Queensborough. Confronted with those choices, Schmeller removed eleven names from the docket, and in late November the board granted tenure to the forty-eight candidates still under consideration.

The "Queensborough eleven," the faculty members deleted from the initial list of recommendations, filed grievances, which under the contract were subject to binding arbitration. At CUNY, the authority to recommend tenure rested with the college presidents, and the authority to confer tenure rested with the Board of Higher Education. The recommendations were transmitted to the board via the chancellor. Although the chancellor could withhold endorsement of a president's recommendations, the chancellor could not withhold the recommendations. In the opinion of the arbitrator, the imposition of guidelines by Bowker and a *committee* of the board violated the board's bylaws, which specified that the chancellor's office may not "compromise or detract from" the duties and responsibilities of the board or the college presidents. The arbitrator ruled that quotas or guidelines could be a legitimate exercise of academic judgment (not grievable under the contract) *as long as* the college president *chose* to implement restrictions. Had Schmeller or the board as a whole established the guidelines, a different decision surely would have ensued. Indeed, in a companion case, the same arbitrator upheld guidelines voluntarily introduced by the president of Manhattan Community College. By contrast, Schmeller's decision to remove eleven names from consideration was regarded by the arbitrator not as an independent academic judgment but as a decision rendered solely in deference to the chancellor's improper directive. In short, while a college president or the board could impose a quota, the chancellor or a committee of the board could not.

As Bowker's successor, Kibbee appreciated both the import of the Queensborough arbitration decision and the limited ability of the chancellor's office to influence tenure decisions. At Kibbee's suggestion, the Council of Presidents created early in 1973 a special committee to examine the issue of academic tenure at CUNY. Although a few departments on some campuses were 90 percent tenured, the committee discerned no pervasive or acute problems. There was general agreement, however, that tenure levels should not be permitted to increase markedly, since an enrollment decline appeared likely after the "open-admissions boom" ended. The committee thus proposed a 65 percent tenure limit for each college.

Widely circulated, the draft report attracted considerable attention and opposition. After considering the responses to the initial draft, the committee submitted formally to the Council of Presidents in September 1973 a revised report, which recommended the development by department of five-year enrollment and tenure projections; a narrative statement of departmental goals and directions; external review of tenure candidates; and a maximum tenure range of 50 to 60 percent, to be applied vigorously to each college. The council endorsed the committee's report on September 10; two weeks later, Kibbee recommended the substance of the report to the Board of Higher Education. Rather than impose a specific, numerical limit on tenured appointments, the guidelines prescribed that a special performance review and statement of justification accompany all recommendations for tenure where the candidate's department was more than 65 percent tenured.

Between the spring and fall of 1973, opposition to the tenure guidelines mounted. The faculty union consistently referred to the guidelines as quotas, an especially astute word choice in a city where "quota" carries a repugnant connotation for members of many ethnic groups. When the board assembled in October to entertain Kibbee's recommendations, the union erected an informational picket line.

Because of significant disagreement within the board about the level and language of the tenure guidelines, the board referred the matter to a special committee comprised of two board members, a CUNY college president, one faculty member, and the chancellor. The board wished to avoid reference to specific numbers and even the mere appearance of a rigid quota. Less than three weeks later, the board reconvened to consider a slightly revised proposal that would require special review procedures and statements of justification where "a majority" of the faculty in the department already held tenure. The motion passed. Ironically, then, the concerns for numbers and quotas engendered by opponents of the earlier 65 percent limit contributed to the establishment of a more stringent standard, 50 percent.

Throughout the winter of 1973-74, the faculty union worked to rescind the guidelines. These efforts coincided with and inflamed a political battle between Mayor Abraham Beame and Governor Nelson Rockefeller over the size, composition, and control of the Board of Higher Education. On December 31, 1973, the old twenty-one-member board ceased to exist and the next day a new ten-member board was constituted. In response to pressures from the union and the new board's desire to end the controversy over the quotas, the chancellor recommended in late February that the guidelines be suspended. The board approved Kibbee's recommendation in April and established a commission to review the issues. In October 1974, the board approved the commission's recommendation to revoke the guidelines and reinstitute prior practices. So ended CUNY's brief encounter with tenure quotas.

Reflecting on these events a year later, Kibbee told us that he had without contradiction supported both the original resolution to establish guidelines and the subsequent motion to rescind them. "The new system had been tried for six months," the chancellor observed, "but had produced no substantial changes in the patterns of tenuring." Since the results were largely insignificant, "there seemed to be no point in continuing

the experiment." The data on tenure decisions for 1973-74, the
year the plan was in effect, do not support Kibbee's contention.
Eighty-one percent of the candidates (88/108) in departments
with *less* than a majority of the faculty tenured earned tenure,
whereas in departments with *more* than a majority of the faculty tenured, only 53 percent of the candidates (62/117) gained
tenure. Apparently, the special review procedures for departments more than 50 percent tenured had a decided impact. Had
these special review procedures been continued, CUNY's tenure
success rate, and perhaps the university's tenure level, might
have dropped. A blend of political and academic considerations,
however, persuaded the chancellor and the board that, while
guidelines might lower tenure levels, the same policy would also
heighten tensions and increase strife. The trade-off was not acceptable.

New Jersey State Colleges

Across the Hudson River from CUNY, there was also an
infatuation with tenure guidelines. Not long after Bowker's
foray, the New Jersey State Board of Higher Education considered the imposition of tenure quotas on the eight state colleges.
At the board's request, Chancellor Ralph Dungan prepared a
staff paper on tenure at the state colleges. Completed in June
1972, the report reaffirmed the need for tenure but called for a
balance between tenured and untenured faculty and a balance
between stability and flexibility, so that the colleges could respond to changes in student markets, programmatic needs, and
societal goals. The report noted that, contrary to a national
norm of a 50-60 percent tenure ratio, 72 percent of the faculty
at the state colleges held tenure in 1972, an increase of nine percentage points over the previous year. The report concluded
with recommendations that the board set a 60 percent limit on
tenure and enact procedures to assure that successful tenure
candidates demonstrate significant potential for continued development as well as satisfactory performance to date.

The board discussed the report over the summer of 1972
and in September adopted a resolution embodying the report's

major recommendations. The resolution directed the board of
trustees at each state college to take the following steps:

1.   Prepare and update annually a ten-year plan indicating the
     steps it would take to achieve a balance of faculty in which
     no more than a "reasonable proportion" are tenured.
2.   Adopt internal policies imposing either specific restrictions
     or more intensive and rigorous review procedures for any
     tenure appointment that raises the current tenure level.
3.   Offer tenure only to faculty members who possess an ap-
     propriate terminal degree or its equivalent.
4.   Award tenure only to those teachers whose performance
     clearly indicates evidence of ability and willingness to make
     a significant and continuing contribution to the growth and
     development of the college.
5.   Award tenure on the basis of positive evidence of excel-
     lence in teaching, research, and contribution to college and
     community, and not simply because negative evidence is
     not presented.
6.   Establish a procedure for regularly evaluating tenured fac-
     ulty.

In October 1972, the board extended this resolution to apply to
the state's two-year county colleges as well.

   To block these directives, the faculty unions for the state
and county colleges sued on grounds that the board had (1) failed
to observe certain procedural requirements of state law; (2) violated the state Employer-Employee Relations Act by altering the
terms and conditions of employment without negotiating with
the union; and (3) exceeded its authority by adopting regulations
that illegally impair the tenure rights of the faculty. The last allegation specifically challenged the board's right to mandate the
establishment of tenure quotas (or a "reasonable proportion" of
tenured faculty), to require more rigorous review procedures for
some candidates, and to order regular reviews of tenured faculty.
In March 1974, the New Jersey Supreme Court unanimously affirmed the lower court's decision that all the actions taken were
within the board's prerogative and authority.

To win the case is not, necessarily, to win the war. Some colleges balked, others dawdled, and still others submitted ludicrous plans to control or reduce tenure levels. One college, for example, commissioned an art professor to design a schematic representation of tenure levels for a twenty-five-year period, fifteen years more than the board had requested. Largely unintelligible even to the senior officers of the college, the chart reflected assumptions based less on realities and more on prayers, such as constant enrollments over the next quarter century and a 5 percent increase in faculty at the graduate level. To the credit of the plainly ingenious professor, the chart displayed a continuous downward slope, which disguised the fact that the tenure level started at 69 percent, increased over the first four years to 81 percent, and then returned to 69 percent over the next twenty years. Hence, the extra fifteen years; a ten-year plan would have revealed an increase of seven percentage points in the tenure level. Rather than tighten standards immediately, the administration obviously elected to "spare" probationary faculty already on board. The projection was revised slightly in 1975 since the size of the faculty decreased. In 1979-80, the actual tenure ratio was 79 percent.

As far as we can determine, no state college has submitted a ten year plan to the Department of Higher Education since 1972 and we are unaware of any extraordinary measures by the Department to restrain tenure levels. By 1979-80 the tenure level for the state colleges had increased to 74 percent. Perhaps more significantly, the tenure ratios at five of the eight state colleges exceed 70 percent while only one college stands below 60 percent.

Advantages of Tenure Quotas*

Simplicity. Everyone comprehends the concept of a quota: declare an upper limit that may not be exceeded. Whereas alternative approaches to the management of academic tenure

---

*This section and the following one are drawn in part from a study by Chait (1976).

require comprehensive data bases, sophisticated analyses, skill-ful administrators, and responsible faculty, tenure quotas require only that the institution select an upper limit, monitor the tenure ratio, and prohibit any appointments to tenure beyond the allowable maximum. How simple and definitive—qualities especially appreciated by unschooled legislators and exasperated trustees. The tenure debate can focus concretely on a deceptively simple matter, determination of an appropriate percentage, rather than on subtler issues of policy and philosophy.

Flexibility. Coupled with a fixed probationary period, a tenure quota guarantees some turnover, and the turnover guarantees that some slots will be available to introduce new faculty and thus new curricula, to respond to market changes, to add instructors with the most up-to-date preparation, and to appoint persons with a particular expertise not now represented on the faculty. Excessively tenured colleges do not enjoy comparable latitude. Glassboro State College (New Jersey), 90 percent tenured, and California State College (Pennsylvania), 95 percent tenured, cannot, for example, readily shift from a historical mission of teacher education to more popular programs because the colleges employ too many tenured professors of education. Moreover, as the surplus of doctoral recipients peaks in the mid-1980s, these same institutions may lack the flexibility and vacancies needed to enter the marketplace and recruit the strongest candidates from among the thousands likely to be available.

Selectivity. On the eve of the trustees' vote on tenure guidelines, President Bartlett commented, "In making tenure decisions, we sometimes lose faculty who otherwise we could continue to keep. But, to go the other way, and say that we will not be selective, would be a very undesirable policy for our faculty. We need to have selectivity." Obviously, a tenure limit forces a university to be particular, since the fixed number of tenure slots dictates that only so many faculty among those currently and imminently eligible can be accommodated. A quota thus inhibits inclinations to award tenure rather generously, whether to be charitable to one's colleagues, to avert difficult decisions, or to avoid careful comparisons among candidates.

From a tactical standpoint, many department chairmen, deans, provosts, and presidents may welcome a quota as an "excuse" to be rigorous. How much easier it is to explain to a faculty member that the "numbers" foreclosed tenure than to detail the substantive reasons for a negative decision. In that sense, the quota may serve as a useful crutch for weak-kneed administrators.

Prestige. As a by-product, the exercise of selectivity will maintain or restore a measure of prestige to the conferment of tenure. If prestige depends to some degree on scarcity, then the fewer persons tenured, the more prestige the appointment imparts and the more tenure signals an ordination to the priesthood and not merely an entitlement to economic security. Where most of the faculty already hold tenure, the award of tenure can scarcely be regarded as a tribute or a badge of distinction, except at the most elite colleges and universities.

Diversity. The vacancies assured by a tenure limit afford occasions to assemble or maintain a diverse faculty, as measured by sex, race, and ethnicity. For institutions committed to affirmative action—whether as a matter of morality, or mandate, or both—the turnover that tenure quotas compel offers the opportunity to enrich the faculty with a more heterogeneous population.

Economy. As Colgate well realized, tenure guidelines ensure a certain percentage of untenured faculty, presumably at the lower ranks. Since lower ranks generally mean lower salaries, tenure guidelines, together with rank guidelines, have a conservative effect on instructional payrolls. Were most faculty clustered at the senior ranks, either the payroll would balloon or the average salaries for professors and associate professors would not be especially competitive.

On first impression, the advantages offered by a tenure quota may seem rather attractive. Quite understandably, the promise of mandated selectivity and a flexible, diverse, and economical faculty generates considerable support for tenure guidelines, particularly among trustees and administrators. There are, however, disadvantages to be considered; and the closer the tenure level draws to the established limit, the more severe and acute these disadvantages will be.

Disadvantages of Tenure Quotas

Inequity. A tenure guideline adversely affects, at least directly, only untenured faculty. A probationary faculty member's chances for a permanent position are reduced or foreclosed by a set limit on tenure levels. Tenured faculty, on the other hand, suffer no immediate or personal hardships from the establishment of a tenure quota. The burden to resolve an institutional problem thus falls unevenly on a single and already vulnerable segment of the campus community and not, as the AAUP recommends, on "all academic generations"—namely, tenured, probationary, and prospective faculty. As quoted in *AAUP Policy Documents and Reports* (American Association of University Professors, 1977, p. 25), "Equity and institutional morale demand that all or almost all of the burden of satisfying the desired tenure ratio should not be placed upon the probationary faculty." Moreover, as we observed at Colgate, tenure-track faculty suddenly confronted with a newly established tenure limit suffer a particularly harsh penalty. Mindful of that consideration, the Keast Commission urged that the implementation of any tenure guidelines be accomplished gradually, "in order to avoid injustice to probationary faculty whose expectations of permanent appointments may have been based on earlier, more liberal practices" (AAUP/AAC Commission on Academic Tenure, 1973, p. 51).

Deemphasis of Merit. Once reached, a stated maximum tenure level precludes permanent status for a probationary faculty member, no matter how well qualified. Thus, the mere whisper of a strict quota may evoke frightful speculation among faculty that an "Einstein" could be denied tenure on grounds that the tenure limit would be pierced. In short, qualitative considerations will succumb to arithmetic considerations. The prospect that numbers may overshadow worth as the determinative criterion for tenure decisions will deflate faculty morale. Faculty with options may accept positions elsewhere rather than play an academic version of Russian roulette. In part for these reasons, the AAUP prefers that colleges and universities confronted with the need to control access to the tenured ranks develop "over the years" stricter standards rather than impose absolute limits on tenure levels. "But," the association warns, "it is essential to distinguish a deliberate change in standards, retaining a positive probability of an individual's achieving tenure pursuant to well-defined criteria and adequate procedure for evaluation and review, from a situation in which the granting of tenure, for reasons unrelated to the individual's merits, is never a realistic possibility" (American Association of University Professors, 1977, p. 25).

Transiency. Without many or any vacancies in the tenured ranks on a campus with a tenure limit, nearly all probationary faculty members will be transients, escorted through the front door today and ushered out the back door six or seven years from now. Rapid turnover among the untenured ranks, a phenomenon described at Colgate as a "rotating bottom," will lower faculty morale, impede cohesion, and foster discontinuity. The problems of transiency will be exacerbated to the degree that probationary faculty seek positions elsewhere rather than await the nearly certain denial of tenure because of mathematical considerations. (Of course, untenured faculty blessed with alternatives may choose to bypass altogether a college perceived as a way station and locate on a campus more likely to offer permanent quarters.)

As a related matter especially significant at Colgate, some senior professors feared that untenured colleagues, eager to enhance career mobility, would discount local priorities and strive to achieve national visibility as researchers, lecturers, and consultants to the neglect of assignments as teachers and advisers. There was a concern that probationary faculty would single-mindedly pursue professional advancement to the detriment of the character and quality of the university. The concern expressed by these professors probably overstates the "uniqueness" of Colgate's demands on faculty and understates the value most faculty would assign to the achievement of national prominence by a colleague, tenured or untenured.

Controversy. As an administration contemplates or enacts a limit on tenured appointments, management simultaneously furnishes faculty and union leaders with a ready-made issue to rally the forces. At Colgate, the debate occasioned more than a few AAUP smokers and some oblique references to faculty unionism. At CUNY, the second attempt to cap tenure levels precipitated intense and forceful political action that ultimately strengthened the union. The introduction of tenure guidelines at the New Jersey State Colleges helped the faculty union to close ranks and add members. Tenure quotas and guidelines can galvanize opposition as few other issues can.

Whatever percentage or range an administration selects, detractors can assail the limit as arbitrary, capricious, and indefensible. What commends 50 percent more than 60? Two thirds more than three quarters? In short, what commends a quota? While more flexible than quotas, guidelines present similar problems. When the upper limit approaches, the administration faces a dilemma. If it adheres steadfastly to the guideline, the faculty will press for a higher ceiling. If it resists, the faculty will maintain that the guidelines are no more than a thinly veiled quota. If it disregards the guidelines, they will be, in effect, inoperative. Tenure levels may rise, and the board of trustees may demand stiffer measures.

Beyond any allegations of arbitrary and capricious action, the administration may be charged with violations of academic freedom. Under AAUP policy, the probationary period provides untenured faculty with an opportunity to demonstrate worthiness for a permanent position. Any rigid upper limit on tenure levels that precludes consideration of a candidate for tenure, irrespective of the candidate's qualifications, would nullify the intent of the trial period: "To make appointments which are destined to lead to nonretention because of a fixed numerical quota of tenure positions, obviating any realistic opportunity for the affected individuals to be evaluated for tenure on their academic record, is to depart from a basic feature of the system of tenure and thus to weaken the protections of academic freedom. . . . Probation with automatic termination is not probation" (American Association of University Professors, 1977, p. 24). To date, the AAUP has not censured any college or university for the establishment of a tenure limit. Freedom from censure, however, does not mean freedom from controversy, as the three case studies presented earlier well illustrate.

Self-Imposed Constraints. Colgate and the New Jersey State Colleges imposed campus-wide limits on tenure densities. At these colleges, the senior-most administrators and the board of trustees render tenure decisions, as opposed to tenure recommendations. Individual faculty, academic departments, and college committees need not, therefore, adhere to any strictures on tenure levels. Hence, these parties to the review process may pass difficult decisions and enforcement of the quota on to senior managers. Ultimately, then, a campus-wide limitation on tenure represents a self-imposed constraint on managerial prerogatives. Once the tenure limit has been reached, a college will be unable to add new permanent faculty to a department with significant growth potential. Compliance with a quota could force a college president to deny tenure to probationary faculty far stronger than most tenured faculty. Can management not be trusted to exercise discretion and serve the long-term interests of the college without "benefit" of a self-imposed constraint?

Suppose the faculty of a college expressed complete confidence in the administration's ability to modulate the school's tenure level. "We are convinced," the faculty senate resolves, "that the college administration will maintain tenure ratios at appropriate and reasonable levels without the undue restrictions on managerial discretion presented by a tenure quota." How does the administration respond to that vote of confidence? Does the administration admit that tenure quotas are necessary to protect the faculty and the college against managerial nonfeasance?

A tenure quota placed on a department presents a somewhat different case. Under those circumstances, the faculty and the department head must shoulder the responsibility, since the administration could refuse to entertain any applications for tenure that would exceed the departmental limit. (With far greater success than CUNY, the Dartmouth College faculty adopted department-based guidelines of 50-66 percent, with the stipulation that each department would normally be permitted to tenure only two candidates per decade for every ten authorized positions unless the department was less than 50 percent tenured. The number of authorized positions was based on a ten-year forecast, revised at three- to five-year intervals, of curricular requirements. The policy also provided that the guidelines "shall not preclude tenure appointments for those judged to possess truly outstanding qualifications.") While departmental quotas also represent a manufactured constraint on judgment and discretion, at least responsibility and accountability are paired. Under a campus-wide policy, the administration will be held accountable for enforcement of tenure guidelines, even though faculty members are responsible for the recommendations that threaten to overrun the upper limit. If self-restraint cannot operate without some additional controls, then department-based quotas seem more sensible, unless the departments are so small that each person's tenure status dramatically affects the ratio.

An Upward Draft. While we have not collected data to confirm the observation, we wonder whether a tenure quota does not, in fact, legitimate a certain tenure density. To be sure, a tenure quota sends a message to the faculty about expectations and limitations. Does the quota, however, not also communicate to the college community that the administration finds acceptable a tenure level of *x* percent? Where institutions are below that upper limit, one can imagine, if not a rush to fill the void, at least an indifference to the tenure density unless and until that upper limit draws near.

Conclusion

Tenure levels are analogous to weight control. An ideal weight depends on individual characteristics much as an ideal tenure ratio depends on institutional characteristics. To maintain that weight, usually expressed as an acceptable range, most physicians would recommend that the patient fashion a balanced and nutritious diet and assert a modicum of self-discipline. At times, intake may have to be limited or rigorous exercise increased to counter some earlier excesses. The more one relinquishes self-control, the greater the risks and the more severe the corrective measures will have to be. With respect to tenure levels, there will probably be defensible reasons now and then to be slightly "overtenured," just as there will sometimes be sensible reasons to limit intake voluntarily. Consonant with that philosophy, the Keast Commission urged that institutions "express their decisions as to the ratio of tenured and nontenured faculty as ranges or limits rather than as fixed percentages" and also recommended that "the chosen ratios be applied with sufficient flexibility to different instructional units of the institution (departments, divisions, separate schools) to take account of significant differences among them in size, current variations in age composition and tenure mix, varying research and teaching responsibilities, and similar considerations" (AAUP/AAC Commission on Academic Tenure, 1973, p. 50).

As a last resort, a patient with an uncontrollable appetite may ask his doctor to wire his jaw shut. A college that continually "cheats" will probably suffer the consequences sooner or later. In the absence of self-restraint, a bloated tenure profile may result, and drastic measures may be deemed necessary. At Muhlenberg College (Pennsylvania), for instance, the administration in 1973 adopted a seven-year moratorium on permanent appointments until the tenure level, then at 74 percent, receded to at least 66 percent. Incumbent probationary faculty and external appointments to department chairmanships were exempted from the ban. With the college's tenure level currently at 68 percent, a committee has been constituted to consider the continued need for a moratorium.

Some members of a campus community would argue that a 74 percent tenure level hardly presents reason for concern; other people at the same institution might be alarmed. While no universally ideal tenure level can be specified, the Keast Commission in 1973 concluded in a "nearly unanimous judgment" that "it will probably be dangerous for most institutions if tenured faculty constitute more than one half to two thirds of the total full-time faculty during the decade ahead" (p. 50). The commission's advice seems sound for the 1980s and 1990s too. We would, however, exhort faculty, administrators, and trustees not to fix blindly on the tenure level to the exclusion of other performance measures or to rely solely on tenure quotas to the exclusion of other personnel policies. Instead of promulgating a definitive quota, a strict guideline, or, worse, a moratorium, we suggest that a college or university view tenure limits as *one* policy variable among many and view tenure levels as *one* performance index among many. A person's weight provides one means to assess his health. No doctor would determine a patient's condition on the basis of weight alone; similarly, no college should rely entirely on tenure levels to evaluate a faculty's fitness or an institution's flexibility. As Colgate eventually recognized (Nevinson, 1980), all the policy variables must be coordinated and all the performance indexes monitored in order to manage tenure policies and practices effectively. Had Colgate started with that realization, the controversies and anxieties provoked by the tenure guidelines could have been averted or at least muted. In any case, to focus on only one aspect of the multifaceted phenomenon of faculty flow is both short-sighted and ill advised.

In the next four chapters, we offer a prescription for a lean and healthy institutional profile. Tenure quotas are one remedy to consider, although we, like the AAUP, believe that a combination of other treatments holds greater promise. A numerical limit on tenure levels may work, but the central question remains whether such a measure must be enacted to curb a college's appetite for tenured faculty. Chapters Seven through Ten delineate an alternative and, we contend, preferable approach, which captures the foremost benefits of tenure quotas without the attendant drawbacks and adverse side effects.

7.

Sound Tenure Policy

██

We begin this chapter with a puzzle and a confession. First, the puzzle. If tenure is a problem, why do not all colleges have tenure problems? If tenure inexorably leads to a tenured-in faculty, why do many colleges have tenure ratios of less than 60 percent? Are tenure *policies* sufficiently dissimilar from campus to campus to account for the differences, or can most of the differences be explained by different approaches to the administration of similar policies? In other words, the problems typically associated with tenure may be problems of policy execution and not problems of policy per se. A simple illustration may suffice.

Ramapo College and Stockton State College are public four-year colleges opened in 1971 by the New Jersey Department of Higher Education. Both schools are governed by the

142

same tenure statutes and the same collective bargaining agreement. As of September 1979, Stockton's faculty was 38 percent tenured, Ramapo's 80 percent tenured. There may be defensible reasons for Ramapo's higher tenure ratio, but if someone is disturbed by Ramapo's tenure density, should tenure policy be the focal point of criticism? Obviously, administrative practice, and not tenure policy, accounts for the difference. The same principle applies more broadly.

Now the confession. When we first decided to examine alternatives to traditional tenure policies, we assumed, at least tacitly, that we would discover one or several alternatives superior to tenure. We had heard too many criticisms of tenure and read too many indictments to believe that there were not more attractive alternatives. We would discover, analyze, and report these options; as a result, some colleges would abandon tenure. In turn, we would win a niche in academe as dragon slayers.

We were mistaken. The more we examined the alternatives, the less we were persuaded that any were markedly superior to tenure or irresistibly attractive. Instead, we reached essentially the same conclusion as the Keast Commission: effectively administered by a campus community, academic tenure can be an effective policy. To go beyond the work and recommendations of the commission, we decided to examine a few schools where conventional tenure policies seemed to work well. Could we identify certain sound practices at these schools that could be applied elsewhere? There was, however, a prior question: What does "work well" mean?

The question could present a methodological morass. What definition should obtain? What criteria should apply? What evidence should be offered? As with most matters of academic quality, one could develop a standard of proof impossible to attain and then discard the question as unanswerable. Despite the methodological pitfalls, we proceeded. We first established four standards we believed to be broadly indicative of an effective tenure system:

1. The institution enjoys a strong academic reputation and employs a well-respected faculty.

2. Selectivity can be observed, as evidenced by voluntary
    resignations and nonreappointments prior to the tenure de-
    cision, and denials of tenure.
3. No more than two thirds of the total full-time-equivalent
    (FTE) faculty hold tenure.
4. The faculty and administration by and large support the
    tenure system as practiced and regard local tenure policies
    as workable, equitable, and generally rigorous.

After consultation with the chairman of the Keast Commission,
other scholars of academe, and officers of national associations
such as the ACE and AAUP, we settled on three diverse schools:
St. Olaf College, the College of Letters and Science at the University of Wisconsin–Madison, and the Harvard Graduate School
of Business Administration. We then visited these three campuses, interviewed faculty and staff, and examined pertinent
personnel policies and data. These three institutions share certain common approaches and customs, which we believe contribute to the effective operation of the tenure system on each
campus. Administrative details often differed, but the general
aims and practices were quite similar.

The following recommendations for effective tenure policy are based only in part on the experiences of these three
institutions. We rely also on personal experiences as practitioners, consultants, and researchers and on information and observations we collected during the course of this study. What will
work where can best be determined locally. Adapted to local
conditions, we believe that the five policies and practices described below are sound, worthy of imitation, and conducive to
the effective management of a potentially effective policy,
namely academic tenure.

Elements of Effective Policy

Judgment, not Measurement. Faculty performance should
be approached as a matter to be judged rather than measured.
While aspects of faculty excellence may be quantified—student
evaluations, for example—most materials that comprise a candi-

date's portfolio serve to inform qualitative and subjective judgments rendered by professionals. The "Standards for Faculty Evaluation" at St. Olaf states: "The following criteria for judgment are qualitative standards in terms of which candidates will be evaluated." At the other extreme stands a private junior college, where faculty are evaluated—scored would be more accurate—by colleagues and students. On a standardized form (or scorecard), faculty numerically rated and ranked candidates for tenure. All faculty with scores above an acceptable minimum, established by the administration prior to the evaluation, earn tenure. Faculty with scores below the minimum are released. Not unexpectedly, when the minimum was 70 (on a scale to 100), everyone scored at least 70. When the administration raised the minimum to 80, everyone scored at least 80. More important, the administration was obliged to assume a clerical role. The faculty "measured" the performance of colleagues; the administration tallied the scores and notified the winners.

At the exemplary schools we examined, procedures akin to a judicial model apply. Parties to the process collect, present, and review evidence appropriate to the decision at hand. At the first level of review, a "jury of peers" carefully considers the evidence, including the "testimony"of outside experts, and renders a decision or, more properly here, a recommendation. The vote may or may not be unanimous, and the decision may be appealed, remanded, or overturned. Even at the appellate level, there are no assurances of unanimity or scientific objectivity. Judges do not measure or score briefs, oral arguments, or decisions on appeal. Judges render judgments that are based on appropriate evidence and certain judicial standards of proof. Similarly, when faculty performance is being considered, the data should support sound judgments and not determine personnel decisions.

Clear Criteria and Standards. Clear and explicit criteria for promotion and tenure provide faculty with a set of performance expectations. Standards communicate the level of excellence or degree of mastery expected. Unless the nature or mission of the institution shifts, the criteria for tenure should remain unchanged, although the standards will change as a faculty member seeks advancement in rank. To use an awkward analogy, the *criteria* for little leaguers and major leaguers are essentially the same. Coaches and managers assess a player's ability to hit, run, throw and field. These are the skills necessary to play the game. Obviously, though, the *standards* for major leaguers differ from those applied to little leaguers. Similarly, faculty at all ranks in a particular school or department should be judged on the basis of the same criteria: teaching, research, and service. The standards, however, should differ from one rank to another or between tenured and untenured status. Policy at the Harvard Business School, for example, delineates one set of expectations for full professor and another set for colleagues at lower ranks:

> Necessarily, the character and amount of evidence available for the appraisal of a person will change as his career advances. Therefore, for appointments below the level of full professor, it is not anticipated that most individuals will have had sufficient time to demonstrate conclusively either outstanding ability in teaching and competence in research or outstanding ability in research and competence in teaching. Rather, the expectation for appointments below the rank of full professor is that they will show strong promise of developing such abilities by the time they are to be considered for appointment to full professor. Ordinarily, an excellent performance during an individual's first appointment in either teaching or research will constitute evidence of such promise. It will be the aim of the school to provide assignments during a person's second appointment which allow him to demonstrate further his foremost abilities and any other skills essential to his promotion not revealed by the nature of his assignments during his first appointment. By the time an individual is considered for a permanent appointment, he should have demonstrated conclusively the level of performance expected of a full professor; and there should be a

good reason to expect that if he is appointed, his productivity will continue at a high level of quality.

As this statement suggests, not only will standards differ from rank to rank but also the same standards of performance may not apply equally to all criteria. The policy neither presumes nor prescribes that faculty achieve excellence and distinction in all areas and in all endeavors. "For the large majority of its faculty, the [Harvard Business] School seeks persons (a) who demonstrate competence and interest in both teaching and research, and (b) who make outstanding contributions in either teaching or research." The Biological Sciences Division at the University of Wisconsin adheres to the same principle: "The candidate must have demonstrated excellence in teaching or research and show satisfactory performance in the second area and in service."

Both schools, then, within certain institutionally determined limits, offer faculty the opportunity to synchronize interests and commitments. Faculty may apportion work time among teaching, research, and service and be evaluated on that basis. For example, an institution could set the following parameters: teaching, 30-60 percent; research, 30-60 percent; service, 10-20 percent. Three faculty with different talents and inclinations might, after consultation with the department head or dean, choose very different combinations:

(1)	(2)	(3)
Teaching 60%	Teaching 30%	Teaching 40%
Research 30%	Research 60%	Research 40%
Service 10%	Service 10%	Service 20%

Faculty are then evaluated for tenure on the basis of a negotiated allocation of time and attention that enables faculty, as individuals, to fashion a work load consistent with personal interests and aptitudes and consistent with institutional priorities. To attain that objective by no means requires that the administration numerically apportion the work activities of each faculty member. A lucid letter of appointment each year could specify work assignments and convey relative priorities without the rigidities, technicalities, and false dichotomies that precise percentages invite. Even without any such policy, many faculty would allocate a considerable portion of their work time on the basis of interests rather than assignments. How simplistic and monolithic a view to assume that all faculty desire the same mix of assignments or that all faculty perform different assignments equally well. To augment worker satisfaction and to maximize faculty productivity, policies should incorporate the advice offered by Yuker (1976, p. 232): "We should recognize individual differences and operate accordingly. We should accept the fact that many faculty members prefer teaching to research, that some prefer research to teaching, and that some feel impelled to do both. . . . Let us make work-load assignments in such a way that these individual differences are taken into account. This would entail writing individualized faculty contracts that specify the approximate amount of time that the given faculty member is expected to devote to teaching, to research, to administrative work, to committee work, to counseling students, and other types of activity."

There are other advantages to the institution as well. Most universities and colleges seek a diverse faculty: some primarily scholars, some principally teachers, and most distinguished in one role and able in the other. Sensitive to the value of such a mix, the "Guidelines for Promotion and Appointment to Tenure Rank in the Biological Sciences" at Wisconsin states: "The achievement of the mission of each of the biological sciences departments requires a balance of individuals with differing commitments to teaching, research, and service. It is essential for the executive committee [a tenure review board] to be informed of the division of responsibilities of each candidate, so that appropriate weighting can be given to evaluations of different areas of activity. This should be expressed as a percentage of time commitment."

The Physical Sciences Division at Wisconsin goes even further. While the area generally expects "well-balanced accomplishments" in teaching, research, and extension, extraordinary candidates for tenure without that balance may still be acceptable "in cases where the candidate is very clearly exceptional" and "where overall balance within the candidate's department will not be adversely affected." In these instances, the standards are especially stringent. A recommendation based "mainly or entirely on research" must demonstrate that the candidate is one of the very best in the field, that the impact of the work goes beyond the immediate field of expertise, and that the candidate is "exceptionally creative, unusually productive, and unequivocally recognized nationally and internationally."

For a recommendation based "primarily or entirely" on the candidate's record as a teacher, the standards are equally rigorous. There must be evidence that the candidate's work has influenced teaching outside of his department, that the candidate's contribution has influenced the teaching done by the candidate's colleagues and that it has extended beyond the campus (here evidence from outsiders must be presented), and that the candidate, on a long-term basis, will remain current in his field.

The use of clear criteria and differentiated assignments permits and encourages faculty to make vastly different contributions toward the central goal of overall excellence. Where all criteria are not uniformly applied to all faculty, institutions can recognize and reward individual excellence in a particular domain and at the same time maintain an overall balance. Which criteria to apply to what degree must be determined by the university, school, or department.

While we cannot prescribe criteria for a particular campus, in Table 3 we list, for illustrative purposes, some criteria and sources of evidence applied at various institutions. (Standards are discussed more fully in Chapter Eight.)

Whatever the particular rubrics or definitions, the statement of criteria should be public, and it should communicate institutional expectations to faculty. At St. Olaf, the general criteria are priority-listed, and within each criterion subcategories are rank-ordered:

The following criteria for judgment are qualitative standards in terms of which candidates will be evaluated. The goal in applying the criteria is distinction as well as competence. . . . These cri-

Table 3. Criteria for Tenure at Various Institutions

Teaching

Criteria	*Sources of Evidence*
Competence in subject matter and across disciplines	Student evaluation
Ability to communicate effectively	Assessment by colleagues
	Direct observation by colleagues
	Teaching materials
Organization of material	Assessment by teaching assistants
Interest in teaching	Student theses, dissertations
Improvement of course materials	Comparison with teaching performance by others in same/similar courses
Ability to understand, evaluate, and use research	
Ability to evoke student interest	Chronology of student progress
Ability to advise, tutor, and evaluate	Peer evaluation of handouts, exams, syllabi
Application of new knowledge to teaching and teaching techniques	Pre/post tests of students
Ability to challenge and motivate students	
Stimulation of independent work	
Adherence to high standards of student performance	

Research

Criteria	*Sources of Evidence*
Ability to stimulate intellectual development of colleagues	Participation in professional programs
Ability to add new knowledge of significance to field	Receipt of grants, fellowships, scholarships
Capacity to develop significant findings from investigation	Critical acclaim or citation by other scholars
Ability to synthesize, criticize, and theorize in an original way	Books, monographs, articles, papers, exhibitions
Ability to clarify extant knowledge	Research awards
Competence in research methods	Professional honors
Ability to relate one's research to applied problems	Terminal degree

teria are neither inclusive nor exclusive, nor is their priority binding with equal force in all disciplines; exceptions may be justified by unusual circumstances, and the listing of these criteria shall in no way preclude a warranted exception.

1. Effective teaching
   a. Extent of mastery of subject matter.
   b. Ability to stimulate the intellectual development of students in the area of one's own discipline; effectiveness in communicating the skills, methods, and intellectual content appropriate to one's discipline.
   c. Effectiveness in classroom teaching, in informal academic contact with students, in supervision of tutorials and independent study, in advising students on their academic programs, and in evaluation of student work.
   d. Demonstrated concern for the role of one's discipline in liberal education, for its relationship to other intellectual perspectives, and, where appropriate, for its bearing on questions with moral, social, and religious dimensions.
   e. Ability to relate professional goals to the needs and goals of one's students as whole persons.
2. Significant professional activity
   a. Excellence and extent of public professional activity (publications, lectures, performances, exhibitions, leadership in professional organizations, and so forth); other evidence of research, scholarship, and creative activity.
   b. Ability to relate scholarship, research, and creative activity to effective teaching.

        c.   Success in stimulating the intellectual de-
           velopment of one's colleagues.
   3.   Other contributions to the purposes of the col-
      lege
        a.   Contributions to department and college
           planning and administration.
        b.   Contributions to the life of the college as a
           community and leadership in achieving the
           goals of the college.
        c.   Contributions to extending the resources
           of the college to the wider community.

The *Faculty Information Manual* at the Harvard Business School contains a ten-page, single-spaced statement on "policies and procedures for appointments and promotions" (reproduced as Appendix I of this volume). After reading the document, one has little doubt about the criteria, standards, and processes that govern tenure decisions. And that is as it should be.

Interim Evaluations. Taken alone, criteria and standards for evaluation serve a useful, but limited, purpose as a statement of institutional norms. To be far more valuable, criteria and standards must be *applied* to personnel decisions. For tenure to work well, the criteria should be clear and evaluations should occur regularly and not merely at the time of tenure decisions. Annual evaluations for untenured faculty, especially during the early years of probation, are advisable. Normally, these evaluations should be conducted by the department chairman, although some may involve the dean or an associate dean. Evaluation conferences typically provide an occasion to review past performance, chart progress, and plan future activities on the course to tenure. In that sense, the annual reviews are developmental or formative. As with most performance appraisals, however, these reviews also serve an evaluative or summative function. While both facets of evaluation are important, for immediate purposes we concentrate on the latter aspect.

The principal observations and conclusions of an evaluation review should routinely be made a matter of record, as a standard and prudent practice and as a precautionary measure should grievances or lawsuits be filed. We recommend that the department chairman or dean provide the faculty member with a written summary of the conversation. That summary, of course, should reflect the supervisor's view of past performance and a mutually acceptable plan for professional improvement and development. The faculty member should also be free to submit a self-assessment.

Where weaknesses are identified or doubts exist, the supervisor and faculty member should forge a specific plan and timetable to overcome deficiencies. The goal of the evaluation session should be a concrete and practical plan and not a list of vague aspirations and elusive hopes. Nor should the goal be a "new spirit" or a "new dawn." What is needed is an action plan —unless, of course, performance to date does not warrant continued employment. The Harvard Business School's *Faculty Information Manual* succinctly states the fundamental premise: "It is the normal practice of the school to appoint more individuals to nontenured positions than can possibly be promoted to professor," the only tenured rank at the school. Necessarily, then, with a fixed probationary period and without extraordinary voluntary attrition, some faculty will be terminated. The question, then, is not whether individuals will be released but rather who and when.

At the exemplary institutions we visited, a significant number of faculty members leave prior to the tenure decision. To use the academic vernacular, some faculty are "weeded out" through the consistent enforcement of stringent standards. Annual or interim evaluations or a comprehensive "threshold" review will help a college eliminate clearly unqualified faculty before they are considered for tenure.

Consider the record at St. Olaf, a college with a seven-year probationary period. As former president Sidney Rand explains, St. Olaf attempts to "make the tenure decision without making it a tenure decision." After a faculty member has served three or four years, the college undertakes a more "thorough, conscious, and heightened" review. Usually, these evaluations are forwarded to the division head, the dean, and the president for a "breakpoint" review of the candidate's performance and prospects for tenure. Faculty members with little or no chance for tenure are, at this juncture, issued a terminal one-year contract. Faculty are not permitted to continue with faint hopes and false expectations. Between 1973-74 and 1976-77 at St. Olaf, a college with about 190 faculty, twenty-five persons were either not reappointed or else resigned after being told that their long-term prospects for tenure were dim. The college has considered the introduction of comprehensive reviews, though still within the department, after the second and fourth years. Many faculty, however, fear that extensive evaluations would then occur too frequently.

In the College of Letters and Science at the University of Wisconsin, the record across departments was more uneven. One department took action on twelve faculty members between February 1972 and October 1977. Of the seven denied tenure, the average number of years on tenure track was 4.5. In other departments, the averages were 6.4, 4.2, and 6.0. These data are not very reliable for two reasons. First, data were not available for all departments. Moreover, as Dean E. David Cronon commented: "Even then, you would not have a complete picture. For example, it is not at all uncommon for departments to convey informally [to a probationary faculty member] that he or she is unlikely to be reviewed favorably for tenure. In a number of such instances, the individual seeks another position without formally being denied tenure or reappointment" (Letter to authors, July 10, 1978).

At the Harvard Business School, interim evaluations are an established norm. First, the area chairman offers, at least annually, to discuss overall performance with each untenured faculty member. The faculty member decides whether to accept that invitation. Normally, at the conclusion of the second year of an initial three-year contract, untenured faculty are reviewed by the area's senior faculty. While not as extensive as a review for promotion or tenure, these sessions determine whether faculty should be terminated at the end of the third year or renewed, most often for two years. For faculty reappointed, the next major review usually occurs in the fifth year. Here the decision will be promotion (generally to associate professor) or termination. The promotion review process differs little from the tenure review process described later. Associate professors usually serve another five to six years before the tenure decision. Thus, in addition to the voluntary annual reviews, there are threshold reviews after the second and fifth year and then again at the time of the tenure decision. At each checkpoint, some faculty are weeded out; the others are provided a summary of strengths and weaknesses and are encouraged to develop, with the area chairman and the senior associate dean, a plan to overcome deficiencies and further buttress areas of achievement. While the Business School would not make available disaggregated data on attrition among untenured faculty, the gross figures suggest considerable "weeding out." In the 1970s, only 40 percent of the assistant professors attained the rank of associate professor and only 36 percent of the associate professors attained the tenured rank of professor. While attrition undoubtedly occurs for many reasons, we believe it is safe to assume that nonreappointment was the major factor.

To cite one more example, longitudinal studies conducted at Dartmouth College reveal that among a cohort of assistant professors about one third ultimately receive tenure. By the time of tenure review, one third of the cohort will have departed through voluntary or involuntary attrition; for those who remain, there is, at that point, a 50-50 chance for tenure.

Not all colleges and universities are so selective. A national survey conducted by the American Council on Education (Atelsek and Gomberg, 1980, p. 16) revealed that comparatively few faculty members are released without formal consideration for tenure. In 1978-79, only 1,313 of 56,566 (2.3 percent) tenure-track faculty were removed before the tenure decision (see Table 4). Even though the respondents were asked to exclude voluntary resignations for reasons other than anticipation of nonreappointment, the proportion of faculty released prior to the tenure decision still seems quite small.

To summarize, we believe that interim evaluations and "weeding out" contribute significantly to effective tenure systems and to a healthy faculty profile. In many cases, conspicuously unqualified faculty can quite easily be distinguished

Table 4. Untenured Faculty Released Before Tenure Decision, 1978-79

	Number Released	As Percentage of Untenured Tenure-Track Faculty
Universities		
Public	322	1.8
Private	116	1.7
Four-Year Colleges		
Public	438	2.6
Private	437	3.0

from the rest. At that time, the college should cut its losses. To retain persons unlikely to present a persuasive case for tenure delays and makes more difficult the decision to separate these individuals from the institution at a later date. Moreover, the presence of these marginal candidates could, by comparison, make otherwise very ordinary candidates appear to be quite acceptable. Worse, after six, seven, or eleven years, as loyalties and sympathies mount, the college runs the risk that the truly marginal candidates will, in fact, not be released. We doubt that faculty will find the decision any easier to accept after six years than after three, and we do not know whether faculty denied reappointment will find a new position any more easily than faculty denied tenure. These questions can be answered only after more data are collected on a case-by-case basis.

We can, however, assert that schools that "weed out" junior faculty will have more flexibility and, of course, fewer tenure decisions. In cases where many or most faculty members never complete the probationary period, the percentage of candidates eligible for tenure actually awarded tenure may have little significance. If five faculty from a cohort of twenty reach the tenure decision and all five earn tenure, the percentage of eligible candidates awarded tenure would be 100 percent. At another institution, where all twenty faculty members reached the tenure decision and ten were awarded tenure, the percentage would be only 50 percent. Which college was more selective? Thus, institutions should monitor both the rate of tenure awards among those eligible and the proportion of a cohort that reaches the tenure decisions. Both data sets are important be-

cause institutions should exercise selectivity en route to and at
the time of the tenure decision.

Institutional Context. Tenure decisions should encompass
at least two dimensions: individual merit and institutional
needs. Historically, colleges and universities have concentrated
on the former and neglected the latter. Thus, portfolios for tenure decisions typically include reams (even pounds) of information about the individual: publications, reviews of those works,
letters of reference, student evaluations, course syllabi. By contrast, portfolios most often contain scanty information about
the institution: tenure levels, enrollment and placement patterns, affirmative action plans, manpower and program needs,
financial statements.

Although many faculty members see themselves as self-
employed professionals, faculty do work within an organization. Personnel decisions, therefore, must be placed within that
larger context. For example, a very talented philosopher, an individual with a strong record of achievement and considerable
potential, may be under consideration for tenure. On merit
alone, the faculty member may deserve tenure. Yet, the college's enrollments in philosophy have plummeted, and projections suggest even greater market deterioration. In addition, the
college already employs an ample number of tenured, middle-
aged philosophers, each with underenrolled courses. To make
matters worse, perhaps the college has decided to shift from the
more traditional liberal arts toward some vocational and pre-
professional programs. Under these circumstances, the college
may properly elect not to tenure an able and gifted professor.
The "fit" between individual merit and institutional need would
not have been a good one.

To be sure, evaluation starts with the quality of the
candidate under consideration. The evaluation, however, must
not end there; the process must assure that individual strengths
are assessed within the context of institutional priorities. In that
regard, St. Olaf has developed commendable policies and practices. The *Faculty Handbook* lists, in descending order of priority, three areas of concern for tenure decisions: (1) the candidate's qualifications, (2) consideration of personnel needs with-

in the candidate's department, (3) consideration of the number of tenured personnel in the candidate's department. The dean of the college prepares a Faculty Staffing Plan, which serves as a backdrop for consideration of institutional needs. Revised annually by a planning committee and based on information furnished by the departments, the plan encompasses the goals of the college, expected enrollments, allocation of resources, program changes, and staffing requirements. The plan projects manpower needs under various sets of assumptions about enrollments, attrition, and faculty turnover. The dean makes the plan available to all faculty.

Perhaps more impressively, each department also develops a long-range plan. Although the content of these plans differs, each begins with a statement of goals for the department and occasionally with a statement of goals for student majors. Departments estimate manpower needs based on different enrollment projections, class sizes, and faculty/student ratios. The history department even disaggregated enrollment data by levels and fields to understand better the department's future needs. Its plan also provides for each faculty member such obvious data as tenure status, scheduled leaves, and retirement dates and less obvious, yet equally valuable, information such as an inventory of courses taught at St. Olaf, courses taught elsewhere, and future teaching and research interests. After presentation of the data, the history department's plan concludes with an analysis of "Flexibility and Growth," an assessment of the congruence between departmental goals and current staff, and a general prognosis of tenure prospects for future faculty.

In summary, all institutions, most especially those with modest resources and limited flexibility, should view tenure decisions within an institutional context. That context should be provided by long-range plans developed at the departmental level and reconciled at the school-wide or college-wide level. To inform and influence promotion and tenure decisions, these plans must, of course, be shared with the parties to those decisions. If faculty committees or boards of trustees are furnished only with information about the individual, then, predictably, the discussion and decision will be solely about the candidate's qualifications.

Some institutions deliberately elect to operate that way. At Chatham College (Pennsylvania), the faculty in the early 1970s secured passage of a policy that ensures, if not a separation of powers, at least a separation of perspectives. The *Faculty Manual* stipulates that "the Promotion and Tenure Committee limits itself to recommendations concerning a faculty member's qualifications and performance. . . . The committee's task is to evaluate a faculty member's professional performance. Determination of the allocation of resources and priorities of the institution is a separate function which must not concern the Promotion and Tenure Committee." As a corollary, the president's judgment must be limited to grounds of institutional priorities. At Chatham, the concepts of institutional priorities and individual merit are so separate and distinct that there are two different grievance procedures for faculty denied reappointment or tenure: a faculty-dominated committee reviews decisions based on individual merit; a trustee-dominated committee hears cases based on institutional priorities.

We do not (nor does the president of Chatham) favor separation of these interrelated issues, although we recognize that some faculty and administrators will see advantages to this division of labor. Faculty can eschew the difficult discussions and decisions on institutional priorities, a particularly unpleasant task during an era of decline. Faculty will not have to write the so-called tombstone list. The advantage to administrators is equally obvious: every personnel decision can be rationalized and defended as a matter of institutional priority. After all, what is not an institutional priority? The policy satisfies sinister motives.

We prefer instead the system used at St. Olaf and at the Harvard Business School, where information and perspectives on both the individual and the institution are integrated throughout the decision-making process and where program and manpower plans provide the scaffolding to build a strong faculty. As guidelines, the plans establish the general principle—that appointments should be consistent with program needs—and simultaneously permit the exception- the appointment of an extraordinarily gifted individual whose interests "do not coincide with the boundaries of the areas of the present faculty organization." We believe that better information makes for better decisions and that faculty and staff should share the responsibility for determining institutional goals and for selecting the mix of individuals best equipped to lead the institution toward those objectives. For those reasons, we cite at length excerpts from the Harvard Business School policy, which reflects the need to achieve a balanced and informed view of individual merit and institutional need:

> Staffing plans need to be built up and reviewed from time to time from the point of view of educational programs as well as subject areas and also from such other perspectives as the distribution of men and women among ranks and among ages. However, the needs of the School as a whole are not necessarily a simple summation of the needs of the parts of its Faculty's organization. It follows, therefore, that the Appointment Committee's advice and the Dean's decisions on specific appointments, though they are importantly affected by the staffing needs of specific Program and Area groups, are not determined by them. The advice and decisions may depart from existing staffing patterns in order to obtain an exceptionally able man or woman, to leave openings unfilled when no candidate of high caliber is available, and to encourage work for which no formal area has been established because the potential for business administration of significant new work is not yet clear. . . .
>
> To help the Faculty Advisory Committee on Appointments and its subcommittees in their deliberations, the Dean, in the early fall of each year, provides the Committee with an overview of its work for the coming year. This overview includes a statement of the Dean's strategy for manning the School with the size and mix of Faculty necessary to accomplish the School's various missions in the foreseeable future. It also includes a statement con-

cerning projected size of the Faculty in the near
term, anticipated openings by relevant categories,
and any other information which the Dean considers pertinent. Finally, it includes the names of all
candidates, to the extent that they are known at
that time of the year, who will be considered for
promotion during the current academic year.

The work of the subcommittees is the painstaking accumulation and weighing of evidence
relative to appointments under consideration. In
this work, however, subcommittee members will
rely in part on information furnished by others.
They should hear from the Dean or Senior Associate Dean for Educational Affairs a thorough review of the anticipated relevant openings over the
next several years, and they should hear from the
Area Chairman a forecast of the teaching and research developments in so far as these can be anticipated. These statements will include a review of
the effects which the appointment being considered is likely to have on the balance between teaching and research in the Area.

Whatever the process, both individual and institutional
aspects of the decision need to be considered. Admittedly, faculty are better positioned to determine individual merit, and
presumably the administration and board of trustees are better
situated to assess institutional priorities. Relative expertise
should not, however, lead to exclusive domains. Each perspective should inform the other, and the decision should reflect
the integration of those perspectives.

One final word on institutional context. Policy statements on criteria for promotion and tenure should state explicitly that institutional needs will be a criterion. In various ways,
faculty handbooks at St. Olaf, the Harvard Business School, and
Dartmouth College make that point. At Colgate University,
however, an otherwise satisfactory set of guidelines for promotion and tenure seems flawed by the omission of any reference

to institutional priorities. On the basis of the current policy statement, naive faculty at Colgate might conclude that distinguished performance alone will be sufficient to procure tenure. At Colgate, as at other strong universities, that is, in fact, not the case. Institutional needs are an important criterion, and faculty should be so informed forthrightly, both as a matter of prudent management and as a matter of fairness.

Multilevel Reviews. For tenure to work well, the review process must cultivate quality control and selectivity, lest the college routinely award tenure to all minimally eligible candidates. To promote quality control, the unit (or individual) that recommends a candidate for tenure must be made answerable to other constituencies with broader perspectives and perhaps more rigorous standards. Accountability can be fostered by multilevel reviews.

While the peer and administrative review procedures at the Harvard Business School, the College of Letters and Science at Wisconsin, and St. Olaf differ, there are also important common elements. We will describe briefly each process and then address the similarities. As noted above, tenure reviews at each of these schools follow and build on interim evaluations at earlier stages of a candidate's progress toward tenure. Thus, we are considering now the culmination of an extensive and systematic process.

At the Harvard Business School (and at Harvard University more generally), the review process rests heavily, almost exclusively, on the opinions and assessments of tenured faculty. While the views of junior faculty may be solicited, only senior faculty vote on the recommendations for promotion and tenure. For each tenure candidate, the dean designates a subcommittee of four to six senior faculty members to gather information and formulate a recommendation. The chairman and at least half of the members of that subcommittee are from academic areas other than the candidate's. The membership of the committee—which may, but rarely does, include faculty not at the school—is confidential. Each candidate may identify professors who "could not dispassionately evaluate his work, and therefore should not be a member of his subcommittee."

The investigative and evaluative work done by the sub-committees is thorough and comprehensive. Faculty and staff, insiders and outsiders, professors and practitioners are all consulted as referees. Scholarly works and instructional materials are carefully scrutinized. The subcommittee then makes a full report and recommendation to the Faculty Advisory Committee on Appointments, which consists of all tenured faculty. After each discussion, which may last an hour or two and sometimes more, the advisory committee casts an "initial and tentative vote by signed and confidential ballot to accept, reject, or modify the recommendation." After this process has been completed for each candidate, the dean requests "final votes" on all candidates. Thus, tenured faculty cast a preliminary vote on each candidate but have an opportunity to reassess their views and change their votes after the entire slate has been presented and considered. In that way, candidates are assessed both separately and comparatively. The results of the votes are not revealed.

Based on the vote of the faculty and the evidence collected by the subcommittees, the dean, "who has sole responsibility," makes his recommendations to the president. As a rule, the dean affirms the majority view of the faculty. The dean discloses his recommendation to the candidate and may, at his discretion, ask an ex officio member of the subcommittee, such as the area chairman or senior associate dean, to share with the candidate the thinking of the subcommittee and the advisory committee.

The College of Letters and Science at Wisconsin organizes academic departments into four divisions: Humanities, Social Studies, Biological Sciences, and Physical Sciences. The initial decision to nominate a candidate for tenure rests with the department—specifically, with the Executive Committee of the department, which is composed of all tenured faculty. The Executive Committee examines formal and informal evidence on teaching competence and research capability. Student evaluations are used to inform judgments of the candidate as a teacher. External experts must be solicited to help assess the candidate as a scholar. After debate, the committee votes.

If the candidate does not receive a favorable recommendation from the departmental Executive Committee, the process ostensibly ends there. Early candidates for tenure may be reconsidered at a later date; candidates at the end of the probationary period are terminated with a year's notice. Even on votes favorable by a narrow margin, the department, in consultation with the dean, may elect not to present the candidate to the Divisional Committee, comprised of twelve tenured senior professors elected by divisional faculty. To be rebuffed by the Divisional Committee would be an embarrassment. Moreover, the Divisional Committee members—typically, the most esteemed faculty—often resurface on the Research Committee, which allocates internal resources for scholarly pursuits. Tainted by memories of a marginally acceptable candidate for tenure, these faculty members may tend to allocate the limited research dollars to other individuals or departments with stronger cases at the time of tenure.

Candidates denied tenure at the departmental level may request a written statement of reasons and ask for reconsideration at an open meeting of the Executive Committee. Alternatively, the candidate may appeal directly to the dean, although as a matter of practice the dean rarely, if ever, overturns a negative recommendation from a department. If the decision leads to termination, the faculty member may also appeal to a university grievance committee concerned principally with the integrity of the process.

When a favorable recommendation reaches the Divisional Committee, the chairman usually assigns two faculty members to review the evidence, to gather additional material as necessary, and to report to the committee as a whole. As at Harvard, the investigations are extensive and the discussions are exhaustive; days on end are devoted to the docket of tenure candidates. Eventually, the committee votes by secret ballot. Three divisions simply vote "tenure" or "deny." In the Humanities Division, faculty may vote "qualified for tenure," "qualified with merit for tenure," or "unqualified for tenure." These gradations help the dean assess a candidate's relative strength. The dean invariably affirms negative decisions and only occasionally reverses positive decisions, and then only those without a decisive majority. From the dean's level upward, the process is typically pro forma—not because the senior administrators are indifferent but because they are confident that quality control has already been exercised.

In the view of Dean Cronon, the Divisional Committees protect strong departments against weaker departments. The Divisional Committees offer the faculty a mechanism to uphold and even upgrade standards. In short, the recommendations of weaker departments are made accountable to the standards of respected faculty from stronger departments.

Reflective of a small liberal arts school, the procedures at St. Olaf differ somewhat from those at Harvard and Wisconsin. The department chairman solicits the opinions of all full-time faculty, tenured and untenured, with at least two years' service at the college. In order to assess teaching effectiveness, the most important criterion, the chairman and at least one other tenured member of the department or division must observe the candidate in the classroom and submit a narrative evaluation of the candidate's performance. "These evaluations shall make reference to student opinion of the candidate's teaching, solicited through discussion with students and student questionnaires."

The next several steps intend to place each candidate within a progressively expanded context. First, the chairman asks all tenured members of the department to rank confidentially all nontenured faculty relative to the candidate for tenure. Concurrently, the chairman may seek the opinions of faculty in other departments at St. Olaf as well as colleagues at other institutions familiar with the candidate's work. The department chairman then meets with the division chairman and presents a recommendation. In turn, the division chairman makes a recommendation to the dean that takes into account the quality of other candidates in that division and information provided by the dean on candidates from other divisions.

By December 15 each year, the dean of the college submits to the Review and Planning Committee all recommendations for promotion and tenure. Among the members of this committee are six faculty members elected at large for three-year terms (at least two must be untenured at the time of election, and no one may serve more than two consecutive terms), the six division chairmen, the president and four vice-presidents, and three students.

As at Harvard and Wisconsin, a subcommittee of professors, three here, examines the performance and portfolio of each candidate for tenure. The subcommittee, which meets at least once with the dean and division chairmen as a group, has full access to the dossiers of all candidates. The subcommittee then makes recommendations to members of the Review and Planning Committee with faculty status. "At a subsequent meeting held at least three days later, the faculty members of the Review and Planning Committee shall, by secret ballot, elect the candidates to be recommended for promotion and tenure." The recommendations are to take into consideration the constraints identified in the Faculty Staffing Plan. During the months when the committee deliberates, the president or the dean of the college interviews each candidate for tenure. By February 15, the dean submits his recommendations to the president.

Should the president intend to make a recommendation to the board of trustees that differs with the committee's vote, he must notify the committee. Upon request, the president must meet with the committee and explain why he reached a decision at variance with its recommendation. Similarly, any candidate at any time may ask to meet with the department or division chairman, the dean, or the president to discuss "the reasons for whatever decisions may have been made."

Elements of Effective Reviews

The review procedures at Harvard, Wisconsin, and St. Olaf exhibit similarities that we believe contribute to effective management of academic tenure. First, and no small matter, there is *an explicit, written procedure.* Tenure reviews are not haphazardly improvised with a new twist or a different process for each case. There are prescribed steps and specific timetables. Second, *the processes are plainly competitive,* and these schools

do not attempt to mute or camouflage that fact. Candidates for
tenure are judged against one another, against future candidates
at the school, and even against potential candidates not currently at the institution. Rather than pretend that the decisions are
not competitive, these schools admit to that reality and then
seek data that will permit a necessarily comparative judgment.
Hence, Harvard faculty vote on candidates case by case and
then again on each candidate as part of the collective. Hence,
St. Olaf asks faculty to rank tenure candidates against others in
the department. It may be genteel to deny or disregard the competitive nature of the decision, and it may be "sophisticated" to
argue that classicists and physicists cannot be compared as
candidates for tenure. It is also naive, mistaken, and unwise.

Third, the *review process* at these schools *places great responsibility on the faculty,* particularly the tenured faculty. In
all cases, a faculty (or faculty-dominated) committee reviews all
candidates for tenure, and a subcommittee investigates each
candidate thoroughly. The committees at Harvard and Wisconsin are composed entirely of tenured faculty. At St. Olaf, only
tenured faculty comprise the subcommittee, and only faculty
members of the Review and Planning Committee vote on tenure
recommendations.

We believe that faculty should be entrusted with the primary responsibility to exercise quality control and select colleagues. As permanent members of the college community, tenured faculty should bear a particular responsibility for institutional quality. In addition to a historical perspective and a
long-term commitment, tenured status affords senior faculty a
special advantage as quality controllers. Tenured faculty enjoy
relative immunity from retribution or retaliation by candidates
denied promotion and tenure, whereas less secure faculty could
be tempted or inclined to forgo rigorous judgments or, worse,
to log-roll.

Wherever possible, the faculty should be empowered to
choose from among the tenured ranks the membership of
school, division, college, and university-wide promotion and
tenure committees. The stronger the traditions of excellence
and self-regulation among the faculty, the more democratic the

selection procedures may be. Where, for instance, quality-minded faculty predominate, an election may be appropriate. At the other extreme, where standard bearers and commitments to distinction are rare, the senior administration may, at least at the outset, have to hand-pick an "elite" committee either to serve as or to select the quality controllers. In any case, we strongly urge that there be college- or school-wide committees, so that departments (or comparable units) are made answerable to a larger constituency of colleagues, who, in turn, are made to feel responsible for the overall quality of the faculty. These committees, comprised of standard bearers, encourage rigor and impart needed legitimacy to the review process.

As noted earlier, the committees must be furnished with adequate and appropriate information. The Harvard Business School and St. Olaf provide faculty committees with pertinent information on the institution, the area or division, the pool of tenure candidates, and the programmatic and financial consequences of various decisions. Providing this information not only aids decision making; it also conveys to the committee that the administration takes seriously both the decisions at hand and the committee's role.

Beyond data supplied by the administration, subcommittees seek and assess still more information, most often on individual merit. The assignment of that task to a small subcommittee helps localize accountability. Subcommittees do not want to present a report found to be weak and insufficient by the larger committee. To do so would embarrass the subcommittee and call into question the wisdom of the recommendation. For these reasons, we recommend the use of subcommittees answerable to the committee as a whole.

Through the search for information and evaluations provided by outside experts, the departmental recommendations can be tested against an even broader constituency than the college-wide committee. Most often, opinions are sought from two principal sources: colleagues at the institution in different fields and colleagues at other institutions in a similar or closely related field. At Harvard generally (with the Business School excepted), the president convenes an ad hoc committee of outside experts to evaluate a particular candidate's work. St. Olaf occasionally consults former students. While the particular audiences consulted may vary, each institution seeks to supplement local views. Such a procedure offers another quality control measure and another mechanism to make faculty test and defend their recommendations. In sum, there should be several levels of review: each furnished adequate information, each assigned a special task, and each sensitive to the larger institutional context.

If these actions do not produce selectivity by peer review, a more drastic measure may be necessary. Universities and larger colleges eager to bolster the peer review process may wish to consider a practice first attributed to the provost's office at the University of Michigan, whereby departments may be required to forfeit the faculty slot occupied by a tenure candidate favorably recommended by the department but rejected *on grounds of merit* at a subsequent level of review. The specter of one less faculty position "encourages" departmental review committees to exercise discretion rather than pass marginal candidates to the next level of review. Where charity or timidity prevails over selectivity at the department level, the position may be confiscated either temporarily or permanently. The "penalty" may be modest for the first mistake and progressively more severe for repeated offenses. When carefully limited to reversals based on the qualifications of the candidate, the policy may effectively deter departments from shirking their responsibilities or passing the buck. For smaller colleges, the policy may be impractical insofar as enrollment patterns, staffing patterns, and curricular balance dictate that departments retain and fill all their vacancies.

The tenure review procedures at the three institutions we examined all *provide some means for the candidate to learn the reasons for a particular decision.* In all cases, faculty may learn the general bases for the decision, sometimes from an administrator, sometimes from a member of a faculty review committee. In no instance, however, are confidences violated. When properly executed, the content of the interim evaluations and the reasons for denial of tenure will, by and large, be one and the same unless the decision rested on institutional priorities rather than individual merit. Providing reasons, therefore, should be more a matter of reviewing earlier evaluations than revealing secrets or unleashing surprises.

There are provisions, formal at St. Olaf and informal at Harvard and Wisconsin, for the college-wide committee to hear first hand why the dean or president reached a decision at odds with the committee's recommendation. This step helps make the administration accountable and helps maintain trust and respect between the faculty committee and the senior officers of the institution.

While such post facto sessions are undeniably valuable, there may be circumstances where these conversations should occur *prior to* the final decision. A university-wide committee or a senior academic officer may, for example, wish clarification of a candidate's record or elaboration of the recommendations offered thus far. Or a decision maker may have reached a tentative conclusion contrary to the recommendations offered at earlier stages of the review process. In all these instances, we would encourage the university-wide committee or the senior administrator to consult before the decision with the college dean, the department head, or the chairman of the review committee. Where questions, doubts, and disagreements exist, why not meet face to face with the persons best acquainted with the candidate, both to learn more and to forewarn the dean or department head, as a matter of courtesy, of the possibility of an adverse decision? Private conversations sometimes can supplement or interpret the written record in important ways. Ironically, in fact, many review committees and senior administrators, especially at large universities, never probe directly the richest source of information: the candidate. Although senior administrators at many institutions often interview candidates for professorships and immediate tenure from outside the institution, far fewer interview candidates from within as part of the promotion and tenure review process. (St. Olaf is an exception.) To enliven the dossier and to gain more insights, particularly where doubts exist, an interview with the candidate could be most useful and profitable.

In addition to these recommendations, two others seem

obvious yet noteworthy. Some individual (or, less desirably, some office) should monitor and ensure the procedural integrity of the tenure review process. Before a recommendation advances from one level to the next, someone should certify that all the procedural requirements have been fulfilled. Second, there should be some officers at or near the top of the organization able to ask penetrating questions about marginal candidates and prepared to say "no" when necessary. We hasten to add, however, that the effective administration of a tenure system requires more than effective administrators. Promotion and tenure processes also engage faculty peers, external referees, and often trustees.* These segments of the campus community, as well as the academic administration, must effectively assume certain roles and responsibilities for tenure policies to operate well. Insofar as shared responsibility accompanies shared governance, the operation of promotion and tenure policies and the quality of promotion and tenure decisions should not be attributed solely to the administration. Successful promotion and tenure practices require an effective *collective* effort that can, unfortunately, be undermined by lapses of any party to the process.

---

*While we concentrated in this chapter on participation by the faculty and administration, Chait (1980) discusses at length the part to be played by the board of trustees.

8.

Evaluating
Tenured Faculty

<hr>

Academic tenure no more constitutes the whole of academic personnel policies than a keystone constitutes an arch. Effective tenure practices necessarily depend on other effective personnel practices, especially faculty evaluation. Too often, perhaps, faculty and administrators focus narrowly on tenure per se and thereby overlook the relationship between tenure and other personnel policies and practices.

In this chapter, for purposes of discussion and consistency, we presume the context of a conventional tenure system and concentrate on tenured faculty. At the same time, we are concerned largely with generic activities, such as evaluation and compensation, inherent to all organizations. Therefore, certain generalizations apply. And even on matters not necessarily intrinsic to all organizations, such as staff development and manpower reduction, some strategies and suggestions transcend the operational differences among employment policies. Thus, the tenor of the comments and recommendations we offer should pertain as well to the administration of term contracts and to the supervision of untenured faculty.

The need for pertinent generalizations would exist even were we to ignore colleges without academic tenure. The approximately 2,600 institutions with tenure systems comprise a heterogeneous lot. There are elite research universities and open-door community colleges, well-endowed private colleges and unendowed state colleges, expansive multiversities and intimate liberal arts colleges. Despite that diversity, certain concepts and actions seem widely appropriate and generally relevant.

The politics necessary to accept and adopt the policy objectives we recommend cannot be as easily generalized. Appropriate strategies and tradeoffs must be determined within the context of local circumstances. An approach suitable for a campus with an active faculty senate and no union may be inadvisable on a campus with a union and no senate. Even confined to a unionized environment, we could not recommend categorically, for example, that management exchange a merit pay provision for annual faculty evaluations or vice versa. Thus, we focus on the policy objectives to be attained and not the negotiating tactics to be employed.

As enumerated by Levinson (1976), a professor at the Harvard Business School, the ultimate goals of any performance appraisal systems are (1) to provide adequate feedback to each employee; (2) to serve as a basis for changed behavior, which leads toward more effective work habits; (3) to provide data for decisions on future assignments, employment status, and compensation. All three goals are significant. While we concentrate on the third objective, we recognize the importance of formative evaluations designed to improve performance. Nevertheless, we are primarily concerned here with those aspects of evaluation that enlighten personnel decisions. In that summative domain, the goals of faculty evaluation have been well stated by the Southern Regional Education Board (1977): (1) to separate superior, satisfactory, and unsatisfactory performers; (2) to

build an evaluation record for each faculty member; (3) to provide due process and fair procedures; (4) to employ an evaluation process acceptable to a large majority of the campus community; (5) to allocate rewards fairly and appropriately.

All these objectives appear to be appropriate at colleges
with contracts and at universities with tenure. For that reason,
many of the elements of effective tenure practices described in
Chapter Seven can be applied to faculty evaluation irrespective
of the particular employment policy in effect. Similarly, the
fundamental approach to faculty evaluation should not change
materially as a function of tenure status; the evaluation of tenured faculty should represent a continuation of prior practices.

Absent *any* data from formal performance appraisals,
evaluation will occur nonetheless. Students and faculty evaluate
one another all the time. Faculty continually assess the work of
colleagues and, at least annually on most campuses, department
heads and deans determine faculty salaries, presumably based to
some degree on past performance. The *practical* questions concern *how* evaluation will be accomplished and, more specifically, whether the evaluation will be formal or informal. Broadly
defined, the "evaluation of tenured faculty" embraces any and
all actions taken now and then to assess the performance of permanent faculty members. To be more precise, we are concerned
with evaluations of tenured faculty which are systematic, summative, and standard procedures applied regularly to all tenured
faculty. The reviews may or may not be linked to other personnel actions, such as salary adjustments or applications for promotions or sabbatical leaves. Among the institutions that meet
this definition of evaluation, we selected Coe College and St.
Lawrence University for closer examination. The somewhat different policies at these somewhat similar schools present instructive comparisons and contrasts.

Coe College

In 1972, about 30 percent of the faculty at Coe College
held academic tenure. Projections prepared by President Leo
Nussbaum revealed, however, that within a few years a relatively

large cohort of faculty appointed in the late 1960s would be eligible for tenure. Unless the historical success rate among tenure candidates declined, the tenured ranks at the college would double. Even that estimate seemed conservative, since Nussbaum expected more and more faculty members to remain at Coe because of the deterioration of the market for academic employment. As one professor observed, faculty now perceived Coe as a "good place to be and not simply a good place to be from." Forecasts of a harsh economic climate, a deficit between $400,000 and $500,000, and steady-state enrollments only compounded the problem. From the president's perspective, the picture was grim. The college was about to lock in old programs and a relatively young faculty while demographic and economic factors locked out new programs and additional personnel.

Nussbaum shared these fears about the college's future with several key faculty members in the hope that some constructive suggestions would emerge. None did. Although concerned, the faculty were not sufficiently alarmed to respond promptly or creatively. Nussbaum then acquainted the executive committee of the board of trustees with the economic, curricular, and human dimensions of the problem as well as the sensitivity of the issue. Implementation of any solution, Nussbaum advised the board, would require a great deal of tact and patience. The faculty would need time to collect data, draft and redraft reports, and consider and reconsider alternatives. To start the process, Nussbaum recommended that the executive committee make known that it was considering the imposition of a tenure quota. As word of that possibility spread, the president conjectured, faculty would recognize the gravity of the problem and begin to search more imaginatively and more urgently for a solution.

Nussbaum's strategy worked. Before long, the entire college community was engaged in an active debate about tenure quotas. Some faculty feared that the proposed quota was the first salvo of a campaign to abolish tenure. In the course of these often intense discussions, Nussbaum gradually unveiled a far less radical proposal, intended to break the deadlock on a tenure quota. The proposal, which Nussbaum had been pondering for several years, stipulated that candidates for tenure submit, along with the usual materials, a ten-year plan for professional growth and development, which would be an additional source of evidence for consideration by tenure review committees. Once granted tenure, faculty members would be obliged to update and extend the plan at least once every five years thereafter, although modifications could be made annually. At the conclusion of each five-year period, the academic dean would conduct an evaluation to determine the degree to which the plan had been fulfilled.

After months of deliberation, Nussbaum's proposal was endorsed by the faculty, despite many questions about the efficacy of ten-year plans. In December 1973, the executive committee of the board officially approved the new policy. From the viewpoint of the faculty, the ten-year plans were "innocuous" and certainly preferable to a tenure quota. The trade-off was not cast subtly in the policy: "As an alternative to setting quantitative limitations on the proportion of the faculty who may receive tenure, qualitative standards will be amplified and clarified." The local AAUP was unenthusiastic yet not expressly opposed. From the perspective of the board of trustees, the ten-year plans, coupled with the establishment of a non-tenure-track system for up to 10 percent of the full-time faculty positions, allayed fears that without a quota everyone would eventually be tenured. An astute bargainer, Nussbaum had constructed a compromise acceptable to both constituencies.

As adopted, the policy stipulates that "Any faculty member eligible for tenure shall submit, at least one calendar year before the tenure decision, . . . a ten-year plan for professional growth and development. This plan shall include: (a) an academic history of the candidate and (b) a prospectus for the decade ahead, in which the candidate indicates what he expects to accomplish in order to further his professional growth and development in a manner consistent with the college's primary emphasis on quality teaching. This plan shall become part of the evidence to be evaluated in making tenure-granting decisions."

Introduced at a weekend conference, with advice on how

to write a ten-year plan, the policy applied immediately to all present and future probationary faculty except candidates under consideration for tenure that year. Tenured faculty under age fifty-five were allowed up to three years to develop a plan; older faculty were apparently exempted.

The provisions for review of the plans and the performance of tenured faculty did not deviate significantly from Nussbaum's initial draft. Five years after the award of tenure, the academic dean, aided by the responsible department head, evaluates the progress made toward achievement of the goals outlined in the plan. The faculty member than revises, as appropriate, plans for the second five years and projects some goals for the five years beyond the original termination date of the plan. "The revisions and the projection shall take into account strengths and weaknesses enumerated in the evaluation of the first five years." Faculty are entitled to a written statement of all evaluations and an opportunity to discuss them with the appropriate administrative officer before the appraisals are entered into the faculty member's personnel record.

With admirable clarity, the policy states that the "ten-year plan and evidence developed therefrom and evaluation of its implementation . . . will be used in making decisions concerning tenure, promotions in rank, sabbatical leaves, and merit increases in salary." These evaluations are supplemented, however, by other assessments of performance by administrators, colleagues, students, and outside experts. "Reliable evidence of a faculty member's performance as a teacher, adviser, and scholar constitutes the essential basis for a *qualitative judgment,* including the credibility of the ten-year plan" (emphasis added).

While the plan and related evaluations inform personnel decisions, the policy does not mention or even intimate that these materials could lead to revocation of tenure. On that score, the policy states: "The grounds and procedures for dismissal for cause are not altered by adoption of this plan." For the faculty, inclusion of that clause represented a significant and hard-won victory, since the *Faculty Handbook* does not list incompetence as a reason for dismissal. (The stated reasons for dismissal for cause are moral or social misconduct, insubordina-

tion, physical or mental incapacity, and program discontinuation.) Originally opposed to the omission of a "detenure clause,"
Nussbaum has since contended that "the system will work better if no one sees the plan as a noose that may fit around his
neck."

Faculty response to the policy has been varied; opinions
ranged from "worthwhile" to "an instrument of the devil."
From the interviews we conducted, we conclude that most faculty acknowledge the value of introspection and planning. On
the whole, such exercises are regarded as a helpful *process,*
probably more valuable than the product—namely, a ten-year
plan. Whether the payoff justifies the effort remains in doubt
for two reasons. First, the conscientious development of a comprehensive plan consumes a great deal of time. Second, some
faculty members believe that the plans are not thoughtfully
considered and constructively utilized by the administration. As
the head of one department remarked, "The administration
drops all those plans into an Orwellian hole." Perhaps for that
reason, a faculty member first submitted a one-sentence ten-
year plan. Through negotiations with the dean, that apparently
pithy statement was expanded.

Although of a somewhat more positive persuasion than
the faculty, the senior academic administrators concede that the
results have been "a mixed bag." Nussbaum freely admits, for
example, that "most plans are trite." Yet, in the president's
view, "Every conference a dean has can be useful in setting a
tone for getting things done." And, indeed, the academic dean
refers to the new system as "primarily a counseling tool."

St. Lawrence University

Unlike the policy at Coe College, periodic evaluation of
tenured faculty at St. Lawrence University can lead to dismissal
for cause. While St. Lawrence reached a different conclusion
than Coe, the origins of a new policy were the same at both institutions: concern among the president and the board of
trustees that the tenure density was about to escalate to an unacceptable level. In 1975, 59 percent of the faculty held tenure.

Projections prepared by the administration forecast that the tenure level would reach 65 percent by 1980 and 73 percent by 1990. (Later estimates revealed that the earlier projections were somewhat exaggerated; the revised estimates predicted that the tenure level would be only 63 percent by 1984-85.)

As an outgrowth of the board's concerns, the trustees requested that a faculty committee explore the strengths and weaknesses of academic tenure and the alternatives of tenure quotas, term contracts, and a nontenure track. Convinced that the alternatives presented decided disadvantages and that "no specific need [existed] at this time" to abandon tenure, the committee reaffirmed a commitment to traditional tenure. At the same time, the committee recognized the need, particularly acute in a steady-state environment, for tenured faculty to remain vibrant. Consequently, the committee recommended in April 1976 that the teaching effectiveness of each faculty member be reviewed by the Committee on Professional Standards every eight years. "The purpose of the review shall be to determine whether there is reason to doubt that the faculty member is a competent teacher. Competency as a teacher shall include adequate mastery of subject matter." Where the Committee on Professional Standards, after a thorough review of the professor's record, observed deficiencies so severe as to constitute incompetence, a written statement of concern would be transmitted to the dean, the president, and the faculty member under review. If discussions between the administrative officers and the faculty member did not yield a "mutual accommodation," a termination hearing would be held before an ad hoc committee of five tenured faculty selected by the Faculty Council.

Not all members of the trustees' Committee on Academic and Faculty Affairs were persuaded that tenure was the "best route" to "acquire and maintain a first-class faculty." Nevertheless, the trustees also discarded the alternatives to tenure as inappropriate and ineffectual and focused instead on a "properly constructed and properly administered tenure system." At the heart of such a system, the board declared, must be "provisions designed to ensure that no tenured position can become a safe haven for the incompetent, the indifferent, or the lazy. As in other walks of life, there must be proper accountability for performance."

(Among the changes in the faculty report made by the trustee committee was the deletion of explicit reference to the 1940 AAUP statement. In the committee's opinion, St. Lawrence University's own statement on academic freedom "should stand wholly on its own feet and incorporate no reference to this or any other extraneous document." The trustees, in short, affirmed St. Lawrence's own "commitment to a principle which no self-respecting educational institution can deny.")

In substantial agreement with the faculty report, the trustees advocated periodic evaluation as the most efficacious means to assure accountability, but the board rejected eight years as too lengthy an interim between reviews. The board committee recommended instead that the dean and department chairman "should review with special attention the performance of any tenured faculty member at the end of every four-year period in which no review of his performance for other reasons has occurred."

In January 1977, the board of trustees adopted a policy of "Continuing Evaluation," effective July 1977. In relevant part, the policy provides:

> It is the obligation of the tenured members of the faculty to continue to maintain their competence in teaching and scholarship. It is the responsibility of the dean of the college, as the principal academic officer of the university, and of department chairmen to ensure that competence is maintained.
>
> If no review of the professional performance of a tenured faculty member has taken place as part of normal promotion or other procedures in the four-year period following his appointment to tenure, the dean and the department chairman shall review the performance of such a faculty member with special attention, and shall continue

to do so at the end of each subsequent four-year period in which no other formal review occurs. Should the dean conclude on the basis of this review that reason for concern exists, he shall discuss it with the faculty member and place a memorandum of the discussion in appropriate files. A copy of the memorandum shall also be furnished to the faculty member. If, after an appropriate interval fixed at that discussion, the cause for concern continues to exist, the dean at his discretion may either request the Committee on Professional Standards to initiate a peer review as a guide to his further action or institute proceedings for termination.

Since adoption of this policy, the tenure level at St. Lawrence has risen to 68 percent. While most of the evaluations tend to be informal and routine, the dean has on two occasions scheduled a more stringent second-year review as a follow-up to the initial assessment. To date, no actions to dismiss a faculty member for cause have been entertained.

Strengths and Weaknesses of Evaluating Tenured Faculty

Periodic evaluations of tenured faculty do not contravene the tenets of traditional tenure, although not everyone subscribes to this view. The Tenure Commission at the University of Pittsburgh, for example, in 1974 rejected "the proposition that the performance of tenured faculty members should be periodically reviewed in the same intense and comprehensive manner in which the performance of a nontenured faculty member is reviewed on the occasion of deciding whether to award tenure. The commission believes that such review would erode tenure, thereby sacrificing the values that tenure confers on the university." We respectfully disagree. In an examination of the precepts and documents on academic tenure, we see no evidence that tenure and rigorous evaluation are incompatible concepts. In fact, meritocracy based on meticulous examination of a professor's work is at the core of academic tenure. Furthermore, neither the 1940 statement by the AAUP nor any other declaration by the AAUP suggests that the evaluation of tenured faculty would be inconsistent with the tenets of academic tenure. Officially, the AAUP has been neutral. Jordan Kurland, associate general secretary of the AAUP, has commented, "We neither endorse nor decry the practice." If, however, a performance evaluation were to be tantamount to dismissal for cause, without opportunity for remediation and due process, then the association would condemn the practice. On campuses concerned with adherence to AAUP policies, the association's neutrality may facilitate adoption of, or at least lessen resistance to, regular assessments of all faculty members.

Periodic performance reviews offer benefits far more important than congruence with AAUP policy. Case studies conducted by the Southern Regional Education Board (1977) emphasize the interrelationships between faculty evaluation and personnel decisions:

> Institutions which have informal, seemingly vague approaches to faculty evaluation tend to have less faculty turnover than those with systematic approaches, and faculty personnel decisions appear to be very difficult to make and are usually put off until the last possible opportunity. Satisfactory faculty performance seems to be assumed in these institutions, with personnel action being taken primarily when adverse circumstances arise. The criteria and standards for promotion are obscure, and many promotions seem to be automatic when a certain amount of time has passed. Salary increases rarely are given for merit, but rather on an across-the-board basis. . . .
>
> [At institutions with systematic and comprehensive approaches to faculty evaluation], the major positive consequence reported was that better personnel decisions are being made, with the result that marginal faculty members are being terminated sooner, strong faculty members are rewarded for

their strengths, and all are stimulated toward improved performance. Administrators at several doctoral-level institutions reported that they believed the overall quality of their faculty has improved, and that faculty tenured before adoption of the present system perform better now than before. Concrete evidence for increased productivity in the area of research and publication is available in some of these institutions [Southern Regional Education Board, 1977, pp. 25-26].

The SREB study, which relied in part on self-reported data, may overstate the benefits that derive from a systematic approach to faculty evaluation. Yet, even were these claims discounted, the general proposition would still hold: Without comprehensive faculty evaluations, prudent personnel decisions are less likely, and uninformed personnel actions are more likely. Evaluative information does not guarantee wise decisions; it only enhances the odds. Given the complexities, subtleties, and perils of personnel decisions, we prefer the most favorable odds possible.

As a general rule, then, regular evaluation of tenured faculty, like regular evaluation of untenured faculty, represents a commendable though imperfect practice. The approach to evaluation adopted at Coe College resembles the growth contracts employed at Hampshire and Evergreen, since both policies rest on the development of a plan for professional growth. In many ways, both designs offer the same advantages: a mandate to consider and, ideally, encounter the future and an "excuse" to converse and confer with colleagues. The evaluation process subtly, almost subconsciously, creates an expectation of progress and advancement. Properly executed, the process also enables individuals and departments to set directions and priorities in harmony with institutional objectives. Several faculty members we interviewed at Coe stressed the value of the plans as a means to orchestrate departmental activities and as a means to learn more about the interests and ambitions of colleagues. At small colleges and large universities alike, colleagues within a department can be remarkably distant and, quite unintentionally, rather private. Frequently, neither time nor circumstance permits the dialogues which the ten-year plans promote.

As individuals develop plans, so too must the institution. Individual and institutional futures must be blended and compromised. Aspirations expressed by individuals often provoke questions about institutional resources and related commitments. The very articulation of individual, departmental, and institutional plans may help identify conflicts and initiate a process to reconcile differences. Unrealistic ambitions or unfeasible plans can be nipped early so as to minimize false hopes and dashed dreams. As one faculty member's plans stated forthrightly, "How much opportunity will Coe afford me to do [what] I want to do and can do best? The indications seem something less than promising." A litany of disappointments and criticisms followed. In conclusion, the professor wrote, "Thus far, I have managed to find or make opportunities to offer the contributions I would like to. I hope that may continue, but it does appear that things may be beginning to close in." These words from a respected faculty member invite management to reflect and respond constructively.

While all growth contract systems stimulate plans and provoke discussions, Coe's particular approach offers additional benefits. First, detached from decisions about continued employment, permanent faculty members can make bolder and more creative plans. Tenured faculty, by definition, are freer to speculate, and the best plans reflect that freedom. A professor of Spanish at Coe contemplated an interdisciplinary pattern of research and instruction that integrates foreign languages and medieval studies. A tenured colleague in chemistry planned industrial work experiences each summer that would enhance his competence as a chemist and as an adviser. (By contrast, the plans of untenured faculty appeared blander, more grandiose and, at the same time, more academically conservative.)

The time demands at Coe may not be quite as onerous as at Hampshire and Evergreen. A restatement and extension of a plan once every five years by a tenured faculty member for purposes of professional development seems to impose a lesser bur-

den than a new plan once every several years by a candidate for
reappointment. (The new ten-year appointment policy adopted
at Hampshire just before this book was typeset may reduce the
work load generated by the review process there.) The very nature of the contract renewal system, more than the requirements of a growth contract per se, accounts for the greater burdens. At Hampshire and Evergreen, the plans are part and parcel
of a process that heavily involves students, peers, administrators, and review committees. Only the review of tenure candidates at Coe consumes as much time as renewals of appointment at Hampshire and Evergreen.

However feasible, Coe's policy suffers some flaws. How
accurately can anyone plan a decade ahead? Necessarily, the
outermost years of the ten-year plans are vague and uncertain.
A five-year span seems more reasonable than ten. Since Coe's
policy already provides for a five-year update, the College could
easily switch to a five-year plan without significantly increasing
demands on the time of faculty or staff.

Second, the policy does not adequately convey what the
components of a growth plan should be or the criteria that will
be used to evaluate it. Consequently, most plans simply adum-
brate routine course revisions, a general research agenda (almost
always centered upon sabbaticals), and proposals for college
service; some plans even stipulate goals for physical fitness, psychological development, and family betterment. Typically,
plans speak of a need "to equip myself more broadly to teach a
wider variety of things"; of intentions "to keep on reorganizing
all of my courses frequently, in an effort to keep them fresh
and timely"; of "developing a number of research studies in
which students can participate as researchers"; of "becoming
more involved in youth activities" in the community. While
nearly all plans proclaim laudable, if unspectacular, goals, very
few map a frontier or bristle with creative energy.

Third, Coe's policy restricts the use of growth plans. The
goal of periodic evaluation should be to identify strengths and
weaknesses and to remedy deficiencies. Information from such
evaluations should enlighten all personnel decisions—salaries,
promotions, sabbatical leaves, terminations for cause. Inadvisably

but understandably, Coe's policies preclude using growth plans as part of any effort to dismiss tenured faculty for cause. Faculty resistance to that provision was too strong to override without substantial risks to the acceptance of the other proposed policy changes.

One final drawback: a benchmark evaluation—every five years, for example—can tempt supervisors to defer informal, day-to-day evaluations or to overlook, at least for the moment, egregious deficiencies. Colleagues and administrators may develop a tendency to keep a list and remain quiet until the "proper time" for evaluation arrives. The faculty member, in turn, may be lulled into a false sense of complacency on the assumption that the absence of criticism constitutes praise. Periodic formal evaluations are not intended to silence criticisms or compliments in the interim or to replace day-to-day feedback. The benchmark evaluation should be a culmination of an ongoing process. With a simple elegance, the *Faculty Handbook* of the University of Oklahoma states: "Faculty evaluation is a continuous process, both prior to and following the granting of tenure. An annual review of each faculty member's performance is the responsibility of the academic deans and the specific academic units."

A Framework for Faculty Evaluation

Like tenure and all other personnel policies, the evaluation process can be no better than the evaluators and the evaluated. To be most effective, the evaluation system should be developed with faculty participation and with the recognition that no evaluation system will satisfy everyone. Once established, the evaluation system must be *used*. Support for evaluation will dissipate quickly if the process appears to be an empty exercise or if personnel decisions frequently contradict or disregard evaluative data. The integrity of the process depends mightily on the integrity of the decision makers. And, we would remind academic administrators that a program to evaluate faculty without an equally rigorous program to evaluate managers invites charges of hypocrisy and undercuts the legitimacy of the policy.

The framework for faculty evaluation developed by the Southern Regional Education Board (1977) contains four components: purpose (objectives, desired outcomes of the program), areas (functions and attributes to be examined), elements (criteria, standards, and evidence), and procedure (sequence of activities). To a considerable degree, we have already considered each of these components in conjunction with our discussions on the evaluation of tenure candidates and tenured faculty. Here, then, we intend only to complete the discussion with some additional observations about areas and, to a greater extent, standards and sources of evidence.

Areas to Be Assessed. Performance appraisals to inform personnel decisions should be related to clearly specified responsibilities, presumably consistent with a faculty member's assignment. Whether through a letter of appointment, a salary letter, or an annual conference, academic administrators and faculty members should share common expectations about the nature and quality of the tasks to be performed. At the very least, faculty should know, broadly and inclusively, what functions and qualities will be evaluated. The work functions normally translate as instruction, scholarly research, university and civic service, and professional activities. (On some campuses, the match between individual talents and institutional needs may be another area of evaluation.) On a departmental or an individual basis, the definitions may be more detailed and more elaborate. For example, relative priorities may be assigned among those functions, or scholarly research may be defined to include (or exclude) pedagogical works. Is academic advising to be regarded and evaluated as an instructional activity? Is work performed as a paid consultant to be considered a professional activity? In the definition of a position, we would avoid the extremes of glib rhetoric and a laundry list of assignments. We would seek instead a lucid statement of expectations and responsibilities to be shared and discussed with each faculty member.

Some special-purpose institutions—military academies or church-related schools, for example—may also wish to include as an area of evaluation attributes as well as functions. Certain qualities, traits, and characteristics may be essential to succeed on that campus. Thus, at Brigham Young University, an institution of the Church of Jesus Christ of Latter Day Saints, the *Faculty Handbook* states plainly that the university requires all employees "to adhere to the highest principles of personal behavior, to exemplify honor and integrity, truthfulness, purity, love, and all the other principles of the Church. They are also required to maintain an exemplary standard of personal appearance." In Levinson's (1976) language, Brigham Young has added a "dynamic" dimension to performance appraisal. The "dynamic" dimension concerns process and manner, *how* one completes the tasks and attains the objectives. The "static" dimension concerns only the tasks and the objectives, *what* needs to be accomplished. To some degree, we suspect, the "dynamic" dimension—personality and style—always enters the equation. In the SREB survey, "personal attributes" ranked fourth among nine areas of evaluation, higher than research and publications. (Doctoral institutions alone rated personal attributes sixth, research second, and publications third. All institutions rated instructional activities first.) Whether desired traits should be detailed as part of a faculty handbook or a letter of appointment or not at all should be decided locally. In any event, to be fair and effective, faculty evaluations must rest on common expectations about the areas to be assessed.

Elements of Assessment. In Chapter Seven, we detailed the criteria, standards, and sources of evidence applied to tenure decisions at the Harvard Business School, the College of Letters and Science at the University of Wisconsin–Madison, and St. Olaf College. In addition, we listed examples of criteria and sources of evidence from a variety of institutions. We wish here to comment further on the matter of standards.

Standards describe the level of performance to be attained for each criterion. How well must one perform? What measure of excellence defines success? Always difficult to devise and apply, standards may be norm referenced or criterion referenced. Norm-referenced standards compare the performance of the candidate (for tenure, promotion, a merit increment) with the performances of other candidates. Some universities, for example, ask external referees where the candidate under consideration ranks among the best untenured faculty in the field; other colleges ask promotion committees to rank-order the candidates under review. Criterion-referenced standards, on the other hand, gauge performance against preestablished levels of accomplishment, without regard for how many faculty fall within any particular category. Students or peers may be asked to rate faculty on a five- or seven-point scale from inadequate to superlative. Although most institutions surveyed by SREB used criterion-referenced standards, few defined the terms—marginal, very good, excellent—in any detail.

Criterion-referenced standards may be either quantitative or qualitative. One preestablished standard for success as a researcher could be, for instance, receipt of $25,000 annually in external funds on average over five years. Alternatively, the standard could be "proven ability to attract outside support" without any stated quantitative dimension.

As a general though not absolute premise, we prefer judgment to measurement and norm-referenced standards to criterion-referenced standards. To the extent that personnel decisions allocate scarce resources—tenure slots, sabbaticals, money—we are inescapably involved in a comparative process. Presumably, not everyone should be granted tenure, promoted, or approved for sabbatical, and not everyone can be awarded an above-average increment. As much as some administrators and faculty seem reluctant to confront that reality, personnel decisions entail competition. The critical consideration concerns definition of the proper reference group to determine the norms. With respect to tenure, most colleges either disdain comparisons or limit them to campus peers. Elite colleges and research universities, on the other hand, gravitate toward regional and national comparisons. While national comparisons may be inadvisable for essentially local colleges, so too may be strictly intramural comparisons. The wider the appropriate reference group can be drawn, the more confidently faculty review committees and administrators can answer the central question: Is the candidate for tenure the best person the institution can attract?

As a first step toward the development of an appropriate frame of reference for normative standards, a college or department might attempt to establish a peer set. Some faculty recruits decline an appointment offer; some talented faculty on board leave. Where do these individuals go? An analysis of faculty recruitment and resignation data may reveal a department or college's counterparts and competitors. How do recent promotion and tenure candidates at these schools compare with local candidates? To reverse the question, colleagues at these other schools could be asked whether the candidate under consideration locally would qualify for tenure (or promotion) at their institutions. Ad hoc committees, in a sense, serve this purpose. Occasionally, a department might even advertise for a tenured position and then compare the caliber of the external and internal candidates. All these actions would provide faculty and staff with some means and norms to assess candidates for promotion and tenure within a context that extends beyond the corners of the campus.

Norm-referenced standards may be painful for department heads and deans to administer and difficult for faculty to accept. Yet they compel discernment and distinctions and thereby encourage faculty and staff to be selective. Selectivity, in turn, promotes institutional improvement. If criterion-referenced standards are to be applied, discrimination and differentiation may not occur. Recall, for example, the experience of the junior college cited in the previous chapter, where peer evaluations always exceeded the minimum scores for tenure established by the administration. The SREB study cites an institution where 90 percent of the faculty scored above the midpoint on evaluations conducted by the department. How useful are these assessments when scarce resources and rewards have to be allocated?

Quantification of standards presents another danger, since numbers can create an illusion of precision and veracity. Without question, quantification of criterion-referenced standards makes sense in certain cases; enrollments and student-credit-hour production, for example, may be appropriate indicators for a standard on instructional productivity. Let us return, though, to the standard of $25,000 a year in external research funds. What if the candidate averaged only $24,000 or attracted $125,000 the first year and nothing thereafter? We are not categorically opposed to quantification, we are, however, wary of the temptation to stretch interpretation of the data beyond the reasonable limits of the information at hand. Harold Leavitt, a professor at Stanford University, has called on American industry to "return to the subtle and the subjective" (Lohr, 1981, p. 51). The same advice applies to personnel decisions at American colleges and universities. Quantitative data, like qualitative data, constitute evidence to be weighed, not gospel to be accepted. When they are treated as gospel, excesses occur. We offer an example.

Effective October 1978, the University of San Francisco adopted a largely quantitative approach to faculty evaluation. A numerical value is assigned to every activity, and the numbers are then converted into letter grades: A = 10 points per annum, B = 8, C = 5. In order for a candidate to attain the rank of full professor, the average of that candidate's annual evaluations from the time of appointment (or last promotion) to the present must equal an A for teaching, an A for research, and a B for service. How does someone average ten points per annum to earn an A? For starters, faculty earn five points for satisfactory performance of a standard work load. "Very low evaluations" by students halve the points earned; "very high evaluations" earn 7.5 points. A modest overload can increase the score by a factor of 1.25, an extreme overload by 1.5. Add a new course (with no apparent reference to the quality of the course) after the first year and earn two points. Attend a professional workshop and gain half a point.

The evaluation of research proves to be a more complex matter. Scores for papers delivered at conferences range from one to four points. The exact number of points depends on the nature of the conference (local, regional, national), the length of the paper, and the quality of the reviews. Published articles are scored on the basis of length, reputation of the journal, and the number of citations elsewhere. Coauthored articles require that the points be "divided by N + 1." Points can be doubled when articles are "reprinted in whole or in substantial part three or more times and cited twelve or more times in reputable books or journals, or given an award by a professional society or discussed as main topic in two or more other articles." Six or more reprints and twenty-four or more citations triple the score. Bad reviews may halve or quarter the score. Short poems? Two to four points. Solo recitals, patents, short stories? Five to ten points. And on the document goes, more like the rules for a game than the guidelines for quality.

In fairness, the designers of the University of San Francisco scheme—able, reasoned individuals and experts on faculty evaluation—are quite satisfied with the system's operation and strongly critical of the subjective peer review process. Admittedly, the peer review process can be abused—for example, if it is used to enforce orthodoxy or to stifle creativity. Despite all its weaknesses, we favor peer reviews over a process that translates standards into numbers and numbers into decisions. In other words, we prefer informed opinions and comparisons by peers and supervisors to numerical displays on desk calculators as the bases for personnel decisions.

As the SREB study concludes, "Standards may be the most difficult element to develop and put into effect at the institutional level. . . . If standards for each criterion cannot be stated or agreed upon, it may perhaps indicate an inappropriate criterion" (Southern Regional Education Board, 1977, p. 42). To develop standards for tenure candidates and tenured faculty, administrators and professors alike and together will have to be persistent, creative, and open-minded. Some standards may be norm referenced, some may be criterion referenced, and still others may be a combination. (For example, policy could stipulate that a criterion-referenced standard, such as "superior," may be assigned by evaluators to a maximum of 25 percent of the candidates under consideration.) We cannot prescribe appropriate standards any more than we can prescribe appropriate criteria. These decisions must be reached by the campus community that has to live with the consequences. We can, however, urge the development of standards, greater reliance on norm-referenced standards, cautious use of quantification, and ample opportunities for informed judgment.

Sources of Evidence. The quality of decisions depends on the quality of the decision makers and the quality of the data available to enlighten the decisions. In Chapter Seven, we listed some possible sources of evidence, mindful of the fact that no documentation will ever be entirely free of defects and biases. In courtrooms, eyewitness accounts, polygraphs, and testimony under oath are sometimes unreliable, imperfect, and inaccurate; evidence to inform academic personnel decisions suffers from the same frailties and flaws. These deficiencies, however, should not deter efforts to accumulate and present proper evidence. To the degree that decision makers can determine what constitutes pertinent information, as well as appropriate application of that information, the evidence gathered should be more useful and less fallible. Against that backdrop, we discuss here several sources of evidence commonly collected yet widely misapplied and misconstrued.

Since the primary function of most faculty is to teach and since nearly every institution rates instruction as the most important area of evaluation for promotion and tenure, an assessment of performance in that dominant activity would seem only logical. After a review of studies of faculty evaluation, Centra (1979) concluded that five conditions were necessary for student evaluations to be meaningful:

1. At least five different courses with fifteen or more students should be evaluated.
2. Decision makers should not fall prey to the micrometer fallacy and assume wrongly that small differences have large meanings.
3. Global questions, which rate the overall effectiveness of the teacher and the course, are by far the most reliable indicators.
4. Standard forms and a common set of ratings are advisable, although individual units may add specific questions.
5. The form should take about ten minutes to complete.

In the interpretation of the results, decision makers should be aware that four factors significantly affect student responses: *class size* (classes with fewer than 10-15 students are most highly rated; classes with 35-100 students are most harshly rated), *mode* (discussion courses are generally better received than lecture courses), *type of course* (slightly higher ratings may be expected for electives and courses in a student's major, slightly lower ratings for courses required to fulfill general degree requirements), and *experience* (first-year teachers consistently do most poorly; teachers with 3-12 years' experience appear to do somewhat better than average; teachers with over twenty years' experience do somewhat worse than average).

With respect to peer evaluation, Centra (p. 75) concluded that classroom observations by peers are not "sufficiently reliable to use in making tenure, promotion, and salary decisions— or would require investing more time in visitations or in training sessions." The questionable value of faculty assessments of classroom performance for summative purposes does not, however, diminish the worth of peer evaluations of other aspects of performance. Colleagues may be able to judge the substance of a course through evaluations of syllabi, objectives, reading lists, assignments, exams, and the instructor's mastery of the discipline.

Even were an institution to devise an evaluation system as sound as circumstances allow, some faculty would voice concern and doubt. What is a good teacher? Is a good teacher necessarily an effective teacher? Is an evaluation of teaching an evaluation of learning? The litany of familiar criticisms and reservations should not, however, forestall the development of procedures to evaluate teaching; and those procedures should, wherever possible, reflect the knowledge we do possess about the elements and limitations of an effective evaluation system. As Lewis (1975, p. 24) has observed: "It would be erroneous to conclude that, because teaching effectiveness is not generally evaluated as adequately as it might be and because our best measures of teaching effectiveness are perhaps invalid, we should not try to distinguish the good, fair, and bad classroom performers. . . . Thus, it seems reasonable to use the best measures of teaching effectiveness we now have at least to weed out the totally incompetent pedagogue."

Unlike the controversies surrounding the evaluation of instruction, most academicians agree that colleagues within a particular discipline or field are best positioned to judge the quality of a candidate's research. Yet the usefulness of evidence furnished by colleagues may vary widely. For more consistently valuable assessments of scholarly research, we recommend the following practices:

1. Peers, especially at the initial level of review, must read and examine, rather than skim or tally, the candidate's work. Assignment of that responsibility to a subcommittee required to provide oral or written reports to the parent committee may promote responsible reviews and informed judgments. The subcommittee should ascertain, for instance, whether the research moves substantially beyond the candidate's doctoral dissertation; whether the seven articles listed are, in fact, one article restated seven ways; and whether the research is original or synthetic, pedestrian or seminal.

2. Distinctions between refereed and nonrefereed journals should be drawn, and the department head, not the candidate, should make the distinctions. At a reputable research university, we observed several instances where articles in nonrefereed journals were listed in the dossier as articles in refereed journals. In one case, *Playgirl* magazine was actually cited as a refereed journal. For the benefit of candidates and reviewers, a list of refereed journals, perhaps even classified by the stature of the publication, should be supplied to all faculty members.

3. If developing and receiving research grants are to be sources of evidence, then the candidate's record should be placed within the larger context of money available in that field of endeavor. The reference group for a philosopher should not include petroleum engineers; comparisons with other humanists on number of grants submitted and dollars obtained would be far more appropriate.

The next several recommendations concern external letters of reference. Lewis (1975, 1980) properly questions the value of many letters of reference (especially letters for female candidates), which tend to be concerned more with personality, style, appearance, attributes, and visibility than with academic accomplishments. Many of the weaknesses of external letters could, we think, be mitigated by careful selection of and better instructions to referees. Properly framed requests to properly selected referees can produce a useful source of evidence to assess research.

4. Someone other than the candidate, most likely the department head or the dean, should select the referees—ideally, respected *peers* knowledgeable about the candidate's research. Unless candidates are expected to attain national eminence as researchers, requests for letters from nationally prominent researchers make little sense. Renowned and prolific scholars should not be expected to be familiar with or to read on request the work of an occasional scholar in order to offer a judgment on a promotion or tenure decision. Testimonials from personal friends and mentors within the profession also offer limited value.

5. The request for a letter of reference should convey clearly the areas of responsibility the referee should address as well as the criteria and standards the university will apply. (Some colleges and universities mistakenly invite external referees to assess the candidate as a teacher, despite the fact that very few referees have any firsthand knowledge of that facet of the candidate's work.) Specific questions should be posed: How does the candidate's research compare with the work of untenured faculty members *A, B,* and *C* at universities *X, Y,* and *Z?* Would the candidate qualify for tenure at your institution? Has the candidate's research been helpful to you in your own work?

6. So as not to prejudice the response, requests for letters should be scrupulously neutral. Statements such as "We are about to recommend *X* for tenure" or "We seek support for *X*'s candidacy for promotion" convey a predisposition to award tenure and intimate that a favorable recommendation would be appreciated and preferred.

Compared to research and instruction, the literature seldom treats problems associated with the evaluation of service. That is probably because service is almost never evaluated. Traditionally, review committees seek only factual information about a candidate's record of service. Dossiers merely list committee assignments, professional memberships, community activities, and consultant work. Rarely do colleges or universities, with the exception of community colleges, require evaluative information about service activities. Was the candidate a conscientious and constructive committee member? Did the candidate ably serve the community or the client? How much time and effort did the candidate devote to volunteer work? We have encountered only one four-year college (no doubt there are some others) that requires committee chairmen to report the attendance and contribution of committee members. Imagine if service on the faculty senate, for example, had to be evaluated rather than simply reported. Perhaps we might have more effective governance systems. In any event, without some evaluative evidence on service, decision makers will be as handicapped as a college admissions officer asked to assess a high school transcript that merely lists the courses taken by the applicant.

In conclusion, sources of evidence about areas of performance as complex and as subtle as instruction, research, and service will always be, to some extent, fragile and flawed. Rather than embrace that hardship as an excuse to forgo the search for evidence, faculty and administrators alike should redouble efforts to collect pertinent information and to apply that evidence responsibly. As a first and minimal step, the campus community must decide what evidence to amass and then communicate that decision to the persons responsible for the development of dossiers. If dossiers are replete with extraneous and useless information, the blame lies less with the candidate than with the cognizant administrator. As a next step, department heads and deans should equip candidates with model dossiers and checklists and then review the documentation for completeness and accuracy. Unnecessary and irrelevant materials should be culled. Some skeptics maintain that the thickness of the dossier and the quality of the candidate are inversely related. That should not be the case; dossiers should be lean and rich. If the faculty review committee needs more information or clearer instructions, the chairman of the committee should so inform the responsible academic administrator.

When all three elements of evaluation—criteria, standards, and evidence—have been defined, a chart can be developed to display, by way of summary, the institution's approach to evaluation (see Table 5). Although only two areas are represented and no norm-referenced standards are cited, the table is nevertheless illustrative and instructive.

Table 5. An Institution's Approach to Evaluation

Evaluation Areas	Criteria	Standards	Evidence
I. Instruction	1. Student learning gains	75% achieve 90% of learning objectives	Pretests and posttests graded by department
	2. Course materials	Clear, relevant, current; behavioral objectives	Submitted to and examined by departmental committee; student ratings
	3. Student satisfaction	80% rate course in top level	Student ratings
II. Research	1. Publications	Specific number in refereed journals	Faculty self-report
		Excellence in quality	Testimony of six outside readers; citations in other works
	2. Grants	$20,000 minimum in grants	Faculty self-report; records

Source: Southern Regional Education Board, 1977, p. 49.

While we consider the SREB framework logical and practical, there are many other commendable models and approaches (see, for instance, Centra, 1977, 1979; McKeachie, 1979b; Miller, 1972, 1974; Seldin, 1980). Any of these works could serve as a point of departure for development of a construct best suited to local goals, needs, and conditions.

9.

Distributing
Rewards
and Applying
Sanctions

𝟪𝟪𝟪𝟪𝟪𝟪𝟪𝟪𝟪𝟪𝟪𝟪𝟪𝟪𝟪𝟪𝟪𝟪𝟪𝟪𝟪𝟪𝟪𝟪𝟪𝟪𝟪𝟪𝟪𝟪𝟪𝟪𝟪𝟪𝟪

Incentive structures are delicate daisy chains that must maintain certain critical linkages. To paraphrase a model of reward practices developed by Porter and Lawler (1968) and Lawler (1971), the linkages are as follows: greater effort by the worker must, as a rule, lead to improved performance; improved performance must lead to greater rewards; and the greater rewards must satisfy the worker's needs and desires. If the incentive structure is to operate effectively, none of these links between effort, performance, rewards, and desires can be severed. Some samples drawn from academic life may illustrate the necessity of these linkages:

Effort and Performance. A university may establish a faculty development program to improve the quality of instruction offered by ineffective teachers. Although Professor Smith participates earnestly in the program, his performance, as measured by student evaluations, does not improve. When practice leads to perfect, or at least to improvement, an incentive to practice exists. When, however, greater effort does not yield improved performance, the motivation to exert greater effort dissipates. Professor Smith quits the faculty development program.

Performance and Rewards. In the mathematics department of a research university, all professors, as a matter of policy, teach one less course a semester than assistant and associate professors, on the premise that professors, as the most active scholars, need release time to pursue research. Despite a heavier course load, Assistant Professor Jones produces far more scholarship than nearly all the professors in the department. In order to be even more prolific, Jones asks to be relieved of one course a semester. The department chairman, a professor, denies the request. The tie between performance (namely, research) and the reward (namely, release time) has been broken, while the relationship between status (or rank) and the reward remains intact. Unpersuaded that better performance will lead to greater rewards and disappointed by that realization, Jones labors less productively.

Rewards and Desires. Brown, the assistant director of a policy research center, performs splendidly. In recognition of that fact and to enhance Brown's professional development, the director asks Brown to attend more national conferences, to visit comparable centers on other campuses, and to cultivate foundation officers, government agencies, and prospective donors. With a young family and a distaste for air travel, Brown would rather stay close to home. From Brown's perspective, the travel demands are onerous, almost punitive. The director, on the other hand, displeased with Brown's work on the road and piqued by Brown's apparent ingratitude, starts to reassess the assistant director's potential. The institutional reward (visibility and professional development through extensive travel) did not meet, and indeed countered, the individual's desires. Worse, the reward, perceived as a punishment, adversely affected performance. The key consideration must be less what the reward costs the organization and more how much the employee values the reward.

How can administrators discover which faculty value what rewards? They can simply ask. Fenker (1977) did just that and discovered that faculty reward preferences differ by age, school, and rank. Of seventeen possible rewards, faculty at the rank of instructor rated a $200 research award eighth, whereas more senior faculty rated the award fifteenth. Faculty at the Divinity School rated travel funds to one conference second only to a sabbatical; faculty at the School of Education rated travel funds ninth. Faculty at the School of Nursing, who shuttle from clinics to classrooms to hospitals, rated a parking place much higher than any other faculty did. In a word, faculty are not monolithic, and therefore the reward structure must be eclectic and personalized. Otherwise, the reward may not, as management would intend, be prized; worse, the reward may be a disincentive.

The goal of any reward system should be to determine what blend of rewards satisfies an individual and then to correlate as closely as possible the *relationship* between work performance and worker satisfaction. The best performers should be the most satisfied and the worse performers the least satisfied. The correlation can be obtained from two data sets: a list of the most and least effective faculty as assessed by the department head or dean, and based in part on peer and student evaluations, and some measure of work satisfaction as self-reported by faculty members. In a well-managed institution, there should be a close correlation between perceived effectiveness and self-perceived satisfaction. To achieve this goal, the total dollar value of the rewards need not change although the distribution curve will. Not everyone will be satisfied by the allocation of rewards; not everyone should be satisfied. But the best should be the most satisfied. This is not inequity; it is good management. Inequities occur when individuals receive the same rewards for different levels of performance.

Extrinsic and Intrinsic Rewards

Like most supervisors, academic administrators usually concentrate on rewards that are within the province of managerial control. These so-called extrinsic rewards may be salaries and fringes or noneconomic commodities such as awards and praise. Intrinsic rewards, by contrast, are essentially self-supplied rewards. No one can allocate such intrinsic rewards as a sense of fulfillment, the excitement of discovery, or the intellectual stimulation of students and colleagues.

As one example of the relationship between intrinsic rewards and worker satisfaction, we note Solmon's (1979, p. 12) conclusion that "faculty who have published more over their careers are more satisfied than others." Yet administrators cannot award or allot publications to faculty; even if they could, the recipients would not enjoy intrinsic satisfaction. That comes from the inherent nature of the research effort and the sense of achievement that accompanies the transformation of ideas and insights into prose. Administrators can, however, help forge an environment conducive to the attainment of intrinsic rewards: "Can faculty behavior be changed? The answer lies not in manipulation of extrinsic rewards such as prizes and honors, although these should not be dismissed. Rather, the answer lies in examining the characteristics of desired faculty activities that can bring satisfaction and in creating situations in which those satisfactions can be found more readily" (McKeachie, 1979a, p. 15).

*Merit Pay.** Merit pay means more money for work well

*Portions of this section first appeared in a study by Chait (1979b).

done. To the extent that colleges and universities adopt formal evaluation systems to inform salary decisions, pay becomes a measure, or more accurately, a reflection of performance. With respect to pay, some will gain more than others presumably because, with respect to performance, some achieved more than others.

In theory, merit pay represents a double-edged sword: a means to reward effective and productive faculty and to penalize ineffectual and inactive faculty. Many faculty members and faculty unions regard merit pay programs as a punitive practice too often intended to discipline outspoken and controversial professors and to reward allies of the administration. Moreover, opponents of merit pay contend, substantial salary increases for a few individuals usually require modest pay increases for many others since the total salary dollars for a fiscal year are, as a rule, fixed. On the other hand, some administrators and trustees consider tenure a shield that insulates faculty from accountability. Merit pay plans offer one of the few means to pierce that layer of protection, to establish performance incentives, and to reward illustrious performers.

The threshold questions are whether the prospect of merit pay will motivate better performance and whether the acquisition of merit pay will satisfy the better performers. Expert opinion on these complex issues differs and sometimes conflicts. Nevertheless, we can distill from research that salaries will motivate employees effectively only if the daisy chain remains unbroken.

First and foremost, the organization must convince the work force that increased effort will lead to improved performance and that improved performance will lead to increased pay. To ensure that linkage, effort must correlate with results and management must conduct performance evaluations, ideally based on objective and clearly communicated criteria. What is more, there would have to be regular, substantive appraisal sessions and explicit discussions between supervisors and subordinates about the relationship between performance and the overall operation of the reward system.

Even were employees to understand and accept the criteria and the process of evaluation, the system would not yet be

validated from the viewpoint of the work force. The employees
must also be persuaded that salary decisions are consistent with
performance appraisals. To achieve that objective requires some
disclosure about salary decisions. If a faculty member does not
know who received what merit increment or how he (or she)
fared relative to specific colleagues, that individual will not
know how well he has done, how fairly the system operates,
how closely pay and performance correlate, and what behaviors
the institution values. To know only that some unnamed colleagues earned merit increments will not be sufficient. Faculty
members need to know who, how much (at least by percentage, if not by dollars), and why. Otherwise, the faculty may
conclude that secrecy serves to conceal decisions based on fa-
voritism or caprice. Worse, faculty intent on self-improvement
would not know which colleagues, at least as perceived by
the administration, are the star performers worthy of emula-
tion.

These circumstances hardly describe the personnel practices of most colleges and universities, where supervision has traditionally been loose and evaluation, particularly after tenure,
sporadic and often unwelcome. The very nature of the academic
profession probably precludes objective, precise performance
measures. As for dissemination of salary decisions, most faculty
and administrators, we suspect, do not support disclosure of salaries or merit pay increments. Divulgence of salaries seems too
crass for the professoriate. Besides, publication of salary actions
may require that faculty compensation committees and administrators explain and defend their decisions. (Regardless of these
concerns, some states require that salaries of all state employees
be publicly available.)

While knowledge of salary decisions about peers will facilitate validation of the system, whether an employee has knowledge of all salary actions or none, the linkage between performance and reward will still be difficult to cement. Merit pay
usually derives from some evaluation by supervisors. Yet studies
reveal that most workers, most notably in unionized settings, do
not believe that their supervisors' evaluations are either accurate
or valid. Small wonder, since most employees rank themselves

as above-average performers. At General Electric, on a 1-100 scale, the average self-evaluation was 77. Whereas 90 percent of the respondents had a self-assessment above the midpoint on the scale, only 2 percent were below. In another study of some 1,110 professionals and managers, 47 percent placed themselves in the top 5 percent and another 36 percent placed themselves in the top 10 percent. No one offered a self-evaluation below the upper quartile on the scale (Meyer, 1975, pp. 43-45). Faculty appear to be no more modest. As discussed later, three separate surveys report that more than 90 percent of the respondents were by self-estimation "above-average" teachers.

By definition, only half of any population can be above average. If, however, most employees have self-perceptions as above-average performers, then inevitably many workers will be disappointed with an average or below-average pay increase. Typically, the employee's response will be to denigrate the supervisor and the importance of the work activities under review. The script for a typical diatribe might be as follows: "The administration always stresses good teaching as the key to success around here. I'm a devoted and talented teacher and what does it get me? A modest, average salary increase. I'll tell you what: either the dean doesn't know a good teacher when he sees one or the college really doesn't give a damn about good teaching. Probably both. In any case, hard work and good results don't pay off around here. Why make the extra effort?" From this professor's viewpoint, there was no correlation between performance and payoff.

Even where performance and reward are aligned, merit pay will not motivate or satisfy an employee unless that worker regards pay as an important and desirable reward. Although money is certainly important to everyone, some people value it less than others do. Considerable research (Lawler, 1971; Herzberg, 1968) suggests that supervisors consistently overestimate the value that subordinates assign to pay, and limited research (Solmon, 1979; McKeachie, 1979a) suggests that professors do not attach as much significance to money as workers in the for-profit sector do. In a summation of research on faculty motivation, McKeachie (1979a, p. 7) concludes, "Thus, the data from all studies are in good agreement about the major sources of work satisfaction for faculty members. In all studies, intrinsic satisfactions are reported to be much more important than extrinsic rewards." Faculty do value other currencies: work freedom, autonomy, intellectual stimulation, critical acclaim, prestige, challenge, and opportunities for creativity. The research cited by McKeachie and studies by the National Endowment for the Humanities and the National Science Foundation (reported by Solmon, 1979) plainly indicate that academics cherish some intrinsic rewards more dearly than substantial salaries. Undoubtedly, pay is important to professors, especially to faculty members with low salaries, but to the degree that it is somewhat less important than other extrinsic and intrinsic rewards, pay loses some of its ability to motivate.

Finally, merit pay seems to work as a motivator only where pay differentials are substantial. A modest economic distinction between the very best and the very worst does very little to motivate performance. How motivated would a faculty member be to excel if the "payoff" were only an extra 1 or 2 percent over the average increment? As Lawler (1971, p. 173) warns: "Motivating people with financial rewards is not a piker's game. Large amounts of money must be given to the good performers if employees are to place a high value on good performance and the raises to which it leads. . . . If a company cannot afford to do this or is not willing to, it should probably forget about using pay to motivate performance." How much is enough proves difficult to gauge, although some compensation analysts have suggested that the merit pay component of a salary increase at least equal the average percentage increment provided to all employees for continued service. Probably the merit increment should be much more than that. The prospect of an 18-20 percent salary increment where the average increase will be 9 percent could well stir motivation. At most colleges and universities, however, increments of that magnitude would almost surely be financially infeasible and perhaps politically unwise.

Merit pay, moreover, adds to a faculty member's base salary. As a result, the costs of a merit increment are compounded each year. A professor salaried at $30,000 earns an 18 percent increase in year one: 9 percent for continued service and 9 percent for merit. On the assumption that the professor receives only a 9 percent salary increase each year thereafter, the cumulative cost of that one merit increment over the next decade will exceed $40,000.

Bonus payments, one-time salary supplements not added to the base, offer a less expensive alternative rarely used by college and universities and regularly used by industry. In the example cited above, if the faculty member received a 9 percent increase and a $400 bonus annually (or a $2,000 bonus twice), the cost to the university would be nearly $2,000 less. Over three decades, the savings would be even greater. While the costs are unmistakably less, we do not know whether a bonus system would be more or less effective as a motivator or as a source of satisfaction. That question requires additional research.

Some colleges, universities, and professional associations honor distinguished research, teaching, or service with awards that carry a monetary prize. Although these awards are, in effect, performance bonuses, the concept has not yet been extended to annual evaluations or to special achievements such as election to a national academy, authorship of an acclaimed work, or reformation of a disciplinary pedagogy. The development of suitable criteria and the perception that bonus payments are somehow unseemly present formidable obstacles to wider acceptance of this practice. Despite these impediments, we encourage further consideration of the concept.

To summarize, all the conditions and resources necessary for merit pay to motivate are not likely to be present at most colleges and universities. The scarcity of funds, the vagaries of performance appraisal, the privacy of salaries, and the presence of a work force with a greater affinity for intrinsic rewards unfavorably affect the motivational power of merit pay plans. We do not mean to imply that modestly differentiated salary increments hold no value or that merit cannot be rewarded. Rather, we believe that merit pay should be viewed as one means to reward distinguished performance and as an unlikely means to motivate faculty members unless all the aforementioned prerequisites are at hand.

In the final analysis, compensation plans, like all other

personnel policies, require that goals be formulated before policy. Salary systems can serve a variety of purposes: (1) to ensure equity on matters of age, sex, race; (2) to motivate and reward superior performance; (3) to penalize inferior performance (see section on sanctions below); (4) to compete effectively in the marketplace; (5) to provide a decent wage; and (6) to align salaries with the institution's ability to pay. Once the goals have been selected and policies adopted, the institution can begin to devise ways to assess achievement of those objectives. The *Higher Education Salary Evaluation Kit,* produced by the AAUP (Scott, n.d.), offers several methods to uncover salary inequities based on race and/or sex. Whether merit pay, compared with other incentives, motivates faculty can only be determined on a case-by-case basis, perhaps through an interview or questionnaire. A college's ability to compete in the marketplace can be assessed in part by interinstitutional comparisons, although administrators should be wary of the pitfalls of comparisons with AAUP salary surveys (Cliff, 1978). A more reliable procedure would be to limit salary comparisons to a preselected cohort of similar institutions that share the same general definitions and work conditions. In addition, the competitiveness of a salary system can be ascertained by a survey of candidates who declined invitations to join the faculty. Did the compensation package significantly influence the decision, or were other factors and considerations more determinative? Finally, a review of balance sheets, payrolls, and revenue streams should indicate whether an institution's compensation plan strains or exceeds the university's ability to finance that plan.

Faculty Development. Merit pay represents one component of a reward structure, and pay satisfaction represents one element of worker satisfaction. There are incentives and sources of satisfaction other than money. On the basis of empirical research, Porter and Lawler (1968, p. 120) deduced that success may be the principal source of satisfaction: "It appears wise to think of job satisfaction as something that is likely to result *from* performance behavior rather than as the cause of good or bad performance." Satisfaction derives from improved or effective performance because such performance provides a sense of achievement and fulfillment, as well as other intrinsic rewards, and frequently, though not always, leads to increased extrinsic rewards.

In light of that theorem, academic administrators would be well advised to develop programs and strategies designed to maximize opportunities for as many faculty as possible to experience and then sustain success. We would categorize these programs and strategies as faculty development. In an ideal world, all faculty would be equally capable and routinely lavished with extrinsic rewards contributory to effective performance and professional success. Realistically, however, colleges and universities have limited resources to fund extrinsic rewards, and not all faculty perform equally effectively. Should resources be committed mainly to remediate conspicuously incapable faculty or to support demonstrably competent faculty? In our view, extrinsic rewards should, by and large, be distributed among the ablest faculty in order to support still greater self-improvement. Conversely, we would be disinclined to throw too much good money after bad. In other words, we would define faculty development as an opportunity for greater self-improvement (and thus greater self-satisfaction) earned on the bases of performance and potential.

Rather than generate an exhaustive list of extrinsic rewards with a salutary effect on professional development, we prefer to furnish some illustrative examples. While some of these rewards generate substantial expenses for the institution, others carry little or no cost, and in no case does the faculty member realize any direct financial gain. The range of rewards might include new faculty slots to build a critical mass of colleagues; authorization for a new course, program, or degree; research assistants; teaching assistants; more clerical support; additional laboratory or computer equipment; an increased library budget; a reduced course load; smaller (or larger) classes; better students; a more compact schedule; a sabbatical; travel funds, research funds, or funds for a colloquium; and additional space for an honors or tutorial program. Any and all of these "payoffs" create conditions conducive to effective performance and hence intrinsic satisfaction. Academic administrators, therefore,

would do well to devote at least as much attention to the distribution of these rewards as to the allocation of 1 or 2 percent
merit increments. The effect of these noneconomic benefits on
faculty satisfaction should not be underrated. Other extrinsic
rewards and forms of recognition relate more to individual motives. For example, Professor X, a world-class scholar, may derive satisfaction from elevated status. In that case, suitable rewards might include opportunities to offer advice and influence
administrative decisions, appointment to key committees, exposure in university publications, an award (monetary or non-
monetary) for distinguished work, breakfast with the president,
lunch with the executive committee of the board of trustees, or
office appurtenances. If the university values Professor X and
Professor X values status, then these actions may also constitute
appropriate rewards.

The philosophical position we have staked has implications for the design of a formal faculty development program.*
Such a program should be portrayed as a desirable and presti-
gious activity rather than as a merely acceptable endeavor or,
worse, a penalty for ineffective performance. To be so positioned, the program should meet four design specifications consistent with a definition of the concept as earned opportunities:

1. Faculty development programs should build on individual strengths and professional roles and activities normally
associated with faculty status and not on perceived needs identified and articulated by the institution. Programs constructed
around problems and needs—for example, programs to improve
the ineffective instructor, to retrain the underutilized professor,
or to update the outmoded old-timer—are foreign to the self-
perceptions of faculty members as accomplished teachers and
active scholars. Endeavors such as scholarly research, curriculum
development, and attendance at professional conferences are
consonant with faculty self-perceptions and convey a measure

---

*James Gueths, assistant vice-chancellor for academic systems at
the University of Wisconsin–Oshkosh, assisted in the development of this
discussion of program design, parts of which first appeared in an article by
Chait and Gueths (1981).

of prestige. Professional activities reinforce a positive, professional image; therapeutic activities do not.

2. Faculty development programs should assume a constructive, as opposed to corrective, rationale. Whereas corrective or remedial programs invite diagnosis of the problem and a prescribed cure, programs with a developmental or constructive purpose encourage faculty to plan and implement a personal agenda for professional growth. Nearly all faculty would embrace a program designed to extend a self-selected sphere of expertise; far fewer would pursue a prepackaged program expressly designed to overcome alleged weaknesses.

Whether voluntary or mandatory, remedial programs to correct purported problems pose great risks. First, superior faculty may well criticize and condemn such efforts as an inefficient and inequitable allocation of resources and opportunities. Second, participants would, rightly or wrongly, be stigmatized as ineffective performers, an image no one actively cultivates or particularly cherishes. Third, compulsory participation would probably be resented by mistakenly self-assured faculty as unnecessary and coercive. And fourth, voluntary participation may not in any case attract the intended clientele for remediation. After all, why would a faculty member with no self-perceived inadequacies participate in a program to overcome deficiencies? Therein lies the rub, especially for programs to improve instruction. In a study by Blackburn (1980), about 90 percent of the faculty surveyed at twenty-four colleges and universities labeled themselves "above average" or "superior teachers." These results corroborated two earlier studies cited by Blackburn, where as many as 99 percent of the respondents offered a self-assessment of "above average." Thus, Blackburn comments (p. 37), "Faculty relegate to myth the idea that there is an epidemic of poor teaching in higher education. And, although faculty committees may vote for instructional improvement, it is probably not . . . because they feel *they* need one but because they believe *their colleagues do,* who, of course, do not share this assessment."

Like others, most faculty seek professional status and the respect of colleagues. Participants in faculty development programs constructed around professional roles and responsibilities should accrue status and peer recognition. As the program takes hold, faculty will start to inquire of one another: "Did you submit a grant proposal? Was it funded? How goes the project?" Later, others will observe: "I saw your monograph." "I read about your new course." "I heard from a colleague about the paper you delivered." Nonparticipants will not be reprimanded or punished, only excluded, as a matter of course, from the psychic rewards, the professional activities of colleagues, and the excitement and respect that faculty development will generate and the university will publicize. Some of these bystanders may then reconsider and energetically undertake activities that demonstrate a worthiness and a willingness to participate.

If faculty are free to pursue constructive professional activities such as scholarly research, sabbatical leaves, and presentations at conferences, what assurance is there that these activities will lead to better classroom instruction, a primary goal of most faculty development programs? In an evaluation of faculty development programs at some twenty liberal arts colleges, Siegel (1980) concluded that improved instruction will more likely "eventuate" from programs concerned with what to teach, what to require, and what to emphasize than from programs explicitly concerned with how to teach. In other words, development programs concerned with scholarly research and curricular substance proved more successful as a means to improve instruction than programs expressly designed to better the quality of teaching. Faculty surveyed by Blackburn (1980) offered a similar view. While faculty development experts tend to emphasize instructional skills, techniques, and technologies, classroom teachers regarded mastery of subject matter, content specialization, and the ability to stay abreast of the field as the essential elements of superior teaching. Consequently, faculty preferred development programs that stressed leaves and research grants to programs focused on pedagogy. In short, the studies by Siegel and Blackburn confirm the appropriateness of the first two design specifications: professional roles and constructive rationales.

3. As much as possible, resource allocation decisions related to faculty development should be determined by the fac-

ulty and not dominated by the administration. Decisions to approve sabbaticals, underwrite research, or sponsor a colloquium series should be reached through the competitive grant model already familiar to faculty at research universities and elite colleges. Proposals, rationales, and budgets should be submitted to a peer review board, which would assess the quality of the proposal and the performance record of the proposal writer. The strongest proposals then would be funded, and the others would not. Such a review procedure should add credibility and an aura of esteem to the program, strengthen faculty commitment through participation in the process, and produce better decisions. Moreover, rigorous peer review culminates in an *award* of funds, which implicitly carries a measure of recognition, prestige, and honor that should enhance the "positive acceptance" of participants. Administratively dominated processes, on the other hand, culminate in a handout at best and an ultimatum to shape up at worst.

Under faculty control, some rewards may in effect be misappropriated; in other words, performance and rewards may not be perfectly aligned. Of course, the distribution of rewards by administrators presents the same risk. To militate against misappropriation of rewards by peer review committees, the administration should orient committees to the philosophy and objectives of the reward structure and furnish committees with pertinent information about the performance record of each applicant. In addition, senior administrators should, in collaboration with the faculty, develop a selection process most likely to populate review boards with the most respected and most rigorous academicians on campus. The criteria for appointment to peer review panels should emphasize the past performance of the nominees.

Obviously, faculty committees cannot enjoy a totally free rein. Actions to reduce course loads, develop new programs, or purchase computer hardware, for example, directly affect the affairs of a department or college. In these instances, approval by the department chairman or dean should precede submission of the proposal to a peer review panel, and in all cases the opinions of the applicant's supervisor should be a part of the documentation to be evaluated. Finally, as with promotion and tenure cases, faculty review committees should make recommendations, not decisions. From time to time, the executive officers of the institution may reach a decision contrary to the faculty's recommendation, but such disagreements should be relatively rare, readily defensible, and clearly explained to the committee.

4. Faculty development programs should be a budgetary priority and not a peripheral accessory available intermittently as fiscal conditions allow. Financial support for extrinsic rewards should be unmistakably central to a university's budget and funded at a level that communicates an institutional commitment to faculty development. While external funds are undeniably valuable, the continuous appropriation of internal resources speaks more eloquently to commitment and enables faculty to plan developmental activities with the knowledge that funds will be available to support the best proposals. As a matter of policy, 1 or 2 percent of the operating budget might be designated "off the top" each year to underwrite the costs of faculty development, much as corporate pacesetters invest regularly and substantially in staff development. In 1978, International Business Machines (IBM), with 160,000 employees worldwide, expended over $50 million on professional and management development; Digital Equipment Corporation, with about 40,000 employees, commits about $15 million a year (Rappa, 1978). Faculty development activities must be budgeted so as to appear—and, in fact, be—as essential and as normal as the endeavors to be funded. There should be no discrepancy between the espoused urgency of the activity and the actual level of support.

In summary, faculty development programs should be conceived of as earned opportunities for self-improvement, and the array of opportunities available should be sufficiently diverse to match rewards with desires. Formal faculty development programs based on these precepts should adhere to four design specifications: (1) Emphasize professional roles and activities. (2) Assume a constructive rationale. (3) Engage faculty in resource allocation decisions. (4) Furnish ample financial support from internal sources.

Ultimately, we aspire to reach a stage where incentive

structures and strategies are unnecessary, where faculty development prevails because the activities impart inherent satisfaction.
When faculty development programs enable participants to experience the satisfactions inherent in research and in teaching,
then faculty will be self-motivated and reward schemes will be a
distinctly secondary consideration. Academic administrators
bear no greater responsibility than to create environments and
circumstances contributive to activities that promote intrinsic
satisfaction. "To motivate faculty," McKeachie (1979a, p. 10)
counsels, "one needs to consider . . . ways of changing the situation to increase intrinsic rewards and ways of appealing to important individuals."

One final note of caution. Whatever the process, whatever
the payoffs, not all faculty development efforts will succeed,
especially to the extent that decision makers play longshots.
And even when the wagers are placed on the odds-on favorites,
as we recommend, faculty development will still be to some degree a risky investment. The only greater risk would be to do
nothing.

Sanctions

Surely almost every appointment to a college or university faculty carries a hope and maybe even an expectation on
the part of both parties that the employee and the employer
will enjoy, as it were, a good marriage. Despite the best of intentions, though, ineffective performance may require that a faculty member be chastised, penalized, or separated from the organization. No honorable college or university takes such actions
lightly, and no humane administrator relishes the occasion.
Even under optimal circumstances, these steps will be difficult
to take and painful to accept. In some instances, systematic
evaluations may help prevent adversities of this sort, and when
such difficulties cannot be avoided, evaluations should help inform and rationalize the necessary decisions. Hopeful that the
use of such policies will be rare yet mindful that the need for
such policies is real, we shall consider the available sanctions in
a sequence from the least to the most severe.

Lesser Sanctions. Under a system that attempts to correlate "payoff" with performance, the mildest sanction may be average treatment with respect to rewards. Conferred no extrinsic rewards beyond the minimum afforded everyone, a professor may properly interpret that action as tempered criticism or at least as an indication that the immediate supervisor(s) judged the professor's performance to be quite mundane. Thus, an average reward package represents, in effect, a mild rebuke.

Among other lesser sanctions available, there are, of course, all the legendary tactics administrators share informally at professional conventions. Apparent favorites include smaller, colder, and darker offices; less secretarial support; severed telephone lines; and unbearable class schedules. Typically, though, these hyperbolic, and maybe hypothetical, stories describe battles won but wars lost. Churlish actions are more likely to exacerbate tensions than to improve performance. A more refined approach may yield similar results, since the very nature of the controversy generates antagonisms and strains relationships. In all likelihood, however, the animosities should be less severe and the interactions less hostile if the sanctions are more civil. And in any event, the institution has an obligation, whatever the caliber of an individual's performance, to be respectful and courteous.

Proper sanctions extend from mild to severe and from informal to formal. In 1971, a special AAUP subcommittee developed an illustrative list of sanctions short of dismissal:

1. Oral reprimand.
2. Written reprimand.
3. Recorded reprimand.
4. Restitution: payment for damage done to individuals or the institution.
5. Loss of prospective benefits for a stated period; for instance, suspension of "regular" or "merit" salary increments or suspension of promotion eligibility. (The University of Oklahoma adds loss of sabbatical leaves, remunerated consultative privileges, and remunerated private practice privileges.)
6. A fine.

7.   Reduction in salary for a stated period.
8.   Suspension from service for a stated period, without other prejudice.

The list compiled by the AAUP acknowledges the legitimacy of salary reductions, although the association would limit such decreases to a fixed period of time. To clarify a common misconception, academic tenure, as conventionally defined, does not carry an entitlement to a salary increment or a guarantee against salary reduction. An institution could adopt a policy that forecloses decreases, although we would hope not. Dissatisfaction on the part of management with the performance of an employee *should* lead to pay dissatisfaction on the part of the worker. How incongruous the circumstance would be if a faculty member's performance dissatisfied the dean, but the dean's salary decision satisfied the faculty member.

Downward salary adjustments should be more gradual than precipitous. Unless performance improves, increments should trend from average to below average, to a token raise, to none, and finally to a salary reduction. Each action should be accompanied and justified by a written evaluation. If an action to dismiss were necessary, at least the salary record would substantiate the university's displeasure with the person's performance. Where the record shows that a faculty member, purportedly so incompetent as to warrant dismissal, enjoyed a history of average or near average salary increments, the case will be vulnerable to challenge. In fact, the faculty member will probably allege that the raises, proximate to the average, signified general satisfaction with his performance. How far can the salaries of tenured faculty be reduced for reasons of ineptitude? Could an institution, for example, reduce a salary over time by 25 percent or 33 percent? As far as we can determine, no court decision has yet to address that precise question. Most likely, the university's case would hinge on the quality and strength of the evaluative data, the clarity of the admonitions and advice offered to the faculty member, and the procedural fairness of the salary decisions.

The range of lesser sanctions should be designated as a

matter of policy and applied progressively from mildest to harshest. Should moderate sanctions fail to affect performance positively, the institution may have to consider and apply the ultimate sanction, dismissal for cause.

Dismissal for Cause. In theory, gross incompetence, substantiated by regular evaluations, can lead to dismissal for good and just cause at St. Lawrence and many other schools. In practice, however, dismissals for cause appear to be quite uncommon, although no one has collected and analyzed empirical data on the matter. Even the anecdotal data seem contradictory: academic officers at conventions routinely complain or boast about efforts to remove incapable faculty, yet we hear and read precious little about actual dismissals.

Four circumstances may explain the relative infrequency of dismissal actions. First, surveys, admittedly dated, indicate that only about half of all institutions define *cause* or the grounds for dismissal (Shaw, 1971; Byse and Joughin, 1959). Even the AAUP has eschewed formulation of a definition to complement its statement on procedures for dismissal. Instead, the AAUP assumes—wrongly, we contend—that "individual institutions will have formulated their own definition of adequate cause" (American Association of University Professors, 1977, p. 5). (While colleges and universities may demur from definitions of *cause,* the courts, when confronted with the same question, have not. At least as interpreted by the judiciary ["Construction and Effect of Tenure Provisions," 1975, pp. 1033-1035], *cause* has been recognized as "legal cause and not merely a cause deemed sufficient. . . . It must be something of a substantial nature . . . and must touch the qualifications of the officer or his performance of his duties, showing that he is not a fit or proper person to hold office." In a definition of "evident unfitness for service" as a standard for dismissal, *evident* has been interpreted as "clear to the vision and understanding," and *unfit* as "not fit; not adapted to a purpose, unsuitable; incapable; incompetent; physically and mentally unsound," and "not adapted for a particular use of service.")

Second, most institutions probably lack the necessary data to document incompetence, a burden of proof that rests clearly on the institution. Regular and adequate evaluations to establish a record of unsatisfactory performance and a record of admonitions to the faculty member are essential to the presentation of the case both intramurally and extramurally. How long has the professor been incompetent? Were performance standards and expectations clearly communicated? Was the professor adequately counseled about ways to improve? What evidence supports a decision to dismiss? Are other faculty equally inept? An examination of the personnel folder reveals evaluative data from the tenure decision twenty years ago and copies of notices about changes in the university's health coverage and life insurance. With little more than impressionistic and hearsay evidence that the professor has "slipped badly," the university will likely have a weak case, a reluctant attorney, and an unfavorable outcome.

Hand in hand with the lack of sufficient evidence may be the lack of sufficient will. Some skeptics speculate that the paucity of dismissal cases can be tied to the scarcity of steadfast administrators. Without evidence to substantiate the charges against the faculty member, however, an aggressive stance by the administration would seem ill advised and unwarranted. In any event, before we indict all administrators as craven, we should acknowledge that decisions not to proceed may often be based on humane and political considerations.

Finally, abstention from dismissal actions may be motivated by financial factors. The costs of internal reviews and litigation cannot be blithely dismissed, especially when doubts exist about the strength of the institution's case. A tenured professor at the University of Idaho, for example, judged by peer review to be "functionally incompetent" as a teacher, has filed a $1 million lawsuit. The professor was not even dismissed, only removed from the classroom and assigned to a research position ("Idaho Professor Sues . . . ," 1980).

Dismissal for cause of a tenured faculty member represents the gravest sanction a college or university can apply. For that reason, action should be initiated only when the incompetence has been chronic, manifest, and documented; only when lesser sanctions have failed to produce improvement; and only after the case has been reviewed by a board of inquiry or a board of appeals, as both St. Lawrence and the University of Oklahoma provide. (Ellis, 1974, offers several other resourceful and fair-minded procedures to resolve conflicts and hear grievances.) To paraphrase Oklahoma's policy, the faculty has an obligation to recommend dismissal when necessary, and the university has an obligation to accord faculty judgments all reasonable consideration.

In sum, dismissals and lesser sanctions should be exceptional actions. Such steps signify failure, most likely on the part of both the individual and the institution. Regrettably, exceptions and failures do occur, and institutions must be prepared to respond appropriately. To do so requires a definition of cause, a delineation of available sanctions, adequate documentation, a fair process, a courageous decision maker, and a sense of compassion.

10.

Auditing
and Improving
Faculty Personnel
Systems

﷽﷽﷽﷽﷽﷽﷽﷽﷽﷽﷽﷽﷽﷽﷽﷽﷽﷽﷽

Most colleges and universities recognize that fiscal resources must be prudently managed. Toward that end, administrators develop at the very least annual or biennial budgets based on estimates of income and expenses; more sophisticated managers also prepare five- or ten-year financial projections. To monitor financial activity, the business office maintains records and prepares annually a balance sheet and a statement of changes in fund balances. The balance sheet presents a financial picture at a particular moment, and the statement of changes compares current circumstances with conditions twelve months earlier. For further verification, independent external examiners scrutinize the college's financial records and reports as well as its accounting and control procedures. At the conclusion of the review process, the auditors issue an "opinion" on the general accuracy and acceptability of the institution's financial records, statements, and procedures.

In a broadly similar fashion, the management of human resources requires that an institution monitor and audit personnel policies and decisions over the short as well as the long term. Curiously, however, few institutions do so. In this chapter, we shall suggest a general framework to examine and evaluate faculty personnel policies and practices. The essential steps are to (1) collect pertinent data, (2) analyze the data, and (3) change policy as appropriate or (4) change personnel as appropriate.

Collecting Data

An audit of academic personnel systems begins with the collection of data, and the collection of data begins with an analysis of the larger environment. Colleges and universities are not sealed environments unaffected by the national and regional economy, federal and state policy, or regional and local demography. The onset of a recession, the discontinuation of work-study funds, or a deceleration of birthrates markedly influences both the welfare of postsecondary education as a whole and specific institutions as component parts. Within the "industry," the review must encompass market trends among consumers; market responses by competitors; and the supply and demand for faculty, which vary widely from field to field. On matters of academic personnel, comparative data on salaries, fringes, tenure, and rank distribution can be obtained from sources such as the National Center for Education Statistics, the Higher Education General Information Survey (HEGIS), the College and University Personnel Association, and the AAUP. If some data are not available or comparable, a college or university can initiate an informational consortium, such as the Association of American Universities Data Exchange, with a group of similar institutions. Familiar with the larger environment, the "auditors" can then focus sharply on the institutional environment.

General guidelines for the internal audit should be established by the president and the board of trustees after consultation with the faculty and senior staff. An examination of the in-

stitutional environment could be conducted by a faculty/admin-
istration committee, by senior executive officers, by a committee of the board of trustees, or by an external review team. Alternatively, the task could be apportioned among these constit-
uents. Selection of the auditors, preferably by the president and
the board, should be based on the general circumstances of the
college, the specific purposes of the audit, and the capacity of
local personnel to perform the review. (For purposes of con-
venience and illustration, we shall assume that the provost or
academic vice-president bears primary responsibility for a periodic review of academic personnel policies and practices as part
of the overall internal audit.) In any event, the auditors should
collect and analyze documents such as mission statements, financial statements, long-range program plans, enrollment trends,
bylaws, regulations and negotiated agreements, affirmative action goals and timetables, capital budgets, and an inventory of
physical facilities.

While these materials convey an institutional context, the
management or audit of an academic personnel system demands
another data base: an inventory of human resources. For each
faculty member, the personnel data base should contain, at a
minimum, these elements:

Date of initial appointment
Date(s) of promotion(s) in rank
Tenure status (date tenure awarded or tenure decision due)
Departmental/school affiliation
Age and mandatory retirement date
Sex
Race
Academic credentials (level and source)
Record of scholarly publications
Record of external grants (amount, source, date)
Record of sabbatical and other leaves
Record of committee service
History of courses offered (work load).

Without such a personnel data base, the academic manager or

auditor would be as severely handicapped as a financial vice-president or auditor without any fiscal records, statements, or accounts.

At first blush, the compilation and maintenance of a comprehensive faculty data base may appear to be impractical as well as exorbitant. There are, however, any number of computer-assisted programs that allow such data to be easily entered, stored, and retrieved. For example, a personnel and payroll program designed by administrators at Montana State University (and similar systems developed at Purdue and Syracuse) accepts about 150 data elements per faculty member. The data base, updated and revised whenever changes in a faculty member's status occur, can be probed or queried from a remote terminal. With respect to costs, the initial collection of biographical and employment data undeniably represents a substantial investment of man-hours; maintenance of the system does not. And whether a university designs a computer program or purchases a software package, the developmental costs will not be as great as the costs an institution will incur through mistakes attributable at least in part to the lack of a comprehensive faculty data base.

A faculty data base, like a balance sheet, captures the circumstances of a particular moment. In order to permit historical comparisons and multiyear forecasts, the faculty inventory should also contain data for the past five or ten years. Equipped with information about previous personnel actions, administrators and auditors will, as we shall discuss shortly, be better prepared to assess and analyze the operation of personnel policies.

As a supplement to the "census" data on faculty, colleges and universities should periodically collect faculty perceptions about the general work environment and specific personnel policies and practices. A periodic survey at Dartmouth College, while limited to untenured faculty, solicits opinions on matters such as mentor relationships, collegiality, work load, communication, scholarship, and instruction. The spring 1978 poll yielded a 50 percent response rate overall and a 67 percent response rate among women. From the twenty-six-page digest of the responses, prepared by the affirmative action office (Bonz, 1979), we cite for illustrative purposes only a few of the many results with policy implications:

   • Whereas 50 percent of the women and 68 percent of the men considered tenure to be a realistic possibility at the time of appointment, by the spring of 1978 only 9 percent of the women and 30 percent of the men expected to earn tenure.
   • Women placed much greater emphasis than men on the value of a mentor as an aid to success, recognition, and tenure.
   • The respondents perceived no significant differences in work load among untenured faculty.
   • Although respondents, especially the women, agreed that regular performance reviews were essential, many faculty, especially newcomers, criticized the adequacy of the reviews as conducted by department chairmen and senior faculty.

Through these annual surveys, Dartmouth College gains knowledge about how untenured faculty perceive a wide range of issues, from the prospects for tenure to the equity of work load. On the basis of the survey results, the college may, for example, choose to strengthen the faculty-mentor relationship and the performance review process, or the college may explore why women were, in general, more self-critical and less optimistic than men. Whatever course of action Dartmouth pursues to improve the work environment for untenured faculty, the decisions will be enlightened by data on the expressed needs and opinions of the individuals most directly affected.

Faculty surveys offer another substantial benefit. The very process suggests that the administration desires and values comments from the faculty. As long as the questionnaire makes plain that the administration seeks opinions and not necessarily consensus, the process should not generate disillusionment or false expectations among the faculty. In the formulation of academic personnel policies, professors and administrators alike speculate all too often about faculty attitudes or generalize from random encounters with colleagues. Systematic surveys of faculty opinion may offer a more reliable source of information and a more likely source of insight to guide policy deliberations.

Analyzing Data

Data represent raw material that must be refined to be beneficial. Through analysis of data, effective managers convert the raw material into a refined resource vital to the development of sound personnel policies and practices. Examination of the data should help academic administrators comprehend the past, manage the present, and shape the future. To be more specific, academic deans and vice-presidents may learn from the data whether personnel policy objectives, established perhaps five to ten years ago, have been achieved and whether present goals are likely to be realized in the decade ahead. At colleges and universities without stated policy objectives, the data and analyses cannot contribute to an appraisal of whether institutional aims have been or will be attained. Since we cannot prescribe a universal set of policy objectives, we shall concentrate on the questions the college or university should ask and analysis of the data should answer. The campus community must then determine whether the answers are congruent with institutional objectives.

The first questions to be posed concern faculty flow, the movement of academic employees into, up, and through the institution. Collected for each individual, the data should be arrayed by department and college or university-wide.

• What is the age distribution of the faculty? How many mandatory retirements will occur in each of the next ten years? Based on recent trends, what is the probability of voluntary retirement at age sixty (or the earliest permissible date for retirement) and each year thereafter until age seventy?

• As an annual average, what percent of the faculty, by tenure status and rank, depart voluntarily?

· As an annual average, what percent of the probationary faculty do not earn reappointment? After how many years of service?

· What percent of faculty members appointed in the same year reach the tenure decision, and among those faculty members what percent earn tenure?

· What is the average length of time between promotion from assistant to associate professor and from associate to full professor? For each year of service at a particular rank, what is the probability of promotion to the next rank?

· When a faculty member at a particular rank departs, for whatever reasons, what is the probability that the replacement will be (a) an assistant professor, (b) an associate professor, (c) a professor?

Taken together, these data will chart faculty flow and employee turnover. Policies on remuneration may be addressed through an analysis of data on mean and median salaries and compensation by rank, length of service, department, and work load, and through comparisons between performance appraisals by supervisors and pay satisfaction as expressed by employees. Affirmative action may be monitored through data, displayed by sex and race, on appointments, tenure status, academic rank, salary, and total compensation.

With the raw data now aggregated (or disaggregated) so as to convey a historical overview and a factual record of personnel actions, the academic vice-president or provost should understand what *has* occurred, a simple yet monumental accomplishment. Then stark realities may be compared with espoused objectives to determine to what extent institutional aims have been achieved. Were, for instance, the goals of selectivity, early retirement, and salary equity attained? Analyses of pertinent data should provide empirical if not always definitive answers.

To pursue one example in greater detail, consider the goal of institutional flexibility. Virtually every college and university articulates institutional flexibility as an objective, yet few define the term or monitor progress toward realization of that goal. Without relevant data and explicit measures of institutional flexibility, many schools rely exclusively on a single barometer—a tenure ratio. Tenure ratios *may* communicate something about flexibility *if* the bases for the calculation are sound and consistent. In one case, Simpson (1975) manipulated the tenure ratio of a university from 29.5 percent to 73.8 percent through additions to and deletions from the base. When added to the denominator, research assistants, teaching assistants, part-time faculty, visitors, adjuncts, administrators, and librarians will lower the tenure level. At the College of Letters and Science of the University of Wisconsin, where graduate assistants and tenure-ineligible faculty assume a considerable share of the instructional work load, the tenure density can be made to vary from 44 percent to 83 percent. At the Harvard Business School and St. Olaf, where nearly all full-time faculty are on the tenure track, tenure ratios are more meaningful; even at these institutions, however, the tenure ratio can be made to vary from 65 to 72 percent at St. Olaf and from 46 to 53 percent at Harvard.

With adequate data and analysis, flexibility may be measured and monitored in other, perhaps more useful, ways. West (1974) proposed that colleges calculate the percentage of instructional salary dollars committed to tenured and untenured faculty, respectively, since ultimately money, more than positions per se, provides the flexibility necessary to change missions and programs. In a financial shorthand, tenured faculty might be regarded as long-term assets with little liquidity, except as retirement draws near. Untenured faculty on multiyear contracts might be viewed as relatively liquid short-term notes, and vacancies might be perceived as cash on hand. The amount of money freed each year for reallocation largely defines the outer boundaries of institutional flexibility. A college 65 percent tenured where tenured personnel consume only 50 percent of the academic payroll probably enjoys greater maneuverability than a faculty only 50 percent tenured where permanent faculty draw 65 percent of the academic payroll. Thus, tenure ratios should be expressed both as a percentage of payroll and as a percentage of positions (with the denominator properly footnoted) committed to tenured faculty. Table 6 displays such information for one department at a research university that gathers similar data for each academic unit. In the department cited here, 70 percent of the tenure-track faculty hold tenure, but these individuals consume fully 80 percent of the department's permanent payroll. By that yardstick, the tenure ratio by positions overstates the staffing flexibility of the department. If tenure-ineligible and one-year appointments were added to the base, the tenure level by positions would decline to 55 percent and by dollars to 72 percent. These data overstate even more dramatically the department's flexibility, since the faculty outside the tenure stream constitute 21 percent of the positions but only 10 percent of the payroll.

Two other measures of flexibility may be considered: faculty turnover and course turnover. Earlier we specified the data needed to monitor the rates of faculty arrivals and departures. For a second index of turnover, the administration should determine annually the proportion of the total faculty new to the campus. That figure should then be calibrated against a stated institutional objective; for example, no less than 5 percent and no more than 15 percent of the faculty shall be newcomers. To be even more precise, different objectives could be established for full-time and part-time faculty and for tenured, untenured, and tenure-ineligible faculty.

If, as enrollments stabilize, more changes and innovations must be generated by the incumbent work force, then departments and schools might also record how often courses and programs are substantially revised, replaced, or abandoned. Although what constitutes a new or revised program is perhaps a matter of opinion and degree, an institution could develop standardized definitions.

Monitoring tenure ratios by positions and dollars and charting turnover rates for faculty and courses better equip a college or university to measure institutional flexibility. As long as policy makers establish goals or acceptable ranges for these performance indexes, then the rate and degree of progress toward institutional flexibility can be calculated. Should an analysis of the data reveal insufficient progress toward attain-

Table 6. Tenure Ratios in One

Age:	20-29		30-39		40-49	
Position	N	Payroll	N	Payroll	N	Payroll
Professor						
Tenured	0	0.0	0	0.0	7	314.3
Associate Professor						
Tenured	0	0.0	2	56.4	5	156.2
Untenured	0	0.0	1	24.0	0	0.0
Assistant Professor						
Untenured	0	0.0	9	189.1	0	0.0
Instructor						
Tenure Ineligible	0	0.0	0	0.0	0	0.0
One-Year Appts.	1	13.3	2	26.8	0	0.0
Research Assistant						
Tenure Ineligible	0	0.0	0	0.0	0	0.0
One-Year Appts.	2	24.3	1	12.3	0	0.0
Total Tenure Track	0	0.0	12	269.5	12	470.5
Total One-Year Appt.	3	37.6	3	39.1	0	0.0
Total Full-Time Academic	3	37.6	15	308.6	12	470.5
Tenured faculty as percent of tenure-track faculty	0		17		100	
Salaries of tenured faculty as percent of total salaries of tenure-track faculty		0		21		100
Salaries of tenured faculty as percent of total salaries of full-time faculty	0		13		100	
Payroll tenured as percent of total full-time faculty		0		18		100

ment of a policy objective, the first response should be to discover whether some goals are incompatible with others and whether certain procedures are incompatible with certain policies. One aspiration of the Harvard Law School, for instance, may be preeminence; another goal may be flexibility. Almost

Department of a Research University

50-59		60-61		62-64		65+		Total	
N	Payroll	N	Payroll	N	Payroll	N	Payroll	N	Payroll
4	160.6	1	35.5	2	79.6	0	0.0	14	590.0
2	57.5	0	0.0	0	0.0	0	0.0	9	270.1
0	0.0	0	0.0	0	0.0	0	0.0	1	24.0
0	0.0	0	0.0	0	0.0	0	0.0	9	189.1
0	0.0	1	19.6	0	0.0	0	0.0	1	19.6
0	0.0	0	0.0	0	0.0	0	0.0	3	40.1
1	12.6	0	0.0	0	0.0	0	0.0	1	12.6
1	13.9	0	0.0	0	0.0	0	0.0	4	50.5
6	218.1	1	35.5	2	79.6	0	0.0	33	1,073.2
1	13.9	0	0.0	0	0.0	0	0.0	7	90.6
8	244.6	2	55.1	2	79.6	0	0.0	42	1,196.0
100		100	100	100	100	0		70	
	100		100		100		0		80
75		50		100		0		55	
	89		64		100		0		72

by definition, esteemed faculty deserve tenure. Thus, a truly exceptional law school staffed by peerless professors may be "excessively" tenured, perhaps at the expense of some flexibility. Indeed, in June 1978, fifty-three of fifty-nine tenure-track faculty at the Harvard Law School held tenure. Would the law school somehow be better if the tenure ratio were only 50 percent? Would the low tenure ratio be a mark of success if brilliant and renowned faculty were denied permanent positions? Would there be cause for celebration if the school's tenure level dropped because the best professors departed for other universities? To cite a more typical example, a state college faced with enrollment declines and little faculty turnover may wish to add more women and blacks as senior faculty and at the same time not exceed current tenure levels. In these two illustrations, the policy objectives are incompatible and perhaps mutually exclusive; some policy trade-offs will be required.

Compromises may also be necessary where procedures thwart some policy objectives and concomitantly support others. A university may, for instance, develop elaborate procedures to assure that candidates for promotion and tenure will receive equitable treatment. The procedures, however, may be so rigid and time-bound as to preclude a speedy counterproposal to a valued faculty member suddenly offered a better position at a better institution. Unable to plead a special case for promotion or tenure outside the prescribed sequence of events, whereby a decision would be rendered six months hence, the university loses a gifted faculty member. Presumably, promotion and tenure policies serve to attract and retain the ablest faculty. In the immediate case, procedures designed to ensure equity inadvertently prevented achievement of that goal.

Policies and procedures may also fail to produce the desired outcome because the policies are unclear, unknown, or unavailable. The institution can remedy these problems rather easily through clarification, dissemination, or formulation of policy. By contrast, when goals require modification, when policies do not support goals, when policies and procedures conflict, or when the faculty as a whole does not accept a policy, the college faces a significantly more difficult task, since each of these conditions requires some policy changes.

In summary, an analysis of data germane to faculty personnel systems should help academic administrators and auditors (1) profile the current inventory of faculty resources; (2) highlight trends, patterns, and changes with respect to faculty flow; (3) chart progress toward stated policy objectives; (4) assess the degree of adherence to policies and procedures; (5) identify any conflicts between and among goals, between goals and policies, and between policies and procedures; and (6) determine whether policies and procedures are clear, available, and understood.

Changing Policy

Although an analysis of faculty "census" data for the past five to ten years should reveal trends, patterns, and changes relative to faculty flow, the past may not always be prologue to the future, especially where circumstances shift abruptly. In the 1980s, for example, economic considerations may curtail early retirements, market conditions may restrict faculty turnover, and financial exigency may, as a practical matter, minimize promotions to tenure. Over the near and intermediate terms, different and even unprecedented circumstances may produce different and even unprecedented results. New policies may be needed to meet a new environment. The threshold questions are: What policies should be changed, and what will be the impact of those changes?

While no one can foretell the future, academic administrators can, with the aid of computer-based models, simulate the future. Programs have been devised by William Massey at Stanford, Robert Linnell at the University of Southern California, Christopher Nevinson at Colgate, Carl Patton at the University of Illinois–Urbana, and George Lamson at Carleton College, to name only a few. (For one example of a faculty flow model, see Appendix B.) Despite some differences, the models are by and large quite similar. Two principal elements comprise the data base: current faculty "census" data and personnel policy parameters. The programs allow the user to manipulate or "perturb" the several policy variables that affect faculty flow—variables such as success rates for promotion and tenure, average length of the probationary period, retirement probabilities, replacement policies, compensation plans, and affirmative action goals and timetables. With remarkable rapidity, the computer calculates and simulates the effect of the proposed policy changes on faculty flow annually for as many as twenty years. Thus, policy makers may observe and evaluate the likely consequences of policy changes *before* the changes are enacted—a rather decided advantage. These programs can answer questions such as these:

> • If the probability of tenure for assistant professors were decreased from .6 to .4, what would the effect be on turnover rates and tenure levels?
> • How would a nine-year probationary period affect the tenure success rate and tenure ratio over the next decade?
> • If the probability of promotion from associate to full professor were decreased from .5 to .2 for the first six years after attainment of the associate rank and increased from .2 to .7 thereafter, what would be the effect on rank and salary structures?
> • Under present tenure success rates, how many women would have to be appointed before the percentage of tenured female faculty doubled?
> • How many vacancies can be anticipated in a particular department or throughout the university over the next ten years?
> • Under current policies, what will be the age distribution of the faculty in 1990? How would a change in policy that increased the probability of retirement from .2 to .5 for faculty members between ages sixty-two and sixty-eight alter the age profile of the faculty in 1990?

To exploit fully the capabilities of these models, an institution must, of course, be able to articulate present policy and future goals. The goals should be realistic and whenever possible measurable. For example:

> To achieve minimally x percent faculty turnover.
> To maintain a tenure level above x percent and below y.

To increase by x percent the proportion of women and minorities on the faculty.

To tenure, on average, no more than x percent of a faculty cohort.

To shorten the mean length of employment from x years to y.

To reduce the rate of growth of the faculty payroll by x percent.

Necessarily, these statements represent so-called micro-objectives or subgoals. Computer-based models cannot measure current or future attainment of macro-objectives, such as a stronger faculty or a livelier intellectual environment, although academic administrators may conclude that particular activities monitored by the model constitute bellwether components of certain broader objectives. Models simulate the effects of designated personnel policy changes on operations; managers must then evaluate the relationship between those expected changes and the achievement of larger institutional objectives.

In like manner, simulations are forecasts, not guarantees. The validity of the prognostications furnished by the computer depends primarily on the accuracy of the data and the validity of the policy assumptions entered into the program. If the assumptions are erroneous, or the new policies are quickly discarded, the predicted and actual outcomes will bear no resemblance to one another. Despite these limitations, we recommend computer-based models as a stimulus to formulate policy objectives and as a tool to evaluate *beforehand* the consequences and wisdom of contemplated policy changes.

Policy changes, then, should be preceded by (1) a statement of present policy, (2) a statement of the goals to be achieved by a new policy, (3) an enumeration of the policy alternatives, and (4) a simulation of the probable results each alternative portends. Even after all that, there are no assurances that a proposed policy will in fact ameliorate a stated problem. Unfortunately, colleges and universities rather regularly adopt solutions unrelated to the problems at hand (Cohen and March, 1974). The collection and analysis of data and the simulation of results produced by policy changes should, however, reduce the frequency and margin of error.

The need for perspicacity when policy changes are under consideration mandates consultation with the faculty. Neither administrators nor trustees have cornered the market on acumen. Consultation with the faculty, therefore, may well produce better policy. Furthermore, the consultative process improves the likelihood that the change will be effectively implemented, especially in those instances where the faculty will actually be called on to apply the new policy, such as revised criteria, standards, or procedures for tenure.

Beyond questions of process lie matters of substance, specifically coverage and content. When policies are to be changed or modified, the college must decide whether the new policy shall apply to all faculty or whether some shall be exempted by a "grandfather clause" and whether to compose the new policy locally or to import word for word a "model statement" developed by a professional association, most often the AAUP.

On the issue of coverage, definitive answers are, with a few exceptions, rather scarce. A university may not unilaterally adopt policies that alter the terms and conditions of employment incorporated in a collectively negotiated agreement. Nor, as Bloomfield College learned so painfully, may an administration unilaterally abolish tenure (*AAUP* v. *Bloomfield College,* 129 N.J. Super. 249, 322 A.2d 846 (1974); *affirmed* 136 N.J. Super. 249, 346 A.2d 615 (1975)). To do so would abrogate the contractual rights and privileges of tenured faculty.

These one-sided preemptive actions present extreme and therefore comparatively simple cases. There are, however, gradations of change and subtler issues than violation of a contract or the elimination of tenure. There are circumstances where policies can be amended or revised, particularly where the university reserves the right to amend or where there has been mutual consent and due consideration. Whether a university may adjust a professor's terms and conditions of employment subsequent to the initial appointment, to what extent, and by what process depend substantially on local bylaws, handbooks, and contracts. As an illustration, Case Western Reserve University and Providence College both lowered (prior to the revision of the Age Discrimination in Employment Act) the mandatory retirement age for faculty. Despite the basic similarity of the cases, the courts reached quite different decisions. In *Rehor* v. *Case Western University,* 331 N.E.2d 416 (Ohio 1975), the Ohio Supreme Court afforded Case Western considerable latitude to modify policy, since the university had expressly retained the right to change the rules and regulations that governed tenure and related matters. In the opinion of the court, the wages and benefits accepted each year by the plaintiff constituted due consideration. In *Drans* v. *Providence College,* 338 A.2d 1033 (R.I. 1978), a more recent and better-reasoned decision, the Rhode Island Supreme Court ruled that the college may have the right to alter retirement policy but that changes may not be adopted unilaterally or without due consideration beyond the mere fact of continued gainful employment.

Can a university impose a tenure quota, lengthen the probationary period, or adopt new criteria for evaluation and apply these policies to currently employed probationary faculty? So far, no court of law has been presented with these precise questions. (In *Association of New Jersey State College Faculties, Inc.* v. *Dungan,* 64 N.J. 338, 316 A.2d 425, 1974, the Supreme Court ruled that the establishment of the tenure quota was within the prerogative of the state, but the matter of the rights of untenured faculty was not expressly addressed.) Can a college unilaterally impose a program to evaluate tenured faculty periodically? Again the answer will likely be determined by interpretation of local documents.

While no universal principle can be espoused to cover all contemplated policy changes, where the change concerns academic tenure or related issues, legal counsel should be obtained before the policy changes are enacted. In many, though not all, instances, a grandfather clause may be prudent or even essential, particularly where the policy change diminishes the procedural or substantive rights of faculty. In any case, colleges would be well advised first to obtain an informed legal opinion and then to define appropriate coverage, instead of defining the coverage and then awaiting a legal challenge.

Although important considerations, the determination of a university's authority to act and the determination of appropriate coverage are, in fact, only precursors to the fundamental task at hand: to write policy. The translation of policy objectives into policy statements can be an onerous and complicated assignment. Policies can be so broad as to be vague or so specific as to be inflexible. Ambiguous language can obscure clear intentions. Unsure about the most advisable content or the most judicious language and fearful of censure, faculty and administrators often incline to adopt wholesale the recommendations of the AAUP rather than labor locally to draft policies word by word. Is that a wise decision?

Since the early 1900s, the AAUP has purported to serve as the policy maker for the profession and as the guardian of academic freedom. Policy recommendations developed by the AAUP were no doubt carefully crafted. To dismiss cavalierly the advice and counsel of the AAUP would, therefore, be foolish. To adhere slavishly to AAUP policies would be equally ill advised. Drafted in 1940, the AAUP "Statement of Principles on Academic Freedom and Tenure" may no longer be germane or serviceable. Over the past forty years, circumstances have changed a great deal and AAUP policy comparatively little. Even the interpretations and amplifications issued in 1970 and 1976 are still anchored to the 1940 statement. Moreover, changes recommended by the AAUP, now a labor union, may serve the narrow interests of the rank and file rather than the broader concerns of the institution and industry. (Some policies, such as the seven-year probationary period and the "up-or-out" rule, may disserve the needs of both employees and employers. The faculty member may prefer an extended probationary period to unemployment, and the college may wish to retain the faculty member if a long-term commitment can be averted.)

The AAUP would obviously prefer that institutions adopt its policies wholesale. Indeed, the 1976 "Recommended Regulations on Academic Freedom and Tenure" are intentionally "set forth in language suitable for use by an institution of higher education" (American Association of University Professors, 1977, p. 15). Against that background, Jordan Kurland, associate general secretary of the AAUP, allowed in an interview with us that the association would be "more disposed" to modifications that retain tenure than to alternatives that abandon tenure. Although "committed to tenure as a bulwark," Kurland explained that the association "keeps an eye on the policy function and not on the label." Where the policy fulfills the fundamental purposes of tenure, identified by Kurland as academic freedom, due process, and economic security, the national AAUP would not be prone to intervene or to censure. At least as regards the colleges we visited and studied, the association's response to policy changes was consistent with Kurland's representation of the AAUP's position: The AAUP has not actively intervened as an adversary or censured institutions that have *modified* traditional tenure policies. It has intervened as an adversary where institutions attempted to undo tenure. And it has censured institutions that have abolished tenure.

What about the specter of censure? Censure by the AAUP signifies that the institution has "not observed the generally recognized principles of academic freedom and tenure endorsed by this association." As we observed above, institutions should not casually or defiantly disregard a policy scrupulously composed by thoughtful individuals. By the same token, reasonable people can reach different conclusions, and an institution may conclude, after deliberation, that a policy contrary to AAUP prescription seems advisable and defensible. In those instances, we would counsel an institution to be undaunted by the possibility of censure.

Among administrators particularly, censure seems to be unduly feared, yet few academicians can even name currently censured institutions, a condition that makes difficult boycotts, reprisals, and embarrassment. In any case, a college or university could do worse than to be associated with Arizona State, the University of Maryland, Texas A & M, Marquette University, and the State University of New York, five institutions now censured. Furthermore, as a practical matter, the association cannot censure every institution that deviates from its norms. The list would grow too long; the longer the list, the weaker the impact. As Groucho Marx quipped about a high school di-

ploma, "If I have one, what can it be worth?" If too many institutions are censured, the stigma will unavoidably lose some of
its force.

We are not suggesting that an institution deliberately
court censure or disregard the AAUP. Rather, we are advising
institutions not to allow the threat of censure alone to stymie
an action or a policy decision that, after ample consideration,
seems prudent. As the then provost of Union College commented about the institution's decision to suspend the "up-or-
out" rule, "once we put aside the AAUP guidelines, the world
opened up." We strongly recommend that faculty, administrators, and trustees explore together the universe of policies and
possibilities beyond the AAUP *Policy Documents and Reports.*

However significant the AAUP may be, its recommendations neither govern nor control a university's personnel actions
unless that university adopts by reference or by incorporation
the association's policies. No one should be deluded by academic lore to presume otherwise. (For incisive analyses of the
status of AAUP policy generally and the association's retrenchment policies more specifically, consult Furniss, 1978 and
1976, respectively.) The documents that determine the propri-
ety and ultimately the legality of a college's personnel decisions
are the college's handbooks, bylaws, and common practices as
well as relevant statutes and any collective bargaining agreements in force. At the risk of only slight oversimplification,
what a college can or cannot do—within the limits of law and
union contracts—depends largely on what institutional policy,
not AAUP policy, stipulates. Should litigation arise, the courts
will decide whether the college's personnel actions conformed
to the *college's* personnel policies and whether those policies
conformed to law. As the Iowa Court of Appeals ruled in *Lumpert* v. *University of Dubuque,* 255 N.W.2d 168 (1977), "Each
case is subject to its own contractual provisions." Or to paraphrase a colloquial maxim, "What you write is what you get."
Two cases related to the dismissal of tenured faculty due to apparent financial exigency dramatize the principle at issue.

Creighton University terminated Edwin Scheuer (and
three others), a tenured faculty member in the School of Phar-

macy, which operated at a deficit. The university as a whole was not financially exigent. University policy stated that financial exigency "may be considered to include bona fide discontinuation of a program or department of instruction or the reduction in size thereof." In his suit against Creighton University, Scheuer cited AAUP policy and argued that financial exigency must be university wide before dismissals could occur; the court, however, rejected that argument: "To accept plaintiff's definition would require Creighton to continue programs running up large deficits so long as the institution as a whole had financial resources available to it. . . . We specifically hold the term 'financial exigency' *as used in the contract of employment herein* may be limited to a financial exigency in a department or college. It is not restricted to one existing in the institution as a whole" (*Scheuer* v. *Creighton University*, 199 Neb. 618, 260 N.W.2d 595 (1977); emphasis added). *Browzin* v. *Catholic University*, 527 F.2d 843 (D.C. Cir. 1975), presents a similar decision.

In contrast, consider the fate that befell Bloomfield College in *AAUP* v. *Bloomfield College*, 129 N.J. Super. 249, 322 A.2d 846 (1974); *affirmed* 136 N.J. Super. 249, 346 A.2d 615 (1975). In that case, where the college had attempted to dismiss thirteen tenured faculty members and to place all other tenured personnel on term contracts, the court held the institution to a strict standard of "demonstrably bona fide" financial exigency. Why? First, the *Faculty Handbook,* which, the court ruled, "forms an essential part of the contractual terms governing the relationship between the college and the faculty," established the standard of a "demonstrably bona fide" financial exigency. Throughout the decision, the court repeatedly referred to self-limitations imposed by the college's policies: "*By their choice of preconditions* . . . that the board's action be demonstrably bona fide . . ." (at 855) "If a yardstick, however imperfect, . . . *was agreed upon,* then the court must follow its dictates." (at 855) "Bearing in mind . . . the extremely severe restrictions *which the college has accepted upon its authority to act . . .* " (at 855) "The actions of Bloomfield College with respect to the tenured status of its faculty members . . . overflowed the limits of its authority *as defined by its own policies*" (at 856; emphases added). Unfortunately, Bloomfield College had never really developed "its own policies"; it had adopted wholly the AAUP's policies, the policies of the plaintiff.

Much as financial exigency may be what an institution defines the concept to be, the same proposition holds for concepts such as academic tenure or retrenchment. Tenure may mean a lifetime position, an appointment until retirement, an appointment for twenty years, or a permanent position as long as the institution has need for the individual's services. Likewise, where no statutes or union contracts apply, colleges and universities enjoy great latitude to define the criteria for layoffs of academic personnel. No constitutional precept dictates that either seniority or tenure status must prevail as the bases for cutbacks. In *Johnson* v. *Board of Regents of University of Wisconsin System,* 377 F. Supp. 227 (W.D. Wis. 1974), James Doyles, noted as a liberal judge, wrote:

> Perhaps the next question is whether the federal Constitution requires that the selection be made on one specific basis or another: in inverse order of seniority within a department, for example; or in order of seniority; or in terms of record of performance; or in inverse order of seniority, but with exceptions for the necessity to retain teachers in the department with specific skills or funds of knowledge. I believe that the federal Constitution is silent on these questions and that the identity of the decision maker and the choice of a basis for selection lie within the discretion of the state government [at 238].

Incidentally, the "basis for selection" can range quite far; the court observed that "the Fourteenth Amendment does not forbid judgments about personalities in this situation."

Are colleges obliged to help faculty locate suitable positions elsewhere within the institution? Outside the institution? Are colleges obligated to retrain faculty for new endeavors? To provide severance pay? To guarantee recall rights? To provide at least one year's notice? The answer to all these questions depends on what obligations the college *chose* to assume as a matter of policy. Where policies are clear, the answers will be clear. Where policies are vague or silent, the answers will depend on common practice and judicial interpretation.

We cite at length these examples of institutional definitions and judicial decisions in an attempt to dispel unfortunate and widespread misconceptions about the status of AAUP policy and the relative freedom of colleges to define personnel policies. As institutions contemplate policy changes, the force of AAUP recommendations should not be exaggerated, and the freedom to compose policies locally should not be minimized. Enormous responsibilities accompany that freedom, since the policies a college chooses will be the policies the college must apply and the courts will enforce. Colleges and universities, therefore, must formulate and modify policy with the utmost attention to definitions and details.

As institutions decide independently the elements of sound practice and sensible policy, the administration should not overlook the standards of regional and professional accrediting agencies. While regional associations do not mandate a particular personnel system, many promulgate standards that may relate to a policy change under consideration. These standards may range from the minimum number of full-time faculty to be assigned to a degree program to definitions of a terminal degree. Professional associations such as the National League of Nurses and the National Architectural Accrediting Board tend to articulate even more detailed standards. Lest accreditation be jeopardized, policy makers should ensure that proposed changes do not contravene agency standards.

To summarize, academic personnel policies and procedures should be drafted and enacted in advance of the need to use them. The onset of crisis or confusion is not an opportune moment to formulate or revise policy. When new or modified policies are under consideration, we make the following recommendations:

1. Changes in policy should be preceded by a statement (or restatement) of policy objectives, an enumeration of the

alternatives, and a simulation, whenever possible, of the
probable results.
2.   Faculty should be consulted, especially when prospective
     changes affect the faculty.
3.   Legal counsel should be obtained to ascertain the need for
     "grandfather clauses," especially where the policy change
     may diminish the procedural or substantive rights of the
     faculty.
4.   Policies and procedures should be selected and language
     drafted by the institution. Institutions should not cate-
     gorically adopt the language of the AAUP or any other as-
     sociation, college, or university.
5.   Policy makers should not underestimate the latitude avail-
     able to an institution to develop policies and define terms
     particularly well suited to local conditions.
6.   Policy makers should weigh each word carefully, since local
     policies will govern local employment relationships.
7.   Once enacted, policy changes should be widely publicized
     and disseminated, especially among persons most directly
     affected by the change.

Changing Administrative Personnel

On all campuses, the success of academic administrators,
the "supervisors," depends mightily on the caliber and cooperation of the faculty, the "subordinates." We must be especially
careful, therefore, to distinguish between (1) personnel problems attributable primarily to policy and policy administration
and (2) problems related more directly to the quality of the faculty. In earlier chapters, we attempted to address matters germane to faculty performance, and the preceding section considered issues of policy. We are now concerned with questions of
policy execution.

A college or university would be ill advised to change personnel policies when it should change administrative personnel
or, conversely, to change administrative personnel when it should
change policy. Sometimes both may need to be changed. If
problems persist where policies and procedures are clear, appropriate, and conducive to the achievement of the stated objec-

tives, then very likely the difficulty rests with the people charged to execute policy and not with policy per se. Analysis of policies and procedures should disclose the locus of accountability. Together with the senior academic officers, the immediate supervisor should ascertain whether the performance of the responsible officer, the nature of the situation, or both create the principal problems.

As suggested by Tagiuri (1974), an analysis of the situation should reveal whether the officer has sufficient authority and resources to accomplish the task. A dean without a veto over promotion and tenure recommendations by departmental and college committees cannot easily oblige a policy objective of selectivity. The chairman of a computer science department with inadequate resources and outdated equipment cannot be expected to compete favorably for candidates with earned doctorates, a relatively scarce and precious commodity. However stringent university policy may be about the need for faculty to hold a doctorate, the chairman will probably be compelled to appoint candidates with a master's degree. Where administrative performance proves weak, despite authority and resources appropriate to the position, then perhaps the supervisor's expectations for that position conflict with the expectations of the incumbent or other constituencies the incumbent must serve. The members of an academic department, for instance, may expect the chairman to argue vehemently with senior administrators for the promotion and tenure of every candidate recommended by the department. The dean and provost, on the other hand, may expect the chairman to exercise discretion and remove all marginal candidates from further consideration. Where the department chairman answers in effect to both the faculty and the dean, such conflicts of expectations will impair the chairman's ability to execute policy. The college may need to seek resolution or at least clarification of the role conflicts rather than seek a new chairman. Finally, the supervisor represents a critical element of the environment. Although not readily assessable from documents and data, the supervisory function must be scrutinized to learn whether the supervisor provided proper direction, leadership, and support.

The situation may explain ineffective performance and

insufficient progress toward policy objectives or the problem may, alas, rest with the individual. To return to Levinson's (1976) dynamic evaluation (Chapter Eight), there may be a mismatch between the requirements of the position and the temperament of the incumbent. The position may demand firm, aggressive behavior to reverse, for example, lax enforcement of promotion and tenure standards, yet the incumbent may be passive and indecisive. Administrators with the necessary traits may not possess the necessary talents to fulfill the responsibilities of the position. When a supervisor, after advice and counsel from appropriate sources, determines that an incumbent lacks the ability to acquire and apply these talents, the incumbent should be reassigned or terminated. If, however, an inherently bright but untutored administrator lacks only some professional development to ply the trade of management effectively, then such opportunities should be made available unless the costs are too steep, or the time commitment is too great, or the circumstances require that the officer be immediately productive. Where considerations of time, money, or urgency will not allow a novice to learn on the job, continued employment in that position until some mistake exhausts the supervisor's patience serves little purpose. The individual should either be reassigned or the position restructured so that the bright prospect may be trained and seasoned under less stressful circumstances.

Where chronic and severe problems of policy administration retard achievement of policy objectives, the senior officers (or the board of trustees) should determine whether the problems derive chiefly from the nature of the situation or the performance of the individual. Where the situation presents the basic difficulties, the circumstances should be altered to the extent possible. Where the policy administrator creates the primary difficulties, the individual should be reassigned, terminated, or further trained.

A Final Word

As members of the academic profession, we should not, as we navigate the maze of personnel policies, procedures, and practices, lose sight of the ultimate objective: to help people realize their fullest potential. While all organizations should strive to fulfill that purpose, colleges and universities, as educational institutions, bear a special responsibility for human development.

As we discuss and administer sound personnel policies and practices, we must remember that people are at stake. Faculty are people with individual histories, emotions, mind sets, talents, and needs; faculty are not interchangeable parts of a cold, impersonal machine operated by academic administrators. The actions we take, far more than the policies we enact, will communicate the values we hold. Thus, all personnel actions should be rendered thoughtfully, honestly, and humanely; for all members of the academic community deserve respect, civility, and equity.

Appendix A

Harvard Business School, Policies and Procedures with Respect to Faculty Appointments and Promotions

꘡꘡꘡

1. There follows a statement of factors which bear upon the appointment and promotion of Faculty members and a description of the procedures used in making decisions. This general statement of policy cannot be exhaustive and it should not be treated literally in all cases. The task of building a university graduate school faculty is a creative work which must call for the exercise of judgment on many considerations in a variety of combinations.

2. The document has been written with this basic premise in mind: To maintain leadership in business education, the School must press forward on two related fronts: (a) the quality of instruction, which embraces the development of instructional methods and materials and the development of effective teachers; and (b) the development through research of concepts

249

and knowledge useful to business administrators and the communication of these to others through writing and teaching.
These goals of the School must be reflected in the selection of
men and women for Faculty appointments. We will be a leading
graduate professional school only if we appoint to our Faculty
those individuals who are leaders or potential leaders in their
fields.

Part I. Standards

3. The School seeks to secure individuals for its Faculty
who possess the basic qualities which contribute to excellence
in teaching and research. These qualities include intellectual
ability and curiosity, analytical power, initiative, imagination,
creativity, industry, clarity of expression, integrity, and a sympathetic appreciation of the viewpoints of others. One major
quality is an interest in and enthusiasm for the basic objectives
of the School.

4. In appraising an individual, the School has two sets of
criteria: the record of the person's performance and an assessment of his* basic qualities. Both are important. The mature
person who has high potential but little or no record of performance too often continues to have just that. On the other hand,
a good record alone is not enough. We seek the basic qualities
that are likely to insure intellectual growth and excellence in future work.

5. For the large majority of its Faculty, the School seeks
persons (a) who demonstrate competence and interest in both
teaching and research, and (b) who make outstanding contributions in either teaching or research. Judgments about candidates' teaching and research qualities will be made primarily on
the basis of their performance in School-sponsored or supported

---

*It should be understood that wherever *he, him,* or *his* is used in
this statement to refer to an individual whose sex is not known, the usage
is intended to represent and simplify the awkward form *he or she, him or
her,* or *his or hers.* It is the policy of the School to recruit, assign, pay, and
promote qualified men and women for its Faculty without prejudice with
regard to sex, race, religion, or national origin.

activities, whether in the United States or abroad. Because certain types of consulting work may enhance teaching and research competence and performance, as a secondary consideration, the other professional work of a candidate also will be examined.

6. Necessarily, the character and amount of evidence available for the appraisal of a person will change as his career advances. Therefore, for appointments below the level of full Professor, it is not anticipated that most individuals will have had sufficient time to demonstrate conclusively either outstanding ability in teaching and competence in research or outstanding ability in research and competence in teaching. Rather, the expectation for appointments below the rank of full Professor is that they will show strong promise of developing such abilities by the time they are to be considered for appointment to full Professor. Ordinarily, an excellent performance during an individual's first appointment in either teaching or research will constitute evidence of such promise. It will be the aim of the School to provide assignments during a person's second appointment which allow him to demonstrate further his foremost abilities and any other skills essential to his promotion not revealed by the nature of his assignments during his first appointment. By the time an individual is considered for a permanent appointment, he should have demonstrated conclusively the level of performance expected of a full Professor; and there should be a good reason to expect that if he is appointed, his productivity will continue at a high level of quality.

7. It is difficult to draw clear lines between excellence in teaching, on the one hand, and in research, on the other; and it is not always necessary to do so. Contributions to both have much in common, and those who have outstanding capacity in one often possess considerable competence in the other. Whether in teaching or in research, excellence in these roles rests on the ability to make contributions to the development and exposition of the subject matter of a field of knowledge. Especially, the School seeks persons who understand the practice of management and whose research and teaching activities throw light on, and in other ways contribute to, the understanding of

and dealing with problems actually encountered in the administration of business activities. Because visible products of excellence in teaching occur in different forms from evidence of the same capacity in research, it may be useful to describe, separately, the main products of academic work in which evidence may be found.

8. Evidence of excellence in teaching rests on a candidate's capacity to evoke from students thoughtful, analytical approaches to management decision making, appropriately grounded in understanding of the role of administrators and knowledge of the subject matter of a field of business administration. In judging candidates' teaching, it is relevant to consider their sensitivity to management realities and practices as well as their comprehension of the subject matter of their field and their understanding of students' problems in seeking to learn. As teachers they should understand the literature of their fields; demonstrate an ability to understand and evaluate the importance of the research of others; and, where appropriate, introduce the products of new research in their teaching. They should give promise of an ongoing concern for the literature and research of their fields as well as for the problems of practitioners.

A high order of ability in presenting material to students, although important, is not enough when it rests on outlines and teaching materials prepared solely by others. Candidates must demonstrate their own ability to plan and prepare material for the classroom. Further, they should show a lively interest in the problems students encounter in learning the subject matter of their courses. Candidates should be especially sensitive to any problem that affects the class as a whole, even though the problem may be presented by an individual student.

Evidence of candidates' capacity for teaching may be found in their work in both large and small classes and in seminars and in designing and planning courses, seminars, or programs, or significant parts of them; in new materials they have prepared, such as cases, technical notes, and teachers' guides to the use of such materials; and in course outlines and syllabi, lectures, text and casebooks, collections of readings, and so forth. It may also be found in the way candidates develop attitudes toward discussion and learning among students. Candidates should show a high order of ability to throw light on the problems which students encounter in learning to reach decisions based on the subject matter of their courses. The candidates' work should contribute to the development of new and effective approaches to students' problems and questions, especially to those raised by good students. The candidates should treat effectively questions about the relationship of knowledge to the practice of business administration. In all these senses the candidates' work should yield strongly favorable learning situations for students.

A candidate's capacity to make an intellectual contribution through teaching may also be shown in stimulating colleagues through informal contacts as well as in seminars, lectures, and discussions.

In summary, the School seeks to avoid the appointment of men and women who overemphasize day-by-day classroom teaching to the point where they do not effectively participate in and contribute to the intellectual activity of their fields. Rather, they should in some convincing way have demonstrated, in connection with their activities as teachers, interest and ability to further the development of knowledge related to the practice of business administration through writings, courses, seminars, and other discussions with junior and senior colleagues.

9. Evidence of excellence in research rests on a candidate's capacity to develop significant findings from investigation. Such excellence may be demonstrated through a wide range of efforts to advance knowledge or understanding through specific project research, descriptions, and analyses in depth of management practices in business, and the development or improvement of analytical tools. It may be shown also, in part, through stimulating, guiding, and influencing the research of others.

No attempt will be made here to codify the different research styles that are relevant to the study of business administration or to set priorities for one kind over another. The following may serve as guidelines for judging persons thought to have outstanding capacity for research: they will have demonstrated in some substantial way their ability to add, through study, to knowledge of significance for business administration. At different times and in different studies, for example, their approach may have been primarily intuitive or exploratory with the aim of providing initial insights or classifications of data from which hypotheses may be generated for later analytical study. Or their aim may have been systematic, with the intent to clarify a conceptual framework to be tested through observation and experiment; to confirm specific hypotheses within an existing frame of reference; or to state and test new hypotheses. Or they may seek to modify and extend existing methodology, develop new methodology, and constructively criticize the use of existing methodology for the analysis of business problems. Or they may have used some combination of these other styles of research. Each of these orientations, and others that could be mentioned, has its uses at a particular stage in the development of knowledge in a particular field of administration. A candidate with outstanding capacity for research knows and uses in his work the methodology appropriate to his field and to the problems and questions studied.

A few researchers have very effectively influenced their fields with almost no writing, but ordinarily the products of research appear in the form of published works. Books, monographs, articles, papers, and reports of studies to seminars and other professional groups all show the quality of an individual's intellectual contribution and the intensity of his desire to make it. Both are important: the first for obvious reasons; and the second because without it a sense of striving toward the accumulation of knowledge related to business practice is not present.

Research of the highest quality will generally show a thoughtful awareness on the part of the researcher of the relation between the characteristics and interconnections of the phenomena he studies and his views of them. It will also show an appropriate awareness of the stage in the development of knowledge at which the study was conducted. The outstanding researcher will find means to communicate the findings of his own research and to relate them to the research of others. He will also show capacity to influence and help the research of others.

Just as the School seeks to avoid the appointment of persons who overemphasize day-to-day classroom teaching, the idea of a segment of the Faculty oriented exclusively toward research is also rejected.

10. A member of the Faculty may teach and do research in a single field of business administration, in more than one field, or between fields. The Dean, the Senior Associate Dean for Educational Affairs, and appropriate Area and Program Chairman will help each nontenure appointee plan his activities in a way that will offer him a full opportunity, consistent with the School's resources and needs, to develop and demonstrate his capacity. It is expected that a candidate will usually have demonstrated competence in teaching or research in one area before moving to another.

At the same time, it is recognized that the boundaries of intellectual fields do not necessarily coincide with the boundaries of the areas of the present Faculty organization; nor should they. Therefore, if the development of a candidate's intellectual interests takes him into more than one organizational area, the former, not the latter, shall ordinarily control his assignments and activities, insofar as the School's over-all staffing situation permits. In this respect, it is perhaps worth recalling that a stated objective of the Faculty's plan of organization was to facilitate intellectual activities at the School, not hinder them.

It is in the same sense—that is, with an awareness that a field of intellectual activity in business administration may not exactly coincide with a subject area of the Faculty's organization that Faculty staffing requirements are to be interpreted. Staffing plans need to be built up and reviewed from time to time from the point of view of educational programs as well as subject areas and also from such other perspectives as the distribution of men and women among ranks and among ages. However, the needs of the School as a whole are not necessarily a simple summation of the needs of the parts of its Faculty's organization. It follows, therefore, that the Appointment Committee's advice and the Dean's decisions on specific appointments, though they are importantly affected by the staffing needs of specific Program and Area groups, are not determined by them. The advice and decisions may depart from existing staffing patterns in order to obtain an exceptionally able man or woman, to leave openings unfilled when no candidate of high caliber is available, and to encourage work for which no formal area has been established because the potential for business administration of significant new work is not yet clear.

11. A Doctor's degree is not a prerequisite to appointment at any professorial rank at the School. On the other hand, if a person is a candidate for a doctorate either at this School or elsewhere, it is ordinarily expected that he will complete this work prior to receiving a term appointment as an Assistant Professor. The caliber of his work for the doctorate is given major consideration for this initial appointment. If a person who is being considered for an assistant professorship is not a candidate for the doctorate, it is ordinarily expected that the intensity of his training and accomplishment will be of quality comparable to Doctoral training.

12. Often questions are asked concerning the importance attached to a candidate's record of publications. The School is interested in the quality of the communications and not the number of items published. Those moving toward leadership roles in business education should find ways to communicate with others in their field in the academic and business communities. Among the numerous means of communication to be appraised are the following: reports of project research, including books and articles in professional journals and other media; text and casebooks and particularly the accompanying manuals or supplements that show the author's concepts and teaching methods; and speeches and seminars conducted at or away from the School. Beyond these the School recognizes less formal but telling communication within academic circles and within professional associations. In short, the School seeks leadership and this implies ability in communicating.

13. Earlier in this document (paragraph 5) it is stated that judgments about a candidate's qualities will be made primarily in terms of the caliber of his teaching and research. In evaluating the candidate's teaching qualities, any relevant evidence will be considered that bears on the candidate's probable future teaching performance at the School. The evidence may include, among other things, teaching performance at other

schools in the United States or abroad, or in company and community education programs. The weight of any evidence will depend on the extent to which it can be credibly evaluated and
the extent to which it relates to the criteria of paragraph 8. In
evaluating the candidate's research qualities, evidence from any
source will be regarded as eligible for consideration, provided it
affords a test of probable future research performance at the
School. Professional work other than teaching and research, referred to in paragraph 5, includes any activities that may add to
the candidate's effectiveness in teaching and research at the
School. Such activities may include, among others: participating
in activities of relevant professional associations; participating
or consulting with nonprofit organizations on activities which
demand skills similar to those relevant to business and compati-
ble with an individual's professional interests; participating in
the management of business enterprises or government agencies;
and participating in administrative work at the School of the
sort in which Faculty members normally engage.

14. The Corporation has made repeated reference to the
importance of selecting, from inside or outside the University,
the best available persons to fulfill a particular purpose of the
School. This is emphasized because it means to each candidate
under consideration for appointment and to those who are evaluating him that even though excellence of past performance and
promise of future performance are vital criteria, they alone are
not enough. In addition, the assessment of the person's performance and promise to fulfill the objectives of this School in a
particular appointment must be weighed against an assessment
of the ability of others available to fill the position. Such an assessment, of course, cannot be made in the abstract but must
take into consideration how any candidate would be expected
to perform and grow in the particular environment of this
School. Further, a recommendation for an appointment must
recognize the limitation over time of available openings and the
need to balance the abilities of professors within different areas
and within the School as a whole. If the best person available to
fill a particular position does not measure up to the standards
sought within this Faculty as a whole, it is generally best to
leave the position unfilled. In summary, appointments should

be recommended only when all of the following conditions are met: the individual in question has outstanding ability; his abilities are the best available for this School's purposes; his abilities are those needed to balance the skills of others on the Faculty in the area or areas in which he has chosen to work; an opening exists; and the appointment will not block younger persons of greater ability.

15. It is the normal practice of the School to appoint more individuals to nontenure positions than can possibly be promoted to full Professor. There are several reasons for this practice. Most important is the belief that this practice encourages the selection for tenure positions of those individuals who best fulfill the School's needs. The anticipation of only limited growth in the size of the total Faculty reinforces this practice. As a consequence, a number of Assistant Professors will continue their careers elsewhere. Likewise, an individual appointed at the Associate Professor level is not assured of further promotion here, but promotion to the Associate Professor level is ordinarily made on the basis that an opening at the full Professor level on this Faculty does or will exist for which the candidate is judged to be in a strong competitive position, assuming continued growth and development. Competition for any opening, of course, will come from persons outside this Faculty as well as from those already on it.

16. This statement has gone to some lengths to underline that attrition is to be expected at the nontenure levels. We know that any selection process necessarily creates some doubts or apprehensions, but any practice which did not seek to attract and select on a broad basis would not be in the best interest of the School. An important objective of the School is to provide valuable experiences for all term appointees, and the School will seek wherever possible to balance the School's needs with assignments which will give younger Faculty members the fullest possible opportunities to advance in their careers.

Part II. Titles and Terms of Appointments

17. The first appointment to the senior Faculty for men or women with limited experience is usually as Assistant Profes-

sor. Normally an initial appointment to this rank is for a term of four years. The next higher appointment is as Associate Professor. This appointment is normally for a term of five years, but those with an outstanding record may be reviewed for promotion prior to the expiration of their five-year term as Associate Professor. In exceptional cases there may be reappointments as Associate Professor for a term not to exceed two years. The appointment as Professor carries tenure. The School also will use other titles for term appointments, such as Lecturer and Visiting Professor, to meet the needs of the School and the interests of prospective Faculty members.

Part III. Procedures

18. All appointments are made by the President and Fellows of Harvard College, referred to as the Corporation; appointments for periods of time more than one year must also have the approval of the Board of Overseers. Recommendations for Corporation appointments are the responsibility of the President, but he in turn receives recommendations from the Dean, who makes use of Faculty information and judgment.

19. Tenure holding Faculty members have on-going responsibility for coaching and evaluating both the teaching and research of nontenure men and women working in their Area, and, where practicable, other nontenure Faculty members with whom they work in the School's various educational programs and research projects. Therefore, Faculty members holding tenure positions should, throughout the terms of appointment of nontenure Faculty, periodically visit the classes of such individuals, and evaluate other aspects of their teaching and research. There should be sufficient classroom visits to assess an individual's classroom teaching skills and the progress he is making in the development of those skills. With respect to teaching, these same responsibilities are also borne by nontenure Faculty members who head first-year courses, multisection second-year courses, or who are program chairmen. Written observations on classroom visits are to be submitted to a candidate's Area Chairman.

Responsibility for direction of these coaching and evaluation activities rests with the Area Chairmen. In carrying out these responsibilities, they are expected to confer with nontenure Faculty in their areas concerning the need for coaching assistance. In addition, each Area Chairman should help in the development and evaluation of nontenure Faculty by, at least annually, offering to discuss over-all performance with each nontenure Faculty member.

The preceding paragraph notwithstanding, it is also the responsibility of each nontenure Faculty member to take the initiative in seeking coaching assistance. They may desire to seek coaching assistance from members of the Administration, from the Area Chairman, from other tenure members of the Faculty, or from some of their nontenure Faculty colleagues. It is recognized that sometimes some of the most useful coaching comes from the last mentioned source.

20. A Faculty Advisory Committee on Appointments, consisting of all full Professors, advises the Dean. The deliberations of this Committee are highly confidential; its usefulness would be destroyed if reports of its discussions were communicated. The Committee's purpose is to furnish to the Dean the fullest possible information and judgment about men and women under consideration and alternative candidates.

21. Candidates from each area are evaluated first by a committee of the Faculty Advisory Committee on Appointments for that area. Each subcommittee is appointed by the Dean and consists of four to six members. Generally subcommittee members are appointed for more than one year in order to provide continuity to the subcommittee's deliberations. The Senior Associate Dean for Educational Affairs is ex officio a member of all subcommittees. The Area Chairman is typically an ex officio member of the subcommittee for his area.* The appointed chairman of each subcommittee and no fewer than half the members generally are not members of the subject area of the person being evaluated. Apart from the Senior Associate

---

*If the candidate does not have an area affiliation, the Dean shall appoint another tenure member of the Faculty as an ex officio member of the subcommittee. This individual, whose identity will be known to the candidate, should be familiar with the candidate's professional work.

Dean, the Area Chairman, or some other ex officio member known to the candidate, the identity of subcommittee members is confidential. On occasion, men or women who are not at this School may be asked to serve on or work with subcommittees.

22. Each individual holding an appointment at this School who is being considered for promotion will be told in *advance* by the Senior Associate Dean for Educational Affairs that a subcommittee will evaluate him and be given the opportunities of informing the subcommittee of (a) work which he considers to be particularly significant, (b) the names of people who he thinks can best evaluate his work, and (c) his interests and his plans, including the types of assignments which he thinks, if available, will make the greatest contributions to his development and the development of his field. The candidate will also be informed by the Senior Associate Dean that he may indicate the name of any full Professor who the candidate believes could not dispassionately evaluate his work and therefore should not be a member of his subcommittee. The channel of communication selected by the candidate for response may be through the Senior Associate Dean for Educational Affairs, the Area Chairman, or any full Professor the candidate chooses. This is an option of communicating to the subcommittee, not a requirement.

23. To help the Faculty Advisory Committee on Appointments and its subcommittees in their deliberations, the Dean, in the early fall of each year, provides the Committee with an overview of its work for the coming year. This overview includes a statement of the Dean's strategy for manning the School with the size and mix of Faculty necessary to accomplish the School's various missions in the foreseeable future. It also includes a statement concerning projected size of the Faculty in the near term, anticipated openings by relevant categories, and any other information which the Dean considers pertinent. Finally, it includes the names of all candidates, to the extent that they are known at that time of the year, who will be considered for promotion during the current academic year.

24. The work of the subcommittees is the painstaking

accumulation and weighing of evidence relative to appointments
under consideration. In this work, however, subcommittee
members will rely in part on information furnished by others.
They should hear from the Dean or Senior Associate Dean for
Educational Affairs a thorough review of the anticipated relevant openings over the next several years, and they should hear
from the Area Chairman a forecast of the teaching and research
developments insofar as these can be anticipated. These statements will include a review of the effects which the appointment being considered is likely to have on the balance between
teaching and research in the Area. In addition, the Area Chairman, as a known ex officio member of the subcommittee familiar with the candidate's professional work, should, if the candidate or subcommittee requests it, act as a channel of communication between the candidate and the subcommittee.

The Area Chairman and other members of the Faculty
will furnish specific information relating to the attainments and
abilities of those both at this School and elsewhere who might
reasonably be considered as alternative candidates for an appointment. This information should include the names of the
most qualified women and of the most qualified persons of minority backgrounds, together with the reasons why each of
them is not being recommended, whenever that is the case. The
subcommittee's evaluation should be made within the context
of this information.

25. Reports by subcommittees to the Full Faculty Advisory Committee are, to the extent possible, grouped by rank.
For example, subcommittee reports on all candidates under
consideration for appointment to the rank of full Professor
are read and discussed at consecutive meetings of the Full Faculty Advisory Committee on Appointments.

In each case the subcommittee sets forth the most significant evidence that it has collected, its evaluation of the individual under consideration, and presents a recommendation for
action to be taken. This report is discussed fully by the whole
Faculty Advisory Committee on Appointments.

Upon completion of discussion of the report of each subcommittee, the Dean requests from the Full Advisory Commit-

tee on Appointments an initial and tentative vote, by signed and confidential ballot, to accept, reject, or modify the recommendation of each subcommittee. The outcome of the vote is not announced at this time to the Full Advisory Committee on Appointments. When the reports of all subcommittees reviewing candidates for promotion to a particular rank have been read and discussed, the Dean requests final votes on each candidate from the Full Advisory Committee on Appointments. The results of these votes are also confidential. All evidence, recommendations, views, and votes are taken into account by the Dean, who has sole responsibility for the recommendations made to the President. It is the responsibility of the Dean to disclose his recommendations to the individual candidates. In addition, the Dean, at his discretion, may ask one of the ex officio members of the subcommittee to communicate the thinking of the subcommittee and Full Advisory Committee on Appointments to the candidates. These procedures are designed to encourage thorough and impartial consideration of each candidate and consistent applications throughout the School of the standards for promotion.

26. Subcommittees are concerned principally with contemplated appointments at the Associate and full Professor level. When a person is first considered for appointment as an Assistant Professor, the situation is often such that the Dean must give substantial weight to evidence and recommendations presented by people who are not at this School and by members of the interested subject area here.

Appendix B

Faculty Flow Simulation

The simulation presented here is based on a model developed by Robert Linnell, director of institutional research at the University of Southern California, and modified by Andrew W. Masland, a doctoral student at the Harvard Graduate School of Education.

The simulation models Alpine University, a pseudonym for an actual university with 152 FTE faculty and a liberal arts orientation. Section I states the dimensions and parameters of the personnel policies and practices in effect at Alpine at the time we visited there and collected the necessary data. In other words, the results reproduced below represent projections based on then current policies at Alpine. To gauge the effect of certin policy changes on faculty flow, composition, and compensation, administrators at Alpine could (and did) alter any or all of the nine policy variables tracked by the model. Section II profiles the faculty at present. Section III offers an executive summary of the results of the simulation, and Section IV presents the results in much greater detail. While we selected a ten-year planning period and projected a steady-state enrollment, the program permits up to a twenty-year planning horizon and projections of growth or decline. To protect the identity of the institution, we have deleted the names of the academic departments and the specific time frame of the projections. The computation time for the simulation was 13.48 seconds.

I. Policy Options

A. Retirement Policy: The probability of retirement by faculty between the ages of 62 and 68 will be as follows:

Age	Probability of Retiring	% Remaining
62	0.1	90 %
63	0.1	80.9%
64	0.1	62.8%
65	0.9	7.2%
66	0.9	0.7%
67	0.9	0 %
68	1.0	0 %

B. Voluntary attrition and tenure success rates will be:

	Voluntary Attrition	Probability of Tenure
Full Professor	0	0.9
Associate Professor	0.007	0.5
Assistant Professor	0.034	0.3
Instructor	0.027	0

C. The replacement probabilities by rank will be:

	Probability of Being Replaced By:			
	Full	Associate	Assistant	Instructor
Full Professor	0.1	0.2	0.3	0.4
Associate Professor	0	0.1	0.4	0.5
Assistant Professor	0	0	0.3	0.7
Instructor	0	0	0.3	0.7

D. Newly appointed faculty will have the following character-
    istics:

	Average Age	Probability of Salary Level			Years Until Tenure Decision
		Low	Medium	High	
Full Professor	40	0.2	0.3	0.5	3
Associate Professor	30	0.3	0.5	0.2	3
Assistant Professor	26	0.6	0.2	0.2	6
Instructor	25	0.8	0.2	0	6

E. Promotion policy will be:

Probability of promotion to Professor in first eight years
after tenure is 0.2.
Probability of promotion to Professor after eight years of
tenure is 0.8.
Probability of promotion to Associate Professor without
tenure is 0.1.
Probability of promotion to Associate Professor if tenured
this year is 0.4.
Probability of promotion from Instructor to Assistant Professor is 0.7.
Promoted faculty receive additional 5 percent increase in
salary.

F. Affirmative action:

Probability of hiring female (per two-year interval) for first
ten years: 0.08, 0.08, 0.08, 0.08, 0.08
Probability of hiring minority (per two-year interval) for
first ten years: 0.03, 0.03, 0.03, 0.03, 0.03

G. Full-time faculty required for first ten years of planning
    period (for yearly intervals):
    152, 152, 152, 152, 152, 152, 152, 152, 152, 152
    The % of part-time faculty will be: 3.3.
    The annual cost of one part-time faculty (in terms of FTE)
    will be: $9,000.

H. Annual faculty salary increases will be, on average:

Full Professor	7.9%
Associate Professor	10.6%
Assistant Professor	11.3%
Instructor	11.4%
Part-Time Faculty	7.0%

I. (This model includes provisions for merit pay increases, but Alpine University elected not to use merit pay.)

II. Current Profile of Full-Time Faculty

	Total	Tenured	Male	Female	Minority
Full Professor	48	47	48	0	1
Associate Professor	34	30	33	1	1
Assistant Professor	48	5	40	8	2
Instructor	17	0	13	4	1
All Ranks	147	82	134	13	5

Current faculty cost   = $2,628,800
Average faculty age (years) = 42.9

Current starting salaries:

	Low	Medium	High
Full Professor	17,000	18,000	20,000
Associate Professor	13,500	14,500	16,000
Assistant Professor	11,400	12,000	13,000
Instructor	11,000	11,500	12,000

Current age distribution:

	21-25	26-30	31-35	36-40	41-45	46-50
Full Professor	0.0	0.0	0.0	2.0	5.0	11.0
Associate Professor	0.0	0.0	2.0	7.0	11.0	6.0
Assistant Professor	0.0	10.0	20.0	15.0	3.0	0.0
Instructor	0.0	6.0	7.0	2.0	1.0	1.0
All Ranks	0.0	16.0	29.0	26.0	20.0	18.0

	51-55	56-60	61-65	66-70	71-75
Full Professor	10.0	11.0	7.0	2.0	0.0
Associate Professor	2.0	3.0	3.0	0.0	0.0
Assistant Professor	0.0	0.0	0.0	0.0	0.0
Instructor	0.0	0.0	0.0	0.0	0.0
All Ranks	12.0	14.0	10.0	2.0	0.0

III. Executive Summary

Over the ten-year planning period, 111.4 positions are expected
to be filled with new faculty. The average turnover percentage will be 7.6% per year.

A total of 25.4 positions are expected to open because of faculty resignations, 24.4 positions will open from retirements,
5.4 positions will open due to deaths, and 56.2 positions will
open due to tenure denial.

The average faculty age in year 10 will be 40.3.

In year 10, the average faculty salary will be $31,085.
    Total faculty salary costs will reach $4,658,000 in year 10.

In year 10, 57.5% of the faculty will have tenure. It will require
76.2% of the total faculty salary costs to support the tenured
faculty.

In year 10, 4.3% of the faculty will be minorities and 6.3% of
the faculty will be female.

In year 10, the full-time faculty will be distributed as follows:

Full Professor	45.1%
Associate Professor	17 %
Assistant Professor	32.7%
Instructor	5 %

Faculty changes:

					Year					
	1	2	3	4	5	6	7	8	9	10
Avg # Voluntary Attrition	2.8	2.2	2.6	3.0	2.0	3.6	2.4	1.0	3.2	2.6
Avg # Death	0.4	0.4	0.8	1.0	0.8	0.6	0.2	0.6	0.2	0.4
Avg # Denied Tenure	0.6	3.4	4.0	8.0	4.2	8.2	9.8	8.2	5.2	4.6
Avg # Retire	4.2	2.8	2.8	1.0	1.8	2.6	2.2	1.0	2.6	3.4
Avg # Tenured	1.4	2.6	2.2	4.2	2.0	3.8	4.2	5.8	4.2	5.2
Avg # Promotion	25.0	18.2	15.0	13.6	16.8	13.0	13.4	15.2	15.2	16.0
Faculty Leave	8.0	16.8	25.8	37.0	45.0	56.2	65.2	70.2	73.6	78.0
Cumulative # Hires	8.0	16.8	27.0	40.0	48.8	63.8	78.4	89.2	100.4	111.4

Faculty data (averages):

					Year					
	1	2	3	4	5	6	7	8	9	10
# Professor	56.2	58.0	59.6	60.6	62.2	62.6	63.6	65.8	66.8	66.4
# Associate Professor	26.6	27.6	26.2	26.8	27.6	26.6	24.4	23.8	22.6	25.0
# Assistant Professor	54.4	52.6	53.4	49.8	49.6	47.8	46.8	46.8	47.4	48.2
# Instructor	9.8	8.8	7.8	9.8	7.6	10.0	12.2	10.6	10.2	7.4
# FTE (PT)	5.0	5.0	5.0	5.0	5.0	5.0	5.0	5.0	5.0	5.0
Faculty Required × 10	15.2	15.2	15.2	15.2	15.2	15.2	15.2	15.2	15.2	15.2
Faculty Age	42.6	42.2	41.8	41.5	41.5	40.8	40.5	40.7	40.6	40.4
Salary × 1000	19.0	20.3	21.6	23.1	24.6	25.7	26.7	28.2	29.8	31.1
Total Costs 100K	28.4	30.4	32.4	34.5	36.8	38.5	40.0	42.2	44.6	46.6
% Faculty Tenured	53.3	52.5	51.4	52.8	52.4	52.8	53.7	56.6	57.1	57.6
% Female	9.1	9.1	8.6	9.0	9.3	7.8	7.1	6.4	6.5	6.4
% Minority	3.5	3.5	3.7	3.9	3.7	4.1	4.5	4.6	4.9	4.4
% Tenured of Payroll	63.5	63.3	62.4	64.2	64.3	66.2	69.2	73.7	75.2	76.2

Expected # original faculty by department remaining at university:

Department	Year									
	1	2	3	4	5	6	7	8	9	10
A	9.4	8.8	8.0	7.6	6.8	5.8	4.2	3.2	3.2	3.2
B	12.0	11.8	10.4	9.6	8.6	8.0	7.2	7.0	6.6	5.8
C	5.0	4.2	4.0	3.0	3.0	2.4	2.4	2.4	2.4	2.4
D	3.0	2.8	2.0	1.6	1.6	1.6	1.6	1.6	1.6	1.6
E	13.6	13.2	12.8	12.4	11.2	8.8	7.8	7.6	7.0	7.0
F	4.0	4.0	4.0	4.0	4.0	3.0	2.0	2.0	2.0	2.0
G	8.0	8.0	8.0	7.4	6.8	5.8	5.8	5.8	5.8	5.6
H	6.0	5.2	4.6	3.8	3.6	3.4	3.4	3.4	3.2	2.4
I	5.8	5.2	4.6	4.4	4.4	4.4	3.2	3.2	3.2	3.0
J	8.4	7.2	6.8	6.0	5.4	4.8	4.8	4.6	4.6	4.6
K	5.8	5.8	5.4	5.2	5.2	5.2	4.6	4.6	4.6	4.6
L	5.0	5.0	5.0	3.6	3.4	3.2	3.2	3.2	3.2	3.2
M	9.4	9.0	9.0	9.0	9.0	8.8	8.4	7.8	5.8	5.0
N	6.6	6.6	6.4	6.2	5.0	5.0	4.8	3.6	3.6	3.0
O	2.8	2.8	1.8	1.0	1.0	0.4	0.4	0.4	0.4	0.4
P	9.0	8.0	7.0	6.4	6.4	5.8	5.0	4.4	4.4	4.4
Q	10.6	10.4	9.6	9.4	8.6	6.8	6.6	5.8	5.6	5.2
R	7.8	6.2	5.8	4.2	3.2	3.2	2.0	2.0	2.0	1.6
S	1.8	1.6	1.6	1.6	1.6	1.6	1.6	1.4	1.4	1.2
T	5.0	4.4	4.4	3.6	3.2	2.8	2.8	2.8	2.8	2.8

Expected # cumulative openings by department each year:

Department					Year					
	1	2	3	4	5	6	7	8	9	10
A	0.6	1.2	2.2	2.6	3.4	4.6	6.4	7.8	8.6	8.8
B	0.0	0.2	1.6	2.6	3.8	5.2	6.0	6.2	7.2	8.6
C	0.0	0.8	1.0	2.0	2.0	2.6	2.6	3.4	4.2	4.4
D	1.0	1.2	2.0	2.4	2.6	2.6	3.2	3.2	3.8	3.8
E	1.4	1.8	2.2	2.8	4.0	6.4	8.4	8.8	10.0	10.6
F	0.0	0.0	0.0	0.0	0.0	1.0	2.0	2.0	2.0	2.0
G	0.0	0.0	0.0	0.6	1.2	2.2	2.2	2.6	2.6	3.0
H	0.0	0.8	1.6	2.4	2.6	3.0	3.0	3.6	4.2	5.6
I	0.2	0.8	1.4	1.6	1.6	2.2	3.6	4.0	4.8	5.0
J	0.6	1.8	2.2	3.4	4.2	5.2	5.4	6.2	6.6	7.4
K	0.2	0.2	0.6	0.8	0.8	0.8	1.6	1.6	1.6	1.8
L	1.0	1.0	1.4	3.0	3.2	3.4	3.8	3.8	4.2	5.4
M	0.6	1.0	1.0	1.0	1.0	1.2	2.0	2.8	5.0	6.0
N	0.4	0.4	0.6	0.8	2.0	2.2	2.8	4.0	4.0	4.6
O	0.2	0.2	1.2	2.0	2.0	3.0	3.4	3.4	3.4	3.6
P	1.0	2.0	3.0	4.0	4.0	5.0	6.6	7.6	8.6	9.4
Q	0.4	0.6	1.6	2.0	2.8	4.8	5.0	6.0	6.8	7.4
R	0.2	1.8	2.4	4.2	5.2	5.6	7.4	8.8	9.4	10.4
S	0.2	0.4	0.4	0.4	0.4	0.4	0.6	0.8	0.8	1.0
T	0.0	0.6	0.6	1.4	2.0	2.4	2.4	2.6	2.6	2.6

	Total Fac. Hired over 10 Yrs.	Fac. Cost (1,000s) in Year 10	Avg. Fac. Age in Year 10	% Fac. Tenured in Year 10
Minimum	101.0	4,455.0	39.3	54.4
Mean	111.4	4,658.0	40.3	57.5
Maximum	123.0	4,835.0	41.0	61.2

Average age distribution in year 5:

Rank	21-25	26-30	31-35	36-40	41-45	46-50	51-55	56-60	61-65	66-70	71-75
Full Professor	0.0	0.0	0.0	1.4	7.6	14.4	15.4	11.6	11.2	0.6	0.0
Associate Professor	0.0	4.2	6.8	7.2	6.0	2.2	0.8	0.0	0.4	0.0	0.0
Assistant Professor	5.0	24.0	7.4	7.2	4.2	1.8	0.0	0.0	0.0	0.0	0.0
Instructor	3.4	4.0	0.2	0.0	0.0	0.0	0.0	0.0	0.0	0.0	0.0
All Ranks	8.4	32.2	14.4	15.8	17.8	18.4	16.2	11.6	11.6	0.6	0.0

Average age distribution in year 10:

Rank	21-25	26-30	31-35	36-40	41-45	46-50	51-55	56-60	61-65	66-70	71-75
Full Professor	0.0	0.4	2.2	3.6	6.0	12.6	15.0	16.0	10.4	0.2	0.0
Associate Professor	0.4	7.4	10.4	1.6	3.0	1.4	0.8	0.0	0.0	0.0	0.0
Assistant Professor	5.8	30.2	8.3	0.4	1.4	1.2	0.4	0.0	0.0	0.0	0.0
Instructor	3.4	4.0	0.0	0.0	0.0	0.0	0.0	0.0	0.0	0.0	0.0
All Ranks	9.6	42.0	21.4	5.6	10.4	15.2	16.2	16.0	10.4	0.2	0.0

References

AAUP/AAC Commission on Academic Tenure. *Faculty Tenure: A Report and Recommendations.* San Francisco: Jossey-Bass, 1973.

American Association of University Professors. "Report of the Joint Subcommittee on Faculty Responsibility." *AAUP Bulletin,* 1971, *57* (4), 524-527.

American Association of University Professors. "On the Imposition of Tenure Quotas." *AAUP Bulletin,* 1973a, *59* (4), 428-430.

American Association of University Professors. "Surviving the Seventies." *AAUP Bulletin,* 1973b, *59* (2), 188-213.

American Association of University Professors. *AAUP Policy Documents and Reports.* Washington, D.C.: American Association of University Professors, 1977.

American Association of University Professors. "The Impact of Federal Retirement-Age Legislation on Higher Education." *AAUP Bulletin,* 1978a, *64* (3), 181-192.

American Association of University Professors. "On Full-Time Non-Tenure Track Appointments." *AAUP Bulletin,* 1978b, *64* (3), 267-273.

American Association of University Professors. "Academic Freedom and Tenure: University of Texas at Permian Basin." *Academe,* 1979, *65,* 240-250.

American Council on Education. *1980 Fact Book for Academic Administrators.* Washington, D.C.: American Council on Education, 1980.

Atelsek, F., and Gomberg, I. *Tenure Practices at Four-Year Colleges and Universities.* Washington, D.C.: American Council on Education, 1980.

Berenson, D. "Should Old Engineers Just Fade Away?" *Chemical Engineering,* Sept. 12, 1966, pp. 212-216.

Blackburn, R. T. *Tenure: Aspects of Job Security on the Changing Campus.* Atlanta: Southern Regional Education Board, 1972.

Blackburn, R. T. "Project for Faculty Development Program Evaluation: Final Report." Unpublished paper. Ann Arbor: Center for the Study of Higher Education, University of Michigan, 1980.

Bonz, M. H. "Assessment of Junior Faculty Experience at Dartmouth College." Unpublished paper. Hanover, N.H.: Dartmouth College, 1979.

Byse, C., and Joughin, L. *Tenure in American Higher Education: Plans, Practices, and Laws.* Ithaca, N.Y.: Cornell University Press, 1959.

Carnegie Council on Policy Studies in Higher Education. *Three Thousand Futures: The Next Twenty Years for Higher Education.* San Francisco: Jossey-Bass, 1980.

Cartter, A. M. *Ph.D.'s and the Academic Labor Market.* New York: McGraw-Hill, 1976.

Centra, J. (Ed.). *New Directions for Higher Education: Renewing and Evaluating Teaching,* no. 17. San Francisco: Jossey-Bass, 1977.

Centra, J. A. *Determining Faculty Effectiveness: Assessing Teaching, Research, and Service for Personnel Decisions and Improvement.* San Francisco: Jossey-Bass, 1979.

Chait, R. P. "Academic Tenure and Faculty Unions: On a Collision Course?" In *Proceedings* (of third annual conference). New York: National Center for the Study of Collective Bargaining in Higher Education, 1975.

Chait, R. P. "Nine Alternatives to Tenure Quotas." *AGB Reports,* 1976, *18* (2), 38-43.

Chait, R. P. "Tenure and the Academic Future." In *Tenure: Three Views.* New Rochelle, N.Y.: Change Magazine Press, 1979a.

Chait, R. P. "Faculty Salaries: How Much or What For?" In *Proceedings: Higher Education Legislative Issues for '79.* Atlanta: Southern Regional Education Board, 1979b.

Chait, R. P. "Setting Tenure and Personnel Policies." In R. T. Ingram and Associates, *Handbook of College and University Trusteeship: A Practical Guide for Trustees, Chief Executives, and Other Leaders Responsible for Developing Effective Governing Boards.* San Francisco: Jossey-Bass, 1980.

Chait, R. P., and Ford, A. T. "Can a College Have Tenure . . . and Affirmative Action, Too?" *Chronicle of Higher Education,* Oct. 1, 1973, p. 16.

Chait, R. P., and Gueths, J. "A Framework for Faculty Development." *Change Magazine,* 1981, *13* (4), 30-33.

Cliff, R. "Opportunities and Pitfalls in Faculty Salary Comparisons." Paper presented at 3rd Annual Academic Planning Conference of University of Southern California Offices of Institutional Studies, Los Angeles, Jan. 1978.

Cohen, M. D., and March, J. G. *Leadership and Ambiguity: The American College President.* New York: McGraw-Hill, 1974.

College and University Personnel Association. "Tenure and Retrenchment Practices in Higher Education: A Technical Report." *Journal of the College and University Personnel Association,* 1980, *31* (3-4), 1-226.

"Construction and Effect of Tenure Provisions of Contract or Statute Governing Employment of College or University Faculty Member." *American Law Review,* 1975, *66,* 1018-1068.

Dennis, W. "Creative Productivity Between the Ages of 20 and 80 Years." *Journal of Gerontology,* 1966, *21,* 1-8.

DiBiase, E. R. "Classical Tenure and Contemporary Alternatives: Academe's Principles and Court Decisions." Unpublished doctoral dissertation, Division of Educational Policy Studies, Pennsylvania State University, 1979.

Drucker, P. F. "The Professor as Featherbedder." *Chronicle of Higher Education,* Jan. 31, 1977, p. 24.

Edwards, H. T., and Nordin, V. D. *Higher Education and the Law.* Cambridge, Mass.: Institute for Educational Management, Harvard University, 1979.

El-Khawas, E., and Furniss, W. T. *Faculty Tenure and Contract Systems: 1972 and 1974.* Washington, D.C.: American Council on Education, 1974.

Ellis, J. M. "Grievance Procedures: Real and Ideal." In R. H. Peairs (Ed.), *New Directions for Higher Education: Avoiding Conflict in Faculty Personnel Practices,* no. 7. San Francisco: Jossey-Bass, 1974.

Emenhiser, J., and Chait, R. *Implementing a Tenure Quota: The Colgate Case.* Cambridge, Mass.: Institute for Educational Management, Harvard University, 1976.

Enteman, W. F. "An Attempt to Save Tenure." Speech given to joint meeting of the Association of Departments of English and the Association of Departments of Foreign Languages, St. Louis, Missouri, June 28, 1973.

Enteman, W. F. "Tenure at Union College." *Liberal Education,* 1974, *60* (4), 461-466.

Fenker, R. M. "The Incentive Structure of a University." *Journal of Higher Education,* 1977, *68* (4), 453-471.

Furniss, W. T. "The 1976 AAUP Retrenchment Policy." *Educational Record,* 1976, *57* (3), 133-139.

Furniss, W. T. "Status of AAUP Policy." *Educational Record,* 1978, *59* (1), 7-29.

Grant, G., and Riesman, D. *The Perpetual Dream: Reform and Experiment in the American College.* Chicago: University of Chicago Press, 1978.

Harvard University Committee on Governance. *Discussion Memorandum on Academic Tenure at Harvard University.* Cambridge, Mass.: Harvard University, 1971.

Herzberg, F. "One More Time: How Do You Motivate Employees?" *Harvard Business Review,* 1968, *46* (1), 53-62.

Hruby, N. M. "Life After Tenure?" *AGB Reports,* 1981, *23* (2), 24-27.

"Idaho Professor Sues After Failing Review." *Chronicle of Higher Education,* Dec. 15, 1980, p. 8.

Jenny, H., Heim, P., and Hughes, G. *Another Challenge: Age 70 Retirement in Higher Education.* New York: Teachers Insurance and Annuity Association, 1979.

Kaplin, W. A. *The Law of Higher Education: Legal Implications of Administrative Decision Making.* San Francisco: Jossey-Bass, 1978.

Kerr, C. "Base Point: 1980." *AGB Reports,* 1980, *22* (2), 3-13.

Lawler, E. E., III. *Pay and Organizational Effectiveness: A Psychological View.* New York: McGraw-Hill, 1971.

Levinson, H. "Appraisal of What Performance?" *Harvard Business Review,* 1976, *54* (4), 30-32, 34, 36, 40, 46, 160.

Lewis, L. S. *Scaling the Ivory Tower: Merit and Its Limits in Academic Careers.* Baltimore: Johns Hopkins University Press, 1975.

Lewis, L. S. "Getting Tenure: Change and Continuity." *Academe,* 1980, *66* (4), 373-381.

Lohr, S. "Overhauling America's Business Management." *New York Times Sunday Magazine,* Jan. 4, 1981, pp. 15-17, 42-45, 51, 53.

Luecke, D. S. "An Alternative to Quotas: A Model for Controlling Tenure Proportions." *Journal of Higher Education,* 1974, *45* (4), 273-284.

McKeachie, W. J. "What Motivates Academic Behavior?" In D. R. Lewis and W. E. Becker (Eds.), *Academic Rewards in Higher Education.* Cambridge, Mass.: Ballinger, 1979a.

McKeachie, W. J. "Student Ratings of Faculty: A Reprise." *Academe,* 1979b, *65* (6), 384-397.

Metzger, W. P. "Academic Tenure in America: A Historical Essay." In AAUP/AAC Commission on Academic Tenure, *Faculty Tenure: A Report and Recommendations.* San Francisco: Jossey-Bass, 1973.

Meyer, H. H. "The Pay-for-Performance Dilemma." *Organizational Dynamics,* Winter 1975, pp. 39-50.

Miller, R. I. *Evaluating Faculty Performance.* San Francisco: Jossey-Bass, 1972.

Miller, R. I. *Developing Programs for Faculty Evaluation: A Sourcebook for Higher Education.* San Francisco: Jossey-Bass, 1974.

Moog, F. "Women, Students, and Tenure." *Science,* 1971, *174,* 983.

National Center for Education Statistics. *Salaries, Tenure, and Fringe Benefits of Full-Time Instructional Faculty in Institutions of Higher Education, 1975-76.* Washington, D.C.: U.S. Department of Health, Education and Welfare, 1977.

Nevinson, C. H. "Effects of Tenure and Retirement Policies on the College Faculty." *Journal of Higher Education,* 1980, *51* (2), 150-166.

Oi, W. "Academic Tenure and Mandatory Retirement Under the New Law." *Science,* 1979, *206,* 1373-1378.

O'Toole, J. "A Conscientious Objection." In *Tenure: Three Views.* New Rochelle, N.Y.: Change Magazine Press, 1979.

Patterson, F., and Longsworth, C. R. *The Making of a College.* Cambridge, Mass.: M.I.T. Press, 1966.

Patton, C. V. *Academia in Transition: Mid-Career Change or Early Retirement.* Cambridge, Mass.: Abt Books, 1979.

Porter, L. W., and Lawler, E. E., III. "What Job Attitudes Tell About Motivation." *Harvard Business Review,* 1968, *46* (1), 118-126.

Price, J. L. *The Study of Turnover.* Ames: Iowa State University Press, 1977.

Rappa, J. B. "Professional Development Programs in the Computer Industry: Implications for Academic Management." Unpublished paper. Cambridge, Mass.: Graduate School of Education, Harvard University, 1978.

Scott, E. L. *Higher Education Salary Evaluation Kit.* Washington, D.C.: American Association of University Professors, n.d.

Scott, R. A. *Lords, Squires, and Yeomen: Collegiate Middle Managers and Their Organizations.* Washington, D.C.: American Association of Higher Education, 1978.

Seldin, P. *Successful Faculty Evaluation Programs.* Crugers, N.Y.: Coventry Press, 1980.

Shaw, B. *Academic Tenure in American Higher Education.* Chicago: Adams Press, 1971.

Siegel, M. E. "Empirical Findings on Faculty Development Programs." In W. C. Nelsen and M. E. Siegel (Eds.), *Effective Approaches to Faculty Development.* Washington, D.C.: Association of American Colleges, 1980.

Simpson, W. A. "Tenure: A Perspective View of Past, Present, and Future." *Educational Record,* 1975, *56* (1), 48-54.

Solmon, L. C. *PhDs in Non-Academic Careers: Are There Good Jobs?* Current Issues in Higher Education, no. 7. Washington, D.C.: American Association of Higher Education, 1979.

Southern Regional Education Board. *Faculty Evaluation for Improved Learning.* Atlanta: Southern Regional Education Board, 1977.

Tagiuri, R. *On Dealing with Unsatisfactory Performance.* Cambridge, Mass.: Intercollegiate Case Clearinghouse, Harvard University, 1974.

West, R. R. "Tenure Quotas and Financial Flexibility in Colleges and Universities." *Educational Record,* 1974, *55* (2), 96-100.

Wolf, D. "The Union Plan: A Case Study of the Reform of a Traditional Tenure System." Unpublished doctoral dissertation, School of Education, University of Virginia, 1980.

Yuker, H. E. "Faculty Workloads and Productivity." In T. N. Tice (Ed.), *Campus Employment Relations.* Ann Arbor: Institute of Continuing Legal Education, University of Michigan, 1976.

Index

281

Kormondy, E., 29
Kurland, J., 106, 182, 238-239

L

Lamson, G., 233
Laubach v. *Bradley*, and denial of
  reappointment, 80
Lawler, E. E., III, 199, 205, 206,
  208, 277, 278
Leavitt, H., 191
Levinson, H., 173, 188, 246, 277
Lewis, L. S., 194, 195, 277
Linnell, R., 233, 264
Lohr, S., 191, 277
Lomas, B., 105
Longsworth, C. R., 15, 16, 17, 19-
  20, 278
Luecke, D. S., 109, 277
Lumpert v. *University of Dubuque*,
  and personnel policies, 240

M

McCann, C., 25, 29
McKeachie, W. J., 198, 202, 205-
  206, 215, 277
Manhattan Community College,
  and tenure quota, 127
March, J. G., 41, 235, 275
Marquette University, censure of,
  239
Martin, H., 101
Marx, G., 239-240
Maryland, University of, censure of,
  239
Masland, A. W., 264
Massachusetts, University of, and
  Hampshire College, 15
Massey, W., 233
Merit pay: as awards, 207; as bonus
  payment, 207; issue of, 25; and
  pay differentials, 206-207; as re-
  ward, 202-208; validation of,
  203-206
Metzger, W. P., 13, 14, 92, 277
Meyer, H. H., 205, 277
Michigan, University of, review pro-
  cess at, 169

Middle management, incremental-
  ism among, 46-47
Miller, R. I., 198, 278
Montana State University, person-
  nel and payroll program at, 224
Moog, F., 9, 278
Morris, J., 123-124
Mount Holyoke College, and Hamp-
  shire College, 15
Muhlenberg College, tenure mora-
  torium at, 140

N

National Architectural Accrediting
  Board, 243
National Center for Education Statistics, 8, 10, 222, 278
National Endowment for the Humanities, 206
National League of Nurses, 243
National Science Foundation, 206
Nevinson, C. H., 141, 233, 278
New Jersey State Colleges, and tenure quotas, 130-132, 137, 138,
  237
Nontenure tracks: advantages of,
  80-86; analysis of, 67-90; circumstances for, 86; and clarity and
  certainty, 84-86; at Coe College,
  75-77; and due notice, 85-86; and
  enrichment, 82-83; escape clauses
  for, 84-85; examples of, 77-80;
  and flexibility, 83-84; and freedom from censure, 81-82; policy
  clarification for, 88; policy provisions for, 89-90; political feasibility of, 80-81; recommendations
  on, 86-90; and regular courses,
  86-87; and risk/reward concept,
  73-74; and strategic plans, 88; at
  Webster College, 68-75
Nordin, V. D., 58, 276
Nussbaum, L., 76, 174-178

O

Odessa Junior College, and due process case, 39

Oi, W., 6, 278
Oklahoma, University of: board of appeals at, 220; evaluation of tenured faculty at, 186; sanctions by, 216
Oklahoma State University, nontenure track at, 78
O'Toole, J., 10, 65, 73-74, 278

P

Patterson, F., 16, 17, 278
Patton, C. V., xiv*n*, 233, 278
Pay. *See* Merit pay
Pennsylvania State University, nontenure track at, 78
Performance: effort linked to, 199-200, 203; rewards linked to, 200, 204-205, 213, 216
Perry v. *Sindermann,* and due process, 39
Personnel policies: administration of, 244-246; auditing and improving, 221-247; changing, 233-244; changing, recommendations on, 243-244; coverage of, 236-237; data analysis for, 226-233; data base for, 223-224; data collection for, 222-226; documentation of, 240; and flexibility, 227-232; goals of, 234-235; legal counsel for, 237; objective of, 246-247; and procedures, compromises in, 232-233; statements of, 238-239. *See also* Policy
Pittsburgh, University of, and evaluation of tenured faculty, 181
Policy: administering, 142-171; criteria and standards for, 145-152; effective, elements of, 144-166; institutional context of, 157-162; of interim evaluations, 152-157; judgment, not measurement in, 144-145, 189; on multilevel reviews, 162-171. *See also* Personnel policies
Porter, L. W., 199, 208, 278
Presidents: dilatory policies role of, 103; evaluation role of, 179; and

personnel policies, 222, 223; and tenure policy, 153, 159, 166, 170; and term contracts, 19, 23, 27
Price, J. L., 49, 278
Princeton University: probationary period extended at, 93, 115; tenure slots at, 117-118
Probationary periods, extended: analysis of, 91-100; criteria articulation for, 107-108; evaluation under, 108-109; and faculty anxiety, 111-113; length of, 3, 92-93, 106; objectives of, 95-96; passive advantage of, 109-110; and probability of tenure, 109-111; strengths and weaknesses of, 105-114; at University of Rochester, 93-98; value of, 106-107; variations of, 98-100
Professional development: for administrators, 246; constructive rationale of, 211-212; and evaluation, 153, 176-177, 183-185; examples of, 209-210; faculty role in, 212-214; financial support for, 214; and instructional improvement, 212; and professional roles and activities, 210-211; program components for, 210-214; as reward, 208-215; and term contracts, 28, 33, 44-45, 53-54, 60
Promotion, tenure linked to, 95-98, 113-114
Providence College, and retirement age, 236-237
Provost, and personnel policies, 223, 227, 245
Publications, standards for, 256
Purdue University, personnel policy at, 224

Q

Queensborough Community College, and tenure quotas, 127-128
Quincy, J., 13